2010 Shipwright

2010 Shipwright

The International Annual of Maritime History & Ship Modelmaking

Incorporating

Model Shipwright

Editors John Bowen
Martin Robson

Assistant Editor Michael Leek

CONWAY

A Conway Maritime Book

First published in 2009 by Conway
An imprint of Anova Books Ltd
10 Southcombe Street
London W14 0RA
www.anovabooks.com
www.conwaypublishing.com
www.shipwrightannual.com

Pages 2–3: The main sail of the *Matthew* Replica. *(Conway Picture Library)*

A CIP catalogue record for this book is available from the British Library.

ISBN 9781844861088

Printed and bound by Bangunan Times Publishing, Malaysia.

Distributed in the U.S. and Canada by:
Sterling Publishing Co., Inc.
387 Park Avenue South
New York
NY 10016-8810

Shipwright accepts advertising. For more information please contact:
modelshipwright@anovabooks.com

To receive regular email updates on forthcoming Conway titles, email
conway@anovabooks.com with Conway Update in the subject field.

Contents

Editorial

Welcome to the very first *Shipwright* annual.

Regular readers of *Model Shipwright* will, we hope, welcome the move to a large-format, full-colour annual. We think this provides several benefits. First, due to the increased space there will be no need to run articles over two or more issues thereby removing the frustrating wait for the second part of a fascinating ship modelling description. Secondly, the new format allows plans and images to be presented with enhanced clarity at a larger size. On this point we can also present imagery in full colour – a fantastic development which will really help modellers. Finally, readers will notice that as well as maintaining the high standard of international ship-modelling articles, there are what one might term 'historical contextual' articles. We believe that such articles will inform the subject of modelling and provide interesting research and background material to potential subjects.

Launched to coincide with the publication of *Shipwright* is a brand new website: www.shipwrightannual.com. Readers are invited to log on to this site to download a large-scale plan of this year's Modeller's Draught, to keep up with news and to join the Modeller's Forum. Readers will also be able to order back issues of *Model Shipwright* at a special price, and we hope, at launch, to make a selection of *Model Shipwright* plans and Modeller's Draughts available in downloadable format.

Shipwright remains in the ever-capable hands of John Bowen, with Michael Leek continuing as Assistant Editor. Joining them is Martin Robson, a maritime and naval historian and former Editor at Conway. Together the *Shipwright* team aim to combine loyalty to the history and traditions of *Model Shipwright* while appreciating the need to move the publication forward to meet the needs and interests of today's modellers and maritime historians.

With this in mind, *Shipwright 2010* certainly fulfils the remit to provide high-quality ship-modelling articles written by model-makers. We have selected and presented the contents in order to maximise the many links running through and between articles. They cover a wide range of modelling skills, approaches and subjects – from display models to waterline, kit adaptation to restoration, diorama building to practical tips on materials and tools; all supported by some excellent articles by marine artists and historians.

By way of a preface to this inaugural issue of *Shipwright*, we are delighted to include an exclusive interview with Dr Kevin Fewster, Director of the National Maritime Museum, Greenwich, in which he discusses the running of a major museum and his plans for the future.

We begin the main body with two articles that were originally intended to run over two issues of *Model Shipwright*: 'The Tasmania barque *Nautilus*, 1872-1891', by John Laing and John R. Haynes' article 'USS *Gearing* DD710'. In order to maintain clarity and to take advantage of the move to colour, we have decided to publish them here in their entirety. *Nautilus*, like many barques, was built as a cargo-carrying yacht, and like many hybrid ships had a short but interesting career. With the author's ancestral links to the subject, John Laing has produced a highly detailed and immensely personal account of the building of his 1:96 model. John R. Haynes has rescued the *Gearing* US destroyer class from modelling opprobrium, pointing to the overbearing influence of the more popular *Fletcher*s as subject matter. Both of these opening articles employ different methodologies and approaches to their subject and hence show the range and diversity of the ship modelling community.

The world-renowned marine artist Geoff Hunt has provided an artist's view of how he tackled painting one of the world's most famous ships, the *Mary Rose*, which was commissioned by the Mary Rose Trust. Of particular interest to modellers will be the techniques utilised by Geoff to ensure that his work 'looks right'. How the artist interprets subject matter is also considered by Lloyd McCaffery in his article explaining his approach to marine carving in miniature. Lloyd's work graces several museums and many modellers will be familiar with his book *Ships in Miniature*, (Conway, 1988). Whether you agree or disagree with his statements, we sincerely hope *Shipwright* readers will find much of interest in his very personal account.

Robert A. Wilson takes us back to more traditional subject matter with his waterline model of the composite clipper *Norman Court*. By choosing to model his subject under full sail, Robert has provided an in-depth account of his approach to masting, rigging and providing sails – including the inventive use of an egg. Robert has also contributed a short piece detailing the construction of a device which he uses to represent planking by scoring the decks of his models. Staying with practical guidance, John Dodd describes the advantages of eschewing glue and sticking with traditional methods by creating and using model treenails to fasten together timber.

Alongside new builds, the restoration of existing models is a vital part of the model shipbuilding canon. Bruce Buchanan writes an entertaining account of restoring and then sailing a model fifie. These vessels were developed on Scotland's eastern coast and were used for herring fishing. Surviving examples are quite rare and Bruce was delighted to sail on the restored sailing fifie *Reaper*, owned and run by volunteers from the Scottish Fisheries Museum at Anstruther, Fife (www.scotfishmuseum.org). *Swan*, another example, is owned and run by the Swan Trust (www.swantrust.org.uk).

Research, as highlighted by many of our contributors, is a vital aspect of ship modelling, whether this involves finding suitable plans, investigating ship histories or, as John Bingeman shows us, analysing primary artefact source material. John is the Government Licensee for HMS *Invincible* lost in 1758; her wreck has thrown up a treasure trove of valuable evidence and John has presented here a selection of unusual rigging artefacts. Another wreck, the 70-gun third-rate *Stirling Castle* lost in 1703, provides the background for the fascinating story of a seventeenth-century swingleg table belonging to John Laws, the ship's Gunner.

Moving from the mighty ships-of-the-line down the sailing man-o-war rating system to the smaller end of the scale we have two articles detailing the modelling of two brigs – one fictional and one unnamed. David Mills recounts his project to restore an unidentified 1:48 brig model, originally built by a retired Commodore of the Orient Line, but which had degenerated over the years (the ship not the Commodore!). In his debut article for *Shipwright* John Thompson describes, in meticulous detail, the building of HMS *Teazer*. This ship will be familiar to many readers of the maritime fiction penned by Julian Stockwin, as *Teazer* was the first command of the character Thomas Kydd. As a brig-rigged sloop, *Teazer* was based on the Royal Navy's *Cruiser* class of 1796 and John went to great lengths to ensure that every detail was accurately represented – including many consultations with the author himself.

Another debutant, Rorke Bryan, provides an illuminating historical contextual article examining the US Exploring Expedition of 1838–42, commonly referred to as the 'Wilkes Expedition' after its colourful and controversial commander Charles Wilkes. His squadron included two sloops USS *Vincennes* and *Peacock*, with the *Porpoise* brig and *Relief* store ship. Rorke has included a wealth of information useful for the modeller and some fine images of ship models in the Smithsonian Institute. Continuing the North American theme Jonathan Kinghorn's 'Atlantic Transport Line' provides an overview of this famous shipping company founded in 1881, initially to transport freight and then passengers on the Lon-

don–New York route. One of the ATL ships, *Minnewaska*, is the subject of a short modelling article by John Bowen, originally published in his Miniature Merchantmen series in *Model Shipwright* and presented here in an amended format to complement Jonathan's article. North American waterways provide the context for John Pocius, who reminds us not only of the genius of the naval architect Fred W. Martin, but also of the oft-overlooked skill of diorama construction. This medium allows the modeller to display a number of craft within a chosen situation and show off a range of skills and techniques.

Two short modelling articles round off the annual before coming bang up to date with the Royal Navy's latest warship. James Pottinger has selected a contemporary Scottish fishing vessel, *Prospector* BA 25, for this year's 'Modeller's Draught' while John York recounts his building of a 1:96 model of the ground-breaking SS *Great Britain*. Lt Cdr F. Evans RN and Robert Fosterjohn close the annual with details of HMS *Daring*, welcomed to the fleet on 28 January 2009 as the lead ship of the Royal Navy's new class of Type 45 destroyer. The Royal Navy Philatelic Society released a commemorative limited edition 410 covers to celebrate this auspicious event, which is reproduced here. At the end of the book we have what will become regular sections in the Annual; Book News and 'Shipwright Gallery'.

If you have an article you would like to submit to the annual, a model for inclusion in the 'Shipwright Gallery', or have any queries relating to the submission of material, please contact us at:

Shipwright Editor
Conway
Anova Books Ltd
10 Southcombe Street
London W14 0RA

email shipwrighteditor@anovabooks.com
www.shipwrightannual.com

For detailed information on the submission of articles and images, please visit the website, but as a general guide, all articles should be supplied as a Word document. Digital photographs should be high-quality, high resolution (300dpi) scans in tif or jpg format, with printouts for reference. Scan width should ideally be 16cm in order for us to use them at half-page size or larger. Original prints and photographs are all acceptable.

We look forward to hearing from you!

John Bowen
Martin Robson
Michael Leek

Interview with Dr Kevin Fewster

DIRECTOR OF THE NATIONAL MARITIME MUSEUM, GREENWICH

Conway's Publisher, John Lee, interviewed Dr Kevin Fewster at his office in Greenwich in June 2009. Dr Fewster was previously Director of the Powerhouse Museum, Sydney 2000–2007, and inaugural Director of both the Australian National Maritime Museum, 1989–1999 and the South Australian Maritime Museum, 1984–1989. He was made a Member of the Order of Australia in June 2001 to service in museum administration and to the preservation of maritime history.

JL: You've been Director of the National Maritime Museum for just over eighteen months. How has that time been?

KF: I've been in the job since September 2007, so by the time the *Shipwright Annual* comes out I'll have been at the National Maritime Museum for two years. It was a great honour to take over the job as Director of Greenwich and I'm the first non-British director. I joined just after the Museum celebrated its 70th anniversary and in 2012 – which is a year when there are a few things happening – we'll be celebrating our 75th anniversary. It was also an exciting time to join because the Museum was, and is still, going through a period of amazing growth. In the past year, the financial year 08/09, the Museum received over 2 million visitors for the first time ever. It went up over 21 per cent on the previous year, which meant we had the highest increase of any of the national museums and we're now running Number 8 of the most visited major attractions in Britain.

JL: That's incredible. Maybe top 15, but 8 … When you think about what you're up against.

KF: I think there are a variety of reasons for it. In part, I think it is to do with Maritime Greenwich being given World Heritage status back in 1997, an international seal of approval, a world's best. And it is. I sit in my office and look at the views and the vistas and it is glorious. That recognition has really given the Museum a huge deal. Back in the 90s there were 2

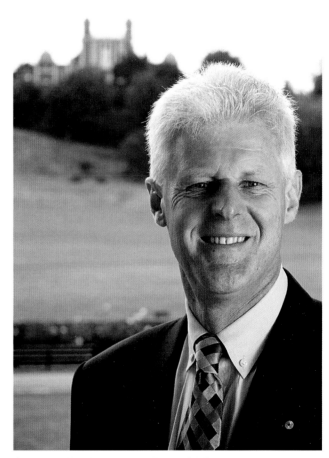

Above: Dr Kevin Fewster in Greenwich Park.

million, or perhaps even less, visitors who came to Greenwich each year. This figure is now running at about 8 million and heading for 10.

Secondly, I think that Greenwich was always perceived as a difficult place to get to whereas in the last 10 years, coinciding with the World Heritage status, was the establishment of the Docklands Light Railway (DLR). This has had a huge impact on making Greenwich feel closer to central London. The opening of the O_2, the former Millennium Dome, and the establishment of fast ferry services on the

Thames Clipper, has meant that the trip from central London is much quicker. Greenwich is receiving much more attention because the O_2 links more people to East London and we have become beneficiaries of that as well. The O_2 announcement was made the day I was interviewed for the job and I said at the interview, of the O_2 opening, I think the river will shrink, that the perceived distance between central London and the east of London will shrink.

And it's happened. The O_2 has become, very quickly, the world's most used concert venue. So, add all those things together and people are now perceiving Maritime Greenwich to be a perfect day out destination – just half an hour from central London – and our market research, our audience research, is showing that last year the number of people coming to Greenwich by river increased: it's now 27 per cent and rising fast.

In terms of the Museum itself, when I came here, I felt the Museum, in a sense, needed to be more integrated with its local community. I often make this point, being an outsider you can sometimes see things others can't – they're too close to it.

To me the key word is Greenwich. This morning I bet you wouldn't have said I'm going to the National Maritime Museum; you would have said I'm going to Greenwich, wouldn't you? Greenwich is the hook, with the Royal Observatory and the Prime Meridian our Number 1 hook. If you look out of the window you will see that most people are heading up to the Observatory. The Prime Meridian – and all that goes with it – is a true international tourist icon and in a funny way the Museum has ridden on the coat tails of the Observatory. Now, I'm trying to change that. I'm trying to build on that popularity and encourage cross-site visits. We've got these great facilities, a great location, and lots of visitation: how can we then fully exploit that to enable people to make the most of their visit to Greenwich and their visit to the Museum and experience as broad a range of things as possible?

JL: How does the experience compare with your time over in Sydney? What are the differences and parallels?

KF: I was the first director at the Australian National Maritime Museum, which opened in 1991, so it's a very young institution compared with the pedigree that Greenwich has, with its scale of collections and length of collecting going back much further here.

Other differences? It's interesting that Greenwich is unusual, although not unique, in being a major maritime museum in the world which does not have water frontage and so does not have anything in the water. Or any large vessels: our small craft are at the Maritime Museum in Falmouth. In Sydney we had vessels in the water as well as exhibit spaces.

Another difference would be the composition of the audience. In Australia it is almost a reversal to Greenwich. Most major museums in Australia – or in Sydney at least – usually work on a mix of around 60 per cent locals and 40 per cent tourists (both national and international), whereas at Greenwich it is pretty much the other way round, particularly for the Observatory where 60 per cent of our audience are international tourists. That impacts on how the Museum operates and what drives programming and such things.

I left the National Maritime Museum in Sydney in 2000 and became director of the Powerhouse Museum, which is a large, very broadly based museum and it had a staff number very similar in size to Greenwich. The Powerhouse Museum also ran, amongst its portfolio of museums, the old Sydney Observatory, which is an 1850s observatory. In a way I had seven years' experience overseeing a historic observatory with all the issues and all the opportunities that that offers. So in terms of the size of the staff and the portfolio, the Maritime and the Observatory, it gave me a really lovely fix between Sydney and Greenwich.

JL: What is the most important or interesting acquisition that you've made since you've been here, for the Museum?

KF: I wouldn't say *I've* made, but has been made since I joined and excited me most: not long after I joined we acquired the Union Flag that was flown as Lord Howe's command flag at the Battle of the Glorious First of June, 1794. The Flag had been placed under export bar, allowing the National Maritime Museum sufficient time to work to raise the funds required to keep the flag in the UK rather than lose it overseas.

JL: It was on display, wasn't it?

KF: We unrolled it in the Queen's House and it is now undergoing conservation. And because it is so massive, how we display it will be a really significant issue for us. When I was in America just a couple of weeks ago, I was in the Museum of American History and they've made the Star-Spangled Banner their key iconic object. They have rebuilt that entire museum and it is fascinating to see how they've made it the centrepiece of the whole museum.

When we unrolled the Union Flag, we received amazing media coverage. It is the sort of object people expect us to have, so when you acquire it, especially as a new director, it is all the more exciting in a sense.

JL: Where did it come from?

KF: It is a classic story, exactly the same as the Star-Spangled Banner. It had been handed on to a family who had an

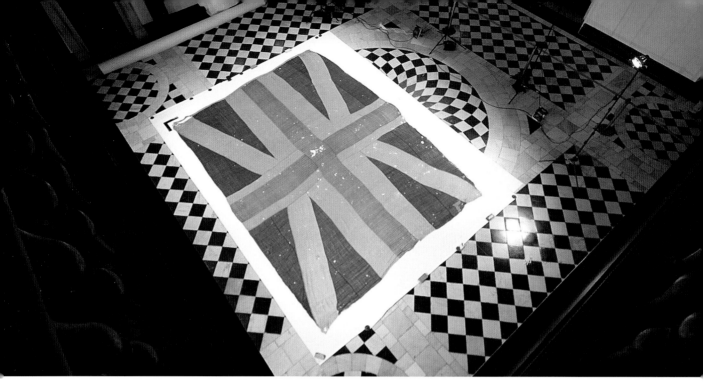

Above: The Union Flag from the Battle of the Glorious First of June rolled out on the floor of the Queen's House.

involvement in the battle. They had packed it in a kitbag and it was up in the loft for the last 50 years, 80 years, 150 years? It's such an incredibly powerful object and it is not like the current Union Flag so you see the history of the nation. It is a breathtaking object.

The other acquisition was an important addition to our Nelson collection. Last year we were presented with one of Nelson's undershirts, which is a vest, if you like. It was part of his kit when he went to sea at Trafalgar although he wasn't wearing it on the day that he died. We showed it in our Nelson exhibition (which is now closed) and when you look at it, you realise what a tiny physique he had.

JL: You have the uniform, obviously, which gives a good indication of his size. That's one of the most surprising things when people see that.

KF: And with the undershirt I think even more so. With the uniform it has the wider shoulders, and the long coat. It's a bigger piece of clothing. But when you see the vest, which was worn next to his skin, it really reinforces just how small he was and that is also very personal. It's that difference between what I said about the Union Flag or his dress uniform coat – they are things for show and prestige – but to see this garment is such a personal thing rather than a matter of symbol.

JL: How do you balance the requirements of being a public institution for research and scholarly endeavour with the need to be a commercial organisation, to bring in numbers, to bring in revenue?

KF: This takes me on to the new Sammy Ofer Wing. When I arrived at Greenwich, the Museum had a project, which had been started but was in its early days, of building a new archive and library. The library, which had been part of the Museum since its inauguration, had grown and expanded, and its facilities were 70 years old. So the museum had commissioned an architect to start designing a new wing for our archive. The space being proposed, which is the south-west corner of the National Maritime Museum's site, is the last corner of this site where we have the potential to do a major redevelopment.

Being a World Heritage Site, we're obviously constrained by all sorts of issues, and for me, the biggest issue confronting this Museum is that we are located in a series of historic buildings. It's the opposite of what I was saying about the glory and the history. Our exhibition buildings in particular are very constrained in terms of their size. The Museum has never had what I call a major temporary exhibition gallery. If you look at other major museums around the world, not just of our stature but well below our stature, they will have a temporary exhibition space of 800–1,000 square metres. So I said we needed to expand what was to be the archive and library into a much broader brief that would give us this proper temporary exhibition space.

Going back to my comment about the Observatory: at present, if you come to the main museum you walk through Greenwich, along Romney Road and then in through the main entrance. And it's not as straightforward as it could be to get from the Museum main entrance to the Observatory or down from the Observatory to the main museum and yet, two out of three of our visitors go to the Observatory first and walk an obstacle course to get down the hill and find the Museum entrance. So it seemed to me that what we should do is design this new wing to take into account the realities of how people come here, which is walking up King William Walk and then up through Greenwich park. We went back to the architects and asked them to revise the whole scheme so that it would include this major temporary exhibition gallery, which is now about 830 square metres – that would be more than double the size of what the Museum had as a temporary space – and to build a new entrance into the new wing which will become the Museum's main entrance. The new entrance will come off the primary approach that people use to get here through the Park from the Observatory and also reduce the barrier between the Museum and the park.

The archive is still a central element, but it is now a much bigger scheme. We started designing within weeks of me arriving followed by an incredible piece of good fortune. A significant figure in the shipping world, Sammy Ofer, stepped forward and offered us £20m towards the scheme. Using that and HLF (Heritage Lottery Fund) support, the capital fundraising for the build, £35m, we were able to put in place within less than a year of me starting.

This is a very long answer, but it's the necessary background. What we're now doing is planning for our major new programme for 2012 when the new wing will be open. What that will mean is we will do many more temporary exhibitions. I also want to see us doing more in the way of sending exhibitions out travelling and bringing exhibitions in from other places. Once you have the right space and the right flexibility it makes it much easier to bring in pre-existing exhibitions, or talk about collaborative programmes with other museums.

For me the question about the public institution for scholarly endeavour versus being a commercial organisation is, in fact, I see the two of them actually coalescing, because as we'll be doing more temporary exhibitions there'll be more of a need for us to link in our research programming and our publications with our exhibition programming. Now that's nothing radical. That makes us like most other major museums around the globe. But I think for us there will be *more* emphasis on that than perhaps there was in the past.

JL: And the library is going to happen in 2012?

KF: The new wing is due to be completed for 2012 before the Olympics. Whether we can do it any earlier than 2012… my hope is we can, but that will all depend on how the work progresses.

JL: Could you outline some of the Museum's future plans regarding actual access and online availability of the model collections.

KF: One of our other big projects that was well underway when I joined the Museum was a three-part partnership between the National Maritime Museum, the Imperial War Museum and Chatham Historic Dockyard to refurbish one of the derelict buildings at the dockyard at Chatham with HLF support and to make it into a store for the ship model collections of the three museums. By far the biggest of these is the Greenwich collection. That project is well advanced. The building work is due for completion around October and it is expected to be open around the middle of next year. It will give Chatham good quality exhibition

Above: Artist's impression of the new Sammy Ofer Wing.

space and temporary exhibition space. The great majority of our models that aren't on display will move to Chatham. We will also have a dedicated research room at Chatham where models can be brought out and made available for researchers. There will be 2,400 models from the Museum's collection moving to Chatham.

JL: And you'll be able to bring some back if there's an exhibition?

KF: Yes, we will be able to bring anything back for an exhibition. Absolutely.

JL: So will the majority of the collection be there?

KF: Certainly the majority will be there and the facilities for researchers will definitely be improved. We are also currently undertaking a major photographic study of the models for our record purposes and that creates the opportunity for them to be put up on the web. There are around 4,000 ship models in the Museum's collection. About 1,200 have already been photographed with another 800 still to be done. I therefore believe that just under 50 per cent of the collection will have an image. All the models that are photographed will be put online by Summer 2010.

JL: That's exciting news. Just in terms of the draughts, though, obviously many of our modellers are looking to get copies. Are there initiatives whereby the actual plans themselves can be made available online?

KF: At present we have material in our collections on site here at the Museum and we also have a large repository for ships plans and photographs at Woolwich. That facility is retained under the new archive proposal, so Woolwich will continue. But we are looking to have more about our material, some of it available here and some of it with our online search engine and upgrading as we go along.

JL: Do you think as a nation we are losing touch with our maritime heritage?

KF: My honest answer on that is yes and no. Yes, in the sense that the number of people who directly work, whether at sea or on the docks, is plainly a fraction of what it once was and nowhere can one be more aware of that than working and living in East London. The challenge for us is to make people aware that the amount of trade that still travels by sea and the importance of maritime trade and maritime experience to this country is no different to what it was. Over 90 per cent of international trade to and from Britain is by sea, and that's pretty common around the world, but because

Above: A 'Zarook' stands propped by for repairs, Ma'alla beach. Its hull is being recaulked and coated with a mixture of lime and fish oil to protect it from ship worm. From *Sons of Sinbad* by Alan Villiers.

most people now travel by air, they assume that everything goes by air, which is not true. So there are misconceptions about that.

On the other side of the coin, soon after I arrived there was a series on one of the TV networks where people were asked to vote for their favourite heritage sites in Britain. For me it was fascinating having just arrived in the country. The Number 1 site, voted for in this national survey, was Stonehenge, which perhaps isn't a surprise. But the Number 2 was *Victory*, and I found that interesting that the maritime significance and symbolism remains as potent as ever. Even though the number of people with that direct family engagement may be a fraction of what it was, the symbolic sense of it and its appreciated value was ranked Number 2 in that national list. And that's a good position to be in, because we can build on that and expose people, I hope, to a broad range of experiences, as well as giving them what they expect.

But, having said that, we should also challenge people and open people up to other things. So in some ways it goes back to what I said about temporary exhibitions. Why I like temporary exhibition programmes is that at any one time you might come and say to me, 'I think it's awful, there aren't as many models here as there used to be'. But then I'd probably say, 'Yes, but we're actually holding an exhibition next year or the year after which is going to have a big focus just on models'. But somebody else might come in when that was on and say, 'Gosh, this place only has models. It doesn't do enough about the merchant marine'. With the exhibition programme you need all those things in the wider sphere.

JL: Have you done any research to see if the type of visitor has changed over the last decade? We talked about the rising numbers.

KF: It's interesting but the demographics haven't changed as much as one might have thought, it's just more of everyone, and obviously free entry introduced in 2001 had a huge impact on this museum as well as museum entry right across Britain. One thing that came out of last year's research was how visitors regard their visit to Greenwich and the Museum. In the past there would been a fairly strong skewing towards people seeing it as earnest and worthy – almost 'you should go there once in your life' kind of thing – whereas last year we had a significant lift in people defining us as a really good day out. For the committed enthusiasts they might see that as a negative, but I see it as a positive, because seeing us as a great day out you're more likely to come back and if you come back a second or third or fourth time, then we have a committed audience of people who engage in it and want to engage in it. That, to me, is a much much stronger position to be in.

JL: I think it's interesting, yes. There's obviously a mix of both and our job and your job is obviously to try and bring in new audiences as well as fulfilling the needs of a loyal, specialist audience, and also challenge the way that people look at things from the start.

KF: For me in my museum career, which goes back a bit now – and the maritime subject is an interesting field for it, because maritime does have a specialist audience – is it possible to mount programmes that appeal to the enthusiast and meet their expectations whilst at the same time engage the general audience? Most people who visit the Museum don't

come as enthusiasts, it's a day out, and so they arrive with a leisure interest rather than a scholarly interest. If one can sense and present programming in its broad sweep: exhibitions and programming, that meet the expectations of both those groups, that for me is what the challenge is all about. So that the person coming here for the day out feels that they have really enjoyed and got something out of it and if you've lifted them to a different plane where they have found it a really satisfying day rather than simply something to do, and at the same time the enthusiast and the expert visit and, through the myriad ways we work, their passion and their hunger is also well and truly met, that's the real trick for a modern museum.

JL: I wondered if there are a few words you could say on the exhibitions for 2010?

KF: Our big exhibition next year is on models. But it's not the models you think. What we are doing – and it's a good example of what I said about working with other institutions – is an exhibition with the Musée de la Marine in Paris. They have a spectacular collection of toy boats. Mainly tin toys. We don't have such a major collection, only a small number of tin boats. I hope we will add some things to it as well because it's a lovely way into that whole sense of models.

JL: To finish on a personal note, I thought I'd ask you what your favourite or most recently read maritime book was.

KF: What I've read just recently, which I really enjoyed – it was one of our publications – just published. A biography of Alan Villiers.

JL: Yes, I know it.

KF: It was interesting for me. There are so many points of personal contact. He was born in Melbourne, where I spent my childhood; his second ship was the *James Craig*, which was a ship that was moored outside my office window in Sydney. He worked on the grain race for years; I've had lots of involvement in that for a variety of historic reasons. He bought and sailed the *Joseph Conrad* around the world; which is now in a public collection at Mystic Seaport. I've worked at Mystic Seaport; I know that vessel well. He was a trustee here at the National Maritime Museum. It was amazing reading this book, getting point after point after point where I had this contact. It was quite extraordinary. A really interesting story and for me at least it was a terrific read.

For further information visit www.nmm.ac.uk

Nautilus (1872-1891)

TASMANIAN BARQUE

by John Laing

Early in 1873 my great-great uncle John Cox signed on as a seaman on the Tasmanian barque *Nautilus* in order to return to England to visit his father's family. Unfortunately he never lived see his English relatives as he fell from the main topsail yardarm during a storm off the Cape of Good Hope and was lost overboard. His death was eventually reported in the Tasmanian newspapers after receipt of a letter from Cape Town setting out the circumstances of the accident.

Having almost completed my first plank-on-frame model, I was looking for a new ship to model and was attracted to the small wooden sailing ships that had been built in Tasmania in the latter part of the nineteenth century. Was the *Nautilus*, connected so tragically with a distant ancestor, one of those ships? If she was, she might be the perfect prototype for my next building task, both the type of ship I was looking for and with a family connection to make the project more personal.

RESEARCH AND PLANS

The first job was to find the right *Nautilus*. *Nautilus* was a fairly common name for sailing ships in the 1870s, but thankfully the newspaper reports of John Cox's death included the name of the ship's Master, Captain Hopkins, and noted that *Nautilus* was a barque. That narrowed the field a bit and with the help of several books on the early maritime history of Tasmania, I soon identified a small wooden barque built in Hobart by Mackey's in 1872.

Next I contacted the Maritime Museum of Tasmania to confirm that my suppositions were correct and I was not letting myself be led astray by wishful thinking. The very helpful folk in Hobart confirmed that I had indeed found the right ship. *Nautilus* was built by the firm of J. & D. Mackey at their Battery Point yard to the order of Mr Henry Hopkins – a prominent Tasmanian businessman. Hopkins had her built as a cargo-carrying yacht with the intention of taking her for a world cruise; the cargo helping to pay the expenses. She was 129ft overall length with a beam of 26ft and a depth of

14ft. She was built from local timbers, with her keel, keelson and stringers all being made from single lengths of timber each 112ft long.

Hopkins sailed to Europe with a cargo of wheat in January 1873 (the voyage that proved so unfortunate for John Cox) and did not return to Hobart until late December (it was, after all, a pleasure cruise), but this was the only voyage on which *Nautilus* was employed as a yacht. Hopkins put her on a regular run to China and she became Tasmania's only regular 'tea clipper'.

On Hopkins' death in 1875 she was sold to another Tasmanian businessman, Hugh Armstrong, who employed her in the colonial trade until he sold her to the Colonial Sugar Refining Company in 1887. She was used by that company for trading to the South Pacific and the end came in August 1891, when she was completely burnt out at Noumea, New Caledonia.

So much for the very interesting history of the *Nautilus*, but was there enough available information to enable me to build a model? There are (one might almost say, 'naturally') no surviving plans for the *Nautilus*. The Maritime Museum of Tasmania has a fine oil painting of her – thought to be painted when she was new – and there is also an unrigged model in the same Museum which shows her on the slips ready for launching; even down to the bottle of champagne at the bow. There is a surviving plan of one of Mackey's ships similar to the *Nautilus* and I also found a postcard of her (taken from another painting) in the State Library of Victoria.

A friend visiting Tasmania was able to photograph the model for me, including an excellent profile view and a full bow view, together with deck details. The (again) helpful folk at the Museum very kindly sketched for me the shape of the bow and stern at deck level. I also obtained copies of the two known paintings.

Armed with all of the above information I was able to draw an accurate outboard profile in both plan and eleva-

Above: Detailed view of the finished model.

tion; but how to turn that into a set of hull lines? I could see the shape of the hull plainly from the photographs of the model, but a shape only visualised is hardly enough to use to draft a set of frames for a plank-on-frame model. I went back to traditional methods and made a half model out of western red cedar built up in seven narrow horizontal lifts to the exact dimensions of the proposed model, and held together with soluble glue. Once the profiles were carved in the block it was simply a matter of carving down the hull until the half model matched the shape I could see on the photographs of the Tasmanian model. The half model was then taken apart and the lifts used as waterlines to draw up the hull lines.

Instead of drawing a fully detailed plan, I drew only the hull lines and had a photographer friend make me an enlargement of one of the paintings so that I could take dimensions directly from that. The photographic enlargement turned out to be not quite the correct size, but it was a simple matter to use a small conversion factor on all dimensions taken off.

THE MODEL

The model was built at a scale of 1:96 ($\frac{1}{8}$in = 1ft), giving a hull length of about 16in (40.6cm). This gave a nice finished size to the model for fitting into the average home without

problems and I find it a nice scale to work with; most detail can be shown and it is a bit of a challenge as well.

THE HULL

The framing was made of pine taken from a 100-year-old table top; milled and sanded to $\frac{1}{8}$in thick. The keel, stem and stern post were hand cut to shape and joined at the correct angles, with weights holding them completely flat when they had been glued. Once the glue was fully cured the joints were dowelled to give them additional strength and the fore and aft deadwoods were built up of small offcuts; glued and dowelled in place. The positions of the frames were then marked on the keel and deadwoods with $\frac{1}{8}$in space between each frame and the rabbet was marked out and cut. Care was taken to ensure that the rabbet was correctly cut across the deadwoods; any error in doing this will mean that the planking will not lie properly across these critical areas.

The completed backbone was placed on the building board and set up between right-angle brackets fore and aft and with chocks on either side of the keel. The building board was a piece of particle board strengthened with metal angles to ensure it remained completely flat. The model remained on this building board until all the frames were in place and the keelson, stringers, deck shelves and rubbing strakes had been fitted, to ensure that it could not warp or twist during these early stages of construction.

Each frame was made up of several short sections of timber to ensure that the grain followed the curve of the frame. Most frames consisted of seven separate sections. Each frame was drawn out on tracing paper and the individual sections were then glued to the paper and to each other. They were held completely flat by weights while the glue dried; they were then drilled and fitted with dowels. When they were quite dry, the frames were cut to shape, bevelled inside and outside, and the mortice for the keel cut.

The bulwark stanchions were included as an integral part of the frames, with a stanchion at every third frame in the general run of the hull, and at every frame in way of the masts. It was thought that this method of construction would result in a much stronger structure at the upper deck, rather than following full-size practice of fitting the stanchions separately.

The aftermost frame was made first as a solid unit and fitted on the fore end of the stern frame. The framing of the counter was then built up using this frame as a support. Once the counter framing was in place a framing jig, cut out of thin MDF board, was made to rest on the aftermost frame and the inboard side of the stem at main deck level. At the position of each frame a notch was cut in the jig so that the frames had positive support at the upper ends while framing was in progress. Many people use an external jig for framing, and this certainly makes the inside of the hull far more accessible for framing, but the internal jig has the advantage of not requiring accurate vertical alignment of the keel assembly and the jig, and also means that the model can be lifted off the building board at any time without having to worry about the jig alignment.

When all the frames had been constructed and glued in place on the keel, the keelson was cut out and laid on top of the frames where it was glued and dowelled to each frame, with the dowels being long enough to penetrate through to the keel. Thin lengths of pine were then bent into place as bilge stringers on each side and glued and dowelled to each frame. This gave the framing a fair degree of rigidity, although the frames were still vulnerable at their upper ends as they were unsupported.

As the height of the deck had been marked on each frame prior to fitting, it was a simple matter to mark in the height of the beam shelf below this. It was then easy to run more thin lengths of pine along each side of the hull as the beam shelves, gluing and dowelling them to each frame. The main deck shelf was run from right forward to one frame abaft the forward end of the poop and the forecastle and poop shelves fitted in their appropriate positions.

Below: Painting of *Nautilus. (Courtesy of the National Maritime Museum, Tasmania)*

The framework was now amazingly strong and rigid, this being helped by the number of glued and dowelled connections throughout the structure. It was now time to consider the planking, but before this was taken in hand the rubbing strake, which could be considered to be a light wale in terms of strength, was fitted to each side of the hull. Again the material was pine and the rubbing strakes were fitted as one piece on each side as far aft as the curve of the counter to give additional strength to the structure. The rubbing strake bent easily to the form of the hull for most of its length, but the sections around the counter required steaming to shape. As the sizes required at this scale are quite small, this was easily done just by boiling them for a few minutes in a saucepan on the kitchen stove, then bending them by hand to the required shape and drying them in the heat of a small electric fan heater. They retained their new shape quite well. (Warning: make sure permission has been given to use both stove top and pan. I have my own pan for this job.)

PLANKING THE HULL

The next job was to plank the hull. Very careful consideration needs to be given to the size of planks and the run of the hull planking if it is to look realistic. I used a nominal plank width of ³⁄₃₂in (9in full size) with the longest planks being 3in

(24ft full size). The thickness of the planks was about 1mm. The hull was divided into five even sections on each side by laying thin battens round the hull and wiring them to the frames after measuring the distances along every fifth frame starting amidships and working fore and aft. These battens were then adjusted by eye until a fair run of planking was achieved along the entire length of the hull. This is easily done by looking at the hull from many different angles and moving the battens slightly to achieve the desired result. It is also necessary to watch the width of the planks at various points along the hull, to ensure that individual planks do not become too wide or too narrow. In the case of the *Nautilus*, with just a little adjustment of the battens, I was able to achieve full runs of planking over the entire hull without the use of stealer planks.

The material used for the hull planking was privet. Both the Chinese privet that grows in old-style hedges and the broad leaf privet produce timber very similar in character to English box if allowed to grow into trees. In some parts of Australia they have become noxious weeds and quite large specimens can be found fairly easily. As they are now (at least where I live) noxious weeds there is no problem about removing them and converting them into first class timber for model making.

Before starting the planking, I drew out a rough planking diagram, which was simply a grid showing each frame and

Below: Lines plan.

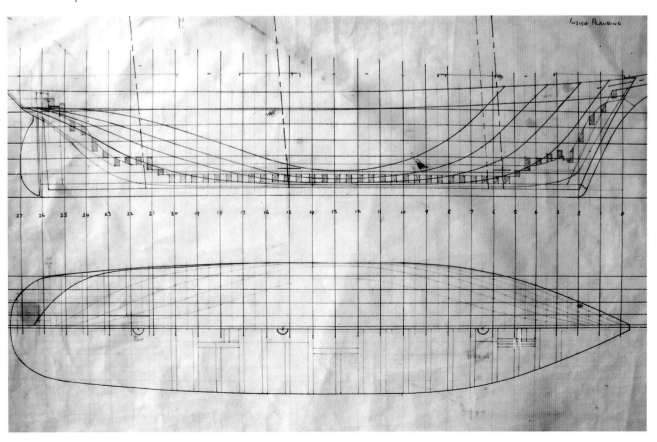

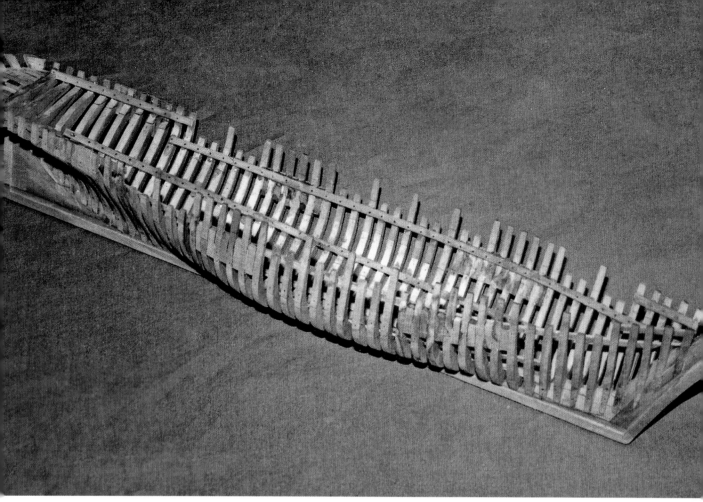

Above: The hull ready for planking.

Below: Hull framing completed

strake of planking as a line. On this grid I could mark in my proposed plank butts to ensure that the planking followed Lloyds' rules for the shift of butts without having to resort to over scale length planks (or to panic when I found the planks on the model getting out of sequence)!

The width of each plank was determined at each frame by the use of proportional dividers. For example, if there were three strakes of planking to fit between the completed planking and the next batten, the proportional dividers were set at position 3 and the distance from the planking to the batten was measured at each frame with the wide end of the dividers and set on the plank with the narrow end. By measuring in this way each plank was the correct width along its entire length and any minor errors in marking or cutting a plank were taken up in the next strake of planking. This ensured that the fair run of planking was maintained throughout.

Planks were fitted alternately port and starboard to ensure that no undue stresses were set up in the hull during building. After cutting, each plank was bent to the required shape to fit the curve of the hull and test fitted for accuracy before fixing with epoxy. Privet is a very friendly timber to work with and can be gently bent and twisted to quite large curves if a little care is used. It has another advantage of retaining its new

shape once bent. All the hull planks on *Nautilus* were hand bent in this manner except for those around the curve of the counter above the rubbing strake, where a little persuasion by boiling was needed.

After gluing, all planks were dowelled (tree nailed) to each frame with bamboo dowels. Bamboo is a good material to use for this purpose when small sizes are needed, as it has very good longitudinal strength down to remarkably small diameters. I was very fortunate in finding an Asian scroll picture at a garage sale that was made from fine

Above: The main deck beams.

Below: Main deck with planking underway

bamboo strands of exactly the right diameter. I now have a lifetime supply.

On completion of the planking up to deck level, the entire hull was given a thorough sanding and several coats of flat polyurethane varnish to protect it before proceeding further.

With the hull planking complete, it was time to begin framing up the deck; but before that was started, I made a very careful review of the model to make absolutely certain that everything was complete inside the hull. This was largely to ensure my continuing peace of mind – when the last deck plank is being fitted is not the time to remember an essential part that needs to be fitted to the inside of the keel.

Once certain that all was correct internally, the framing of the main deck could commence – starting with the positioning of the beams nearest to the fore and mainmasts, as the correct positioning of the masts at deck level was absolutely essential to the final appearance of the model. I fitted simplified mast partners consisting of a block of timber drilled to be a very loose fit, on and for each mast, allowing for final fine adjustment of mast rake and thwartships alignment after the masts were stepped. The partners were housed into their adjacent beams and glued and dowelled in place.

The next beams to be fitted were those framing the hatches; with these in place and with the hatch carlings housed in, the remaining beams were fitted, with the main deck finishing under the break of the poop.

DECK PLANKING

The deck planking of the original ship was of Huon Pine – a very beautiful Tasmanian timber that is now extremely rare (it was almost cut out in the early days of the colony and is now a protected species). A friend had given me a small piece of this timber some years ago and it had been carefully hoarded in the timber box until now. What better use for it than to deck the model in the same timber as the original ship?

The pine was milled and sanded into 1mm thick strips and planking commenced with the laying of a wide margin plank around the edge of the deck – wide enough for it to show inside the covering board. As this margin had to curve around the external shape of the hull and also be housed

Above: Main and poop deck houses.

around the bulwark stanchions, cardboard templates were first made by trial and error fitting for each length of margin plank. Once the margin was complete the deck planking proper was commenced from the centreline working outwards to the margin plank, ensuring that the pattern of plank butts conformed to Lloyds' rules for planking. The planking was dowelled to the beams with bamboo dowels in the same way as the hull planking.

Below: Bow and stem detail.

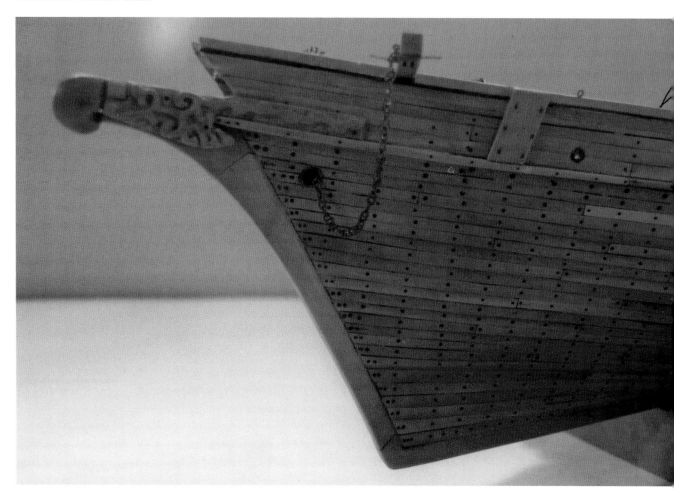

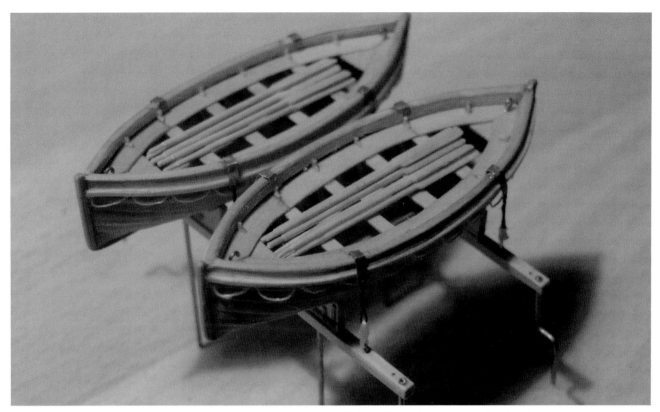

Above: The ship's boats.

Below: Showing the well-detailed fore deck.

Above: The ship's pumps and other deck details

Where the planking met the margin plank at an angle, the planks were joggled into the margin. This was done by shaping the ends of the planks and then cutting out the margin to fit them – a slightly hair-raising process as a slip when cutting the margin plank would mean major problems. Thankfully all went well.

With the main deck planking completed, a covering board (shaped using the same cardboard templates as were used for the margin plank) was laid around the edge of the deck. This covering board was then veneered with a dark timber (unknown species – it was just some dark veneer from the scrap box) to give a contrast to the planking and provide a visual border to the deck.

As on the model, so with my description! I almost forgot the hawse pipes. I was about to start on the forecastle decking of the model when I suddenly remembered that there were as yet no hawse pipes. Thank goodness I remembered in time; it was a timely reminder of the need to always check and to think ahead before starting the next job.

The positions of the hawse pipes were marked on both the deck and the side of the hull and holes drilled from each end to ensure that the openings were in the right place. When drilled, lengths of brass tube were inserted port and starboard and cleaned off neatly with the hull and deck.

With the main deck (and the hawse pipes) completed, the low forecastle and poop deck framing was completed in the same way as the main deck, but the planking was deferred until after the bulwark planking had been completed.

BULWARKS

The bulwarks were now planked using the same shift of butts as the remainder of the hull. This was a straightforward job except for the section around the counter, where the planks had to be steamed to get the required bend. As the planks required at this scale were small, my method of 'steaming' was simply to boil them in a pan on the kitchen stove for a few minutes.

The forward bulkhead of the poop was made from aircraft ply with panelling from thin strips of veneer. Once this

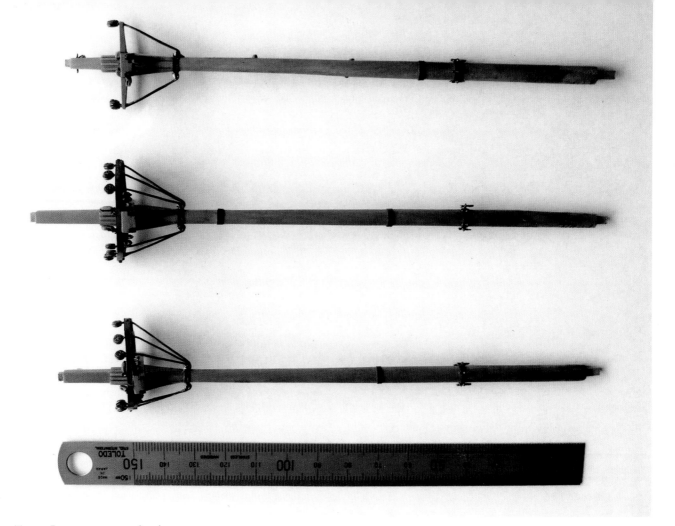

Above: Lower masts completed.

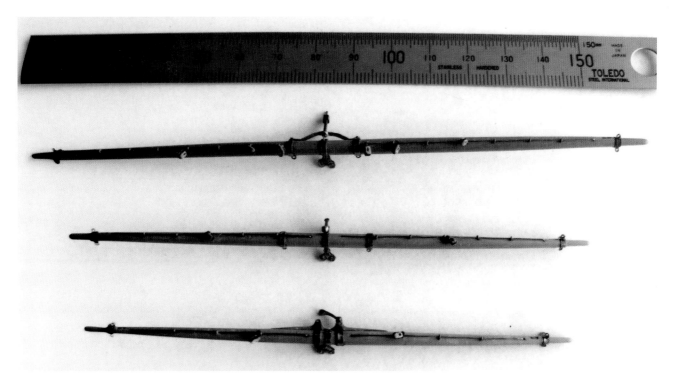

Above: Typical examples of finished yards.

was in place the planking of the forecastle and poop was laid.

The main bulwark capping was at the height of the forecastle and poop, it forms the covering boards on those decks, flowing in a continuous line around the hull. A template for the shape of this rail was made by laying a piece of thin card on top of the bulwarks and drawing around it. The pin rails for the fore and mainmasts were incorporated in this rail as one piece to provide maximum strength. The topgallant rail was made from a narrow piece of pine which was easily bent to the curve of the hull, except around the counter, where it required steaming. There was a dark capping strip fixed to the top of this topgallant rail from the break of the poop forward; the top of the capping being at the same height as the top of the poop rail.

All that now remained to be done on the outside of the hull were the rudder and carvings.

RUDDER

The rudder was made up from planks of pine glued and dowelled together and then cut to the shape of the rudder. The pintles and gudgeons were made up from copper shim and pinned to the rudder and hull with fine copper wire.

Below: The spars laid out for comparison, as mentioned in the text.

CARVINGS

The hull carvings were simple relief work carried out on thin pieces of privet. The individual pieces were cut to fit their locations at bow and stern, and the designs were then drawn on freehand (with much rubbing out and re-drawing involved). The designs were rough cut with small dental burrs in a flexible drive shaft, the finishing done by hand with scalpel blades and a very fine rifler file. The same process was used for carving the name and port of registry on the stern. These carved panels were bent to shape by hand pressure alone and dowelled into position on the hull.

The figurehead was a simple representation of a nautilus shell. This was carved from apple wood.

DECK FITTINGS

Now it was time to turn to the deck fittings and fixtures.

The hatches were the first to be made. The coamings were of mulga, a very hard and dark Australian timber, and the hatch boards of apple. These timbers were chosen for their colour to give some visual contrast on the model. The coamings were simple boxes with half lap corner joints and were a snug fit in the deck openings. On all fittings such as

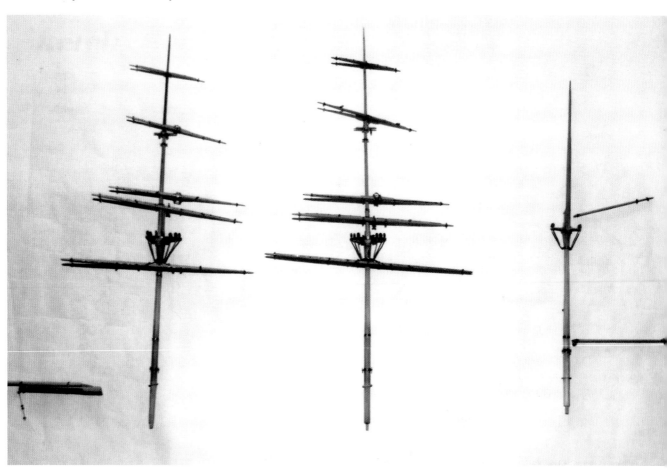

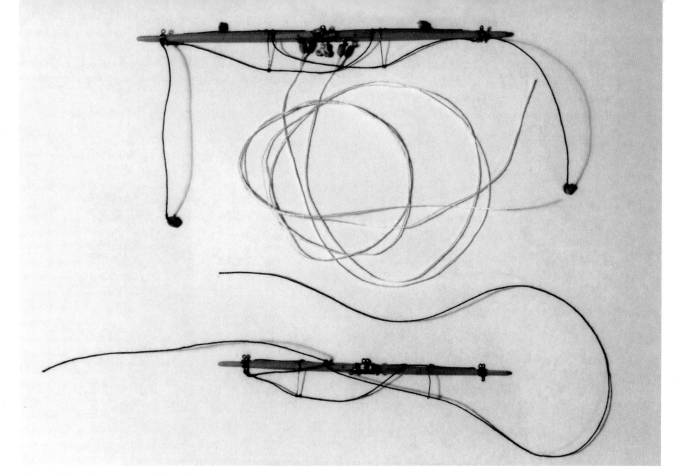

Above: Yards being prepared for rigging.

this requiring square corner joints, I used an engineer's steel square as a jig to hold each corner square while the glue set. There was a shelf set below the top of the coaming to hold the hatch boards, which were made individually with dished holes in the corners to represent the hand holds. [Note: the distance of the top of this shelf below the top of the coaming would be equal to the thickness of the timber used for the hatch boards. Editor] Cleats, to take the battens, and wooden wedges, used to secure the tarpaulins that covered the hatches, were made from copper shim and fitted at intervals of a few feet along the outside of the coamings.

The windlass was not as complicated to make as it looked. The pawl-bitt and the windlass framing of carrick-bitts, knees and strongback were made up from mulga, making sure that the tails of the knees were low enough to fit comfortably under the after beam of the forecastle. A length of pine long enough to make the barrels and warping drums was cut down by hand to a round section and two lengths for the barrels cut off. Three toothed cogs from old clocks and some small washers were found in the scrap box. These were threaded on to a length of copper wire as it was pushed through the hole previously cut in one side of the windlass frame in the following order: barrel, washer, thin cog, washer, thick cog, washer, thin cog, washer, barrel. Finally the wire was pushed through the hole in the other side of the windlass frame and the ends cut off leaving sufficient on which to fix

the warping drums. These warping drums were made by filing a concave shape into the length of barrel timber with a round file and dishing in the ends of the drums with the tip of a drill of the correct size. The drums were then glued to the ends of the wire previously left for them.

The pawl bitt was fitted into the recess left for it in the after end of the forecastle, carefully checked for vertical alignment, and glued into place. The windlass was then positioned hard against it and fixed in position, with the toothed cogs in the centre of the barrel in line with the pawl bitt. The cross-head was built up from scrap copper, soldered together and fixed to the top of the pawl bitt with epoxy. The purchase rods, made up from brass wire, were glued to the back of the purchase rim cogs to keep them in place and the pawl, also from scrap copper, was glued to the after face of the pawl bitt.

DECKHOUSES

The deckhouses were simple internally framed boxes of aircraft ply with thin strips of dark veneer. The veneer was glued and dowelled in place. The door handles were made from pieces of brass wire and the ports from appropriate diameter lengths of brass tubing inserted into the bulkheads and having a film of epoxy spread across them to represent glass. The tops of the deckhouses were planked with Huon

Above: Lower masts and bowsprit rigged.

pine to match the decks; care was taken to camber the tops to the same curve as the deck camber.

The stovepipe on the forward deckhouse was a length of brass tube with a shaped cap from copper shim. The ship's wheel, which protrudes from the poop deckhouse, was laminated from wood shavings around a piece of scrap tubing of the correct diameter, and was built very wide to allow the holes for the spokes to be drilled through. The spokes were cut from privet wood and shaped by hand to their round section and the decorative 'turning' done with small files. The hub of the wheel was made of a small brass washer and a large headed entomological pin. Once the wheel was structurally complete the rim was sanded down to its correct width.

The crew's head on the starboard side of the main deck forward was slightly more complex than the other deckhouses as it had to be made to fit the curve of the deck and also to fit snugly over the covering board and around the main rail. The sides were cut by trial and error and any minor inconsistencies covered by the veneer panelling. The roof was of Huon pine, the individual boards being shaped to fit the double curve of the roof.

The fife rails were constructed from small pieces of pine and privet. Again, the decorative turnings on the posts were cut with small files. The belaying pins were made by filing copper wire to the correct shape. This was not as big a job as it sounds. Once the dimensions had been fixed and a procedure worked out, it was a simple job to file them to the correct shape while holding them in a pin vice with the correct length exposed to work on.

The pump wheels were made in the same way as the steering wheel – by laminating wood shavings around a tube of the right diameter. When the laminating glue had thoroughly hardened, the holes for the spokes were cut and the

Above: Standing rigging completed.

wheels filed and sanded to a round section. The spokes were bent around a former to give them the characteristic 'S' shape and the wheels were then glued together, again using some very small brass and copper washers for the hubs. The remaining parts of the pumps were made up from brass wire and brass tubing.

The poop rail was next but, before anything else was done, a cardboard template of the exact shape of the poop was made and then a second one was made as a precautionary measure in case anything happened to the first one (there would be no chance of making another once construction had begun). The wooden rail stanchions were made from small sections of pine with the decorative turnings cut with small files. Locating pins of fine copper wire were fitted in each end of each stanchion. The rail capping was made from dark coloured veneer cut into sections so that the grain roughly followed the curve of the counter. As a laminate of

veneer would make the capping too thick, fine paper was glued to the back of the veneer to give it a little additional strength as I wanted to complete the capping in one piece. The shape was marked out from the card template and the shape cut with a scalpel and sanded using (very) light pressure from a sanding board. The capping was then laid on the base rail, which was already fixed, and holes drilled in both to accept the stanchion pins. The stanchions and capping rail were then gently assembled and glued.

The last major fittings were the lifeboats and their skids. The two paintings of the *Nautilus* show the boats stowed upside-down on the skids. I decided to stow them right side up. This was partly because I think a model looks better if the details of the boats can be seen and partly because I wanted to see if I could do the job. The skids were a straightforward build of cambered wooden skids with brass wire stanchions. The boat chocks were each made from one piece of pine and scored to look like separate pieces, and with copper wire and shim hinges added. The shape of the top of the chocks could not be finalised until the boats were completed to ensure a good fit.

The boats were built upside down on a wooden former which was much deeper than the depth of the boats. A piece of scrap wood was carved to the shape of the inside of the boats and the line of the boat's gunwale marked around the edge. Small sections of privet were soaked and then bent around the former at 1/16in intervals to form the timbers or frames, and these were glued to the former only above the line of the gunwale. The keel, stem and stern posts were glued to the frames and the boats were then planked with 0.5mm privet planks. Each plank was individually shaped to fit. This was especially important with clinker planking

where the run of the planks was such a noticeable feature of the boat. With the planking completed, the shell was cut from the mould and cleaned up.

Floor boards, thwarts and side benches were made from the same 0.5mm privet and the oars carved from pine. Only six oars were included in each boat as they looked too crowded otherwise. Grab lines were fixed around each boat under the rubbing strake. With the boats completed, the chocks were finished to shape and fixed to the skids; then the boats were glued to the chocks and tied down with gripes over the gunwale.

The anchors were cut and filed from solid brass plate of the correct thickness and the flukes were made separately and pinned and soldered to the ends of the arms. The metal stocks and shackles were from hard brass wire. The anchor

Below: Foremast yards being rigged.

Above: Jig for deadeyes in use.

the right diameter and taper. The shim was rolled around this to form the body of the buckets. The handles were made from bent up pieces of copper wire. As the bottoms of the buckets would not be seen when they were in the racks they were left off.

No lifebuoys were visible in the paintings but, as the ship must have carried them, two were made to hang in brackets on the outboard side of the poop rail right aft. This seems a precarious position for lifebuoys to be stowed but many photographs of colonial sailing ships show lifebuoys carried in just this position. They were made from privet which was quartered and joined into a square so that the grain was running around the circle of the buoy and then carved to shape. The bands are of copper shim with the lifelines worked under them. In order to make detail like this look lifelike, attention should be paid to the way that ropes hang naturally. The upper sections of lifeline hang down over the lifebuoys as can be seen on the full-size articles.

The steering wheel gratings were not very big at this scale, 8mm x 10mm in the case of *Nautilus*. They were made up from small sections of privet with the longitudinal pieces slotted for the half depth cross members as in full-size practice. This can be done at this scale by cutting the pieces to be slotted much longer than required and gluing them down stacked together with spacers between to a piece of scrap wood, ensuring that the glue was outside the proposed line of the completed grating. The slots can then be cut into all pieces at once with a scalpel or very fine escapement file. Once this has been done the cross members can be glued into the slots, the completed assembly cut from the scrap backing, border pieces fixed and the whole assembly sanded smooth.

The skylight and companion for the poop were both made on the simple box principle from aircraft ply with veneer panelling. The roof and sliding top on the companion were single pieces of Huon pine. The lights in the skylight were from Perspex, lightly sanded on the inside to make them obscure. A piece of black paper was also glued across the bottom of the skylight to give it an appearance of depth.

The poop ladders were made from privet without the use of a jig as they are only two treads long and easily held by hand. The fairleads at the after end of the poop were filed up from scrap brass after the inside curve of the leads had been drilled out to size.

The catheads were made from pine and were shaped to fit over the inside of the bulwarks on the forecastle with a shaped chock under them to the deck. The sheaves were dummies. They were drilled out at each end and then filed to shape with a round escapement file.

The bollards fore and aft were from small copper rivets with the heads filed down to the correct size. The bases of the bollards were from thin sections of privet with holes

cables were made up of stud link chain made by bending copper wire in the end on a small pair of long nose pliers which had been filed to the correct shape of the links. Prior to bending each link to shape, the piece of wire held in the jaws of the pliers was filed off to the width of the jaws and became the stud in the link. Quite a lot of chain was required due to the spurling pipes being amidships, but the trick with such jobs is to put a favourite CD on the player and enjoy the music while the length of chain grows.

The fire buckets at the break of the poop were made up from copper shim. I found an old scriber which had exactly

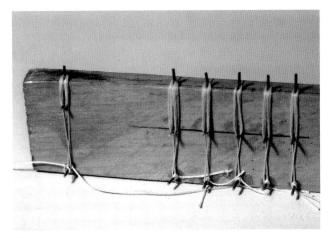

Above: Jig for making rope coils.

Above: Fore cabin fitted.

drilled out to the correct size to accept the rivets.

All wooden parts were finished with matt polyurethane varnish. The metal parts were left natural and over time will weather to a dull, almost black, colour.

Many of the larger deck fittings and fixtures were not fitted at this stage, as their presence would interfere with the rigging process. They were therefore put aside in lidded boxes to keep them dust free until required.

MASTS AND RIGGING

It was now time to start the masting and rigging process, which commenced with making all masts and spars. If all the spars are completed before any are fitted to the model, they can be compared for size relative to each other. This is especially important at smaller scales where the relative size of parts is much more easily noticed.

The dimensions of the masts, bowsprit, jibboom, spanker boom and gaff were scaled up directly from the photographs of the Tasmanian and Melbourne paintings in my possession. I found that both sources agreed almost exactly. As both paintings are in the 'ship portrait' genre they were painted exactly beam on, so taking measurements of these spars was easy. The Tasmanian painting shows the ship from the lee side and the Melbourne painting from the weather side, so that gave additional details of the rigging.

The lengths of the yards could not be taken directly from the paintings as the yards are not shown square to the plane of the painting. Instead they were taken from tables of spar sizes for the tonnage of the ship. The mast lengths compared well in the tables to the sizes measured from the paintings, so the table sizes were used for the yards.

BOWSPRIT, JIBBOOM AND MASTS

The spars were made of pine from the same table top that was used for building the frames but in this case the timber was split along the grain before sawing roughly to size to ensure that the grain would run straight along each spar and thus reduce any chance of later warping. This was felt necessary as some of the spars are less than 2mm in diameter.

All spars were rounded by hand, which is not as difficult as it sounds. A piece of timber is finished square to the largest cross section dimension of the spar and the taper then planed or filed in as needed. Once the taper is complete the square section is reduced to eight sided and then the remaining corners rounded off to complete the round section spar.

The bowsprit and jibboom were tackled first. A rough blank of the bowsprit had been made earlier when constructing the forecastle and this was now finished correctly to size; square at the inboard end and fully rounded from just forward of the stem. The jibboom is a simple round spar, parallel sided for the length of the bowsprit and then tapering towards the outboard end. The dummy internal sheaves on the jibboom for the head stays were drilled through at each end and filed to shape with a round escapement file before any of the bands were fitted. When the jibboom was completed a heel chock of appropriate diameter was made and glued and dowelled to the bowsprit. It is essential that this chock is very firmly fixed as there is quite a bit of pressure exerted by the head stays trying to pull the jibboom inboard.

The bands for both bowsprit and jibboom were made up from copper shim cut wider than required to make fitting the eyes easier and bent around the spar at the band location to give the correct size. Eyes were soldered in at the appropriate places, the band soldered along its joint and the band then cut to the correct width by holding it down on a piece of emery paper with a finger and rubbing until the required size had been reached. The double bands that locate the jibboom were solidly pinned down on a soldering block and the band joints and the two sections of the bands were soldered together at one pass. The martingale brackets were made over-large for ease of fitting, soldered to the martingale and then filed down to their correct size.

The three lower masts are basically the same as each other in construction and differ only in size and in detail of the bands fitted. The mizzen crosstrees are really the same as the fore and main tops, but without the decking or the after crosstree. The main point of caution in making the lower masts is to be absolutely sure that the square on the heel tenon exactly matches the square at the doubling; otherwise the mast will be twisted to one side when the heel tenon is fitted into the mast step.

Each mast blank was measured and marked for length from step to deck, deck to hounds and length of doubling. The blanks were planed to the correct taper for their length above the deck and then shaped round from the hounds down. The heel tenons were cut to fit the mast steps previously fitted in the hull.

The rabbets in the side of the mast for the heels of the cheeks were the next job. When cutting these tenons it must be remembered that the tops and crosstrees lie parallel to the waterline and not at right angles to the mast, so care must be taken to get the angle of the cheek tenons correct.

Once the cheek tenons were cut all the mast bands below the cheeks were fitted, as obviously it would be impossible to fit them over the mast head after the cheeks and tops were fitted. The bands for the mast and also those for the yards

were made from copper shim in the same way as the bowsprit bands. The locations of the bands were easily seen from the paintings. The cheeks were cut from thin pieces of privet and fitted in their rabbets at the correct angle before gluing and dowelling in place. Once the glue had set, the lower ends of the cheeks were faired into the masts using small files.

TOPS FRAMING

The framing of the tops was set out and cut so that they fitted neatly over the lower mast and with the openings for the top-masts of a size for the heels to slide in as a neat fit. The decking of the tops was cut from thin plywood, shaped to go around the openings in the tops, and then dummy planking was scored into it. The decking was then glued and dowelled to the crosstrees, ensuring that each dummy plank was dowelled. The rims were made from copper shim and were glued to the edges of the tops and pinned to the after crosstrees to ensure that they were secure. Once the decking of the tops was fitted the ends of the crosstrees were drilled for the wire futtock shrouds. The completed tops were then fitted on to the cheeks and glued and dowelled in place.

The wires for the futtock shrouds were wrapped tightly around the deadeyes and the ends soldered. Using soft solder

Below: Ship's boats installed.

I was able to get enough heat to the joint to solder without damaging the deadeyes. The futtock shrouds were then fed down through the holes in the crosstrees and soldered to the lugs on the futtock bands. All necessary blocks and eyes were also fitted at this time while the masts were easy to handle.

TOPMASTS AND TOPGALLANT MASTS

The topmasts and topgallant/royal masts were made in the same manner as the lower masts, care being taken to get a good fit of the mast heels in the holes between the crosstrees and trestletrees of the mast below. The fids were made from brass wire and permanently fitted to the mast heels so that the masts would drop into their correct positions as they were rigged. Great care had to be taken with the royal poles, which

Below: Mizzen ready to be rigged.

are less than 1mm in diameter. The mast caps were made up from copper shim and soldered, ensuring that the gap between the two openings was the correct distance for the masts to lie parallel to each other.

BLOCKS AND BELAYING PINS

This might be a good time to digress and explain how the blocks and belaying pins were made as the first of them were required at this time.

The deadeyes were the only item not scratch built for the model. For some strange reason I have an aversion to making deadeyes (an analyst would no doubt have a field day with this!), so I purchased a good supply of excellent 3mm deadeyes from Modeller's Shipyard at Blaxland, near Sydney.

Above: Rigging completed.

The blocks were made from English box salvaged from old carpenter's folding rulers. The wood was cut down to strips of the correct width and depth and the length of the blocks marked out along the strip. Holes were drilled for the dummy sheaves, the sheaves being shaped with a round escapement file and the blocks shaped on the strip with small files before parting off. This sounds like a tedious process, but it is amazing how many blocks can be made in an evening while listening to some favourite music.

The belaying pins were made from copper wire of a suitable diameter. Previously I have made pins of wood at this scale, but the shafts are generally too small to perform adequately when any sort of strain is put on them; hence the copper wire. The pins were made by hand by holding a length of wire in a pin vice with the length of the head protruding and the shape of the head formed by filing. The pin was then reversed and the shaft filed down to the correct diameter. About 150 belaying pins were made, which gave me some spares to replace those dropped or otherwise lost. Again, this was a job for a quiet evening with music.

YARDS

The yards were a fairly straightforward, if delicate, job requiring a straight taper from the shoulders towards each end. The most delicate operation was cutting the shoulder for the yard arm bands, as the slightest extra pressure on the knife saw the yard arm rolling across the work table and another yard in the scrap bin. The lower yard trusses and the lower topsail cranes were soldered up from pieces of copper and brass from the scrap box, the trusses being made non-working and the cranes fixed so they could not swivel at the masts in order to make the final positioning of the yards easier. I had found on an earlier model, at this scale, that fully operational trusses and cranes made correct centring of the yards on the masts almost impossible as the slightest extra pressure on either side would swivel the yard.

The parrel battens for the upper yards were made oversize and cut down to their correct profile once glued and dowelled to the after side of the yards. The parrel gates were made with operating hinges. This makes life easier when rigging commences, as the yards can be left off until required, rather than having to be sent aloft already on the mast in the case of non-opening gates. The hinges are quite

Above: The finished model.

easily made by rolling the ends of the copper shim of the gate around a drill of suitable size (No.75 in this case) before bending the gate to the correct curve. As there is no weight on these hinges in the completed model, I did not solder the hinge joints on any of the yards except the upper topsails, but it would be a good idea to solder them all at larger scales.

The jackstays were made by threading very fine copper wire through a number of stanchions made from the same wire, which were then inserted into holes drilled along the forward quarters of the yards. The stanchions were pushed right in until the ring holding the jackstay was lying against the yard itself. By making the jackstays in this way they do not look over scale, but are still there and provide fixing points for various bits of rigging.

The only other unusual fitting on the yards are the clover-leaf blocks through which the sheets are led. These were made from copper shim, the rough shape of both sides of the block being scribed by hand and the block rough cut as one piece. The two sides of the block were then bent up to make the shell of the block and the 'lobes' drilled for the sheaves, which were simple dummies made from short lengths of wire. With the 'sheaves' securely glued in place,

the shell of the block was filed to its final 'cloverleaf' shape and the blocks fitted under the yards. The spanker boom and gaff were made as simple tapered spars with their various bands and with goosenecks at the heels made from scrap copper.

RIGGING

Before any rigging was commenced I spent some time working through the processes involved and the order of work in my mind. I think that this step is absolutely essential on a model with complex rigging, as some processes that are easily manageable at full size become impossible at model scales if not carried out in the correct order. One example on the *Nautilus* is the main royal stay. The lanyard eyebolt for this stay is impossible to reach once the fore topmast rigging is in place, so the lanyard has to be rigged prior to any fore topmast rigging.

The first items that needed to be fitted were the chain plates. These were made from copper wire by flattening the wire for a length to make the strap and then wrapping the round (i.e. the unflattened) length of the wire around the

Above: Starboard bow of finished model.

deadeye and back to the end of the flattened strap, to which it is then soldered. Holes were drilled through the strap to allow copper pins to be inserted into the hull when the straps were fitted to ensure that there was sufficient strength in the straps to resist the upward pull of the shrouds and stays. The chainplates were aligned with the shrouds and stays with the help of a dummy mast as they were fitted.

Once the chainplates were fitted, a start was made on the rigging. The first step was to lay out all the spars in their proper relationship to ensure that their relative sizes matched. When this had been done, the bowsprit and jibboom were stepped and partially rigged. The main concern at this stage was to tie down the bowsprit and jibboom tightly so that they could resist the upward pull of the fore stays. The jibboom guys were not rigged at this stage as I wanted to leave off the whisker booms for as long as possible since they tend to catch in everything that comes near them.

The mainmast had to be stepped first, as the location of the eyebolts for the main stay close to the foot of the foremast made it impossible for this stay to be set up after the foremast was stepped. All the lower masts were a loose fit at the deck

partners so that the rake could be adjusted accurately. The mainmast was located in its step and wedged at deck level with tiny scraps of wood. When satisfied with the rake, the mast was glued in position and the dummy mast coat slid down the mast and glued over the wedges. The main stay was set up with seizings and the shrouds made ready for rigging – two pairs and a swifter on each side, starting with the forward pair on the starboard side and working alternately side to side until all were set up. Even spacing of the upper deadeyes was achieved by use of a jig that hooked into the holes in the deadeyes and allowed the shroud to be drawn up tight and seized with the deadeye held firmly in place. With all the upper deadeyes seized to the shrouds, the lanyards were set up and lashed above the deadeyes. The ends of the lanyards were left long to allow for final adjustment after all the masts were set up. The other two lower masts were set up in exactly the same way.

The remainder of the masts were rigged in much the same way as the lower masts, except that the fore and main topgallant shrouds were set up with lanyards under the crosstrees rather than with deadeyes. Care needs to be taken on the upper masts to ensure that the rigging goes over the masthead in the correct order since, generally speaking, once above the topmasts the shrouds and backstays are rigged before the forestays. The grommets for the standing lifts must go over the masts before any other rigging.

With the masts rigged the whisker booms could be fitted and the jibboom guys to support and stabilise the head rigging laterally rigged, with the head rigging finished off by rigging footropes. With all the standing rigging now fitted, final minor adjustments were made to the tension of the shroud lanyards and they were then firmly secured and trimmed.

When all this was in place the staysail halliards and downhauls for all masts were rigged, being careful to leave the joining shackles at the foot of each stay where they would naturally be when the sails were unrigged.

The yards were tackled next. Each yard, before being sent aloft, was rigged as fully as possible, including footropes, clew lines, buntlines, sheets and brace pennants. Originally it was intended to rig each mast yard for yard, but by the time the fore yard was rigged it was evident that it would be easier to rig the foremast fully (except for the fore sheets and braces) and then move on to the mainmast. The only exception to this was that it was necessary to rig the main yard before the remainder of the fore yards so that I had space to get in to set up the chain sling on that yard.

When the fore yard had been fixed to the mast by its truss, the running lifts were set up and then the clew lines and tacks, together with pennants for the sheets. These lines stabilised the yard in its position on the mast. The chain sling was then set up and secured to the upper lug of the yard with very fine wire. The buntlines were the last to be rigged. Great care had to be taken in securing the various elements of rigging as it was very easy to pull the yard out of square, or to put too much strain on the yard or truss by over tightening a line.

The upper yards were then rigged in turn, with the halliards of the hoisting yards being loosely gigged until the sheets for that yard were rigged and secured to hold down the yards, after which the halliards were tightened up and secured.

When all rigging for any particular pin rail had been finally secured to the pins, dummy coils of rope were glued over the heads of the pins, being careful to ensure that no false ends were showing below the coil. The coils were made on a simple jig having removable wire pins set at the correct distance to make coils of the right length. When the coils were wound on the jig they were coated with dilute PVA glue (the jig had been waxed first) and left to set. Once the glue was dry the removable pins could be pulled out and the coils removed.

With the yards on the foremast rigged it was time to get on with the ratlines. I know it is accepted wisdom to rig the ratlines before the yards but, on my last model, I had considerable trouble getting to the belaying pins around the ratlines (there is not much space at 1:96 scale) so thought this time I would give myself space to reach things between the shrouds while rigging. I must say that having now done it both ways I am not sure which is the better. Rigging ratlines last certainly gives much more freedom to get at the belaying pins but, on the other hand, the yards do tend to get in the way when trying to install the ratlines.

The sheer poles were made from copper wire and seized to the shrouds just above the upper deadeyes. Initially, the sheer poles were cut much longer than required, then cut to length after being rigged. The ratlines were stitched through the outer shrouds and clove hitched to the inner shrouds. The spacing between each ratline was measured by a length of wood of the correct thickness for the spacing, which was laid along the top of each ratline as the work progressed.

With the foremast completed, the two upper pair of braces (those leading to the deck via the mainmast) were rigged and then the work of rigging yards and ratlines was repeated on the mainmast to complete all of the square yards. Once these were done the main deckhouse was secured in place abaft the foremast and the lower foremast braces together with the fore sheets were rigged. The boats, complete on their skids, were then worked into position between (and amongst) the main rigging and secured in place.

The final jobs were to rig the mizzenmast and fit the deck structures on the poop. The skylight and companionway were glued in place on the deck. As the after deckhouse would interfere with rigging the spanker sheets it was left off until the spanker had been rigged. I then set it in place and glued the two gratings to the deck against the forward end of the house, which gave me the correct position for this deckhouse when fitting it later.

The spanker boom and gaff were very simple to rig. It was just a case of fitting them into their goosenecks on the mast and rigging span, lift, vangs and sheets, together with the outhauls and inhauls for the sail.

When these were rigged the various dummy rope coils were fitted and the after deckhouse slipped into place and was glued against the previously fixed gratings. All that remained to do now was to fit the bumpkins for the remaining main braces and rig the braces.

With the spanker rigging seemingly taking no time at all to complete, the whole project finished with a rush. Several years of effort were over and the completed model could be returned to its display stand and inserted in its permanent display case.

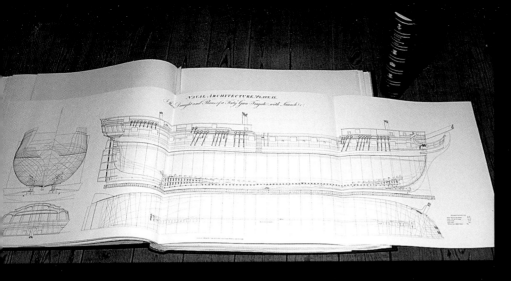

USS *Gearing* DD710

SECOND WORLD WAR DESTROYER

by John R. Haynes

For some reason the US Navy's Second World War *Gearing* class of destroyer has been neglected by modellers and kit makers alike in favour of the smaller *Fletcher* class. The *Fletcher* class hull was slightly widened and used as the *Sumner* class, which in turn was lengthened to develop the *Gearing* class.

As a modeller, and not a naval historian, I will concentrate on the class leader USS *Gearing* DD710 build, leaving the history of their general development for interested readers to investigate.

The armament carried by USS *Gearing* comprised of 6 x 5in/38 guns in twin turrets, 3 x Quad 40mm mounts, 10 x twin 20mm Oerlikons with Mk.14 gunsights, 2 x twin 40mm mounts and 1 x 21in quintuple torpedo tube mounting. The mainmast aerial was SC radar with a Mk.37 main armament director atop the bridge with a Mk.12 and 22 radar antenna. 5 x Mk.51 directors controlled the 40mm guns; two depth-charge rails with two extra storage rails were mounted at the

stern with three depth-charge storage racks fitted each side with the associated K guns.

At 390.5ft long overall, the model hull at my usual scale of $\frac{1}{8}$in = 1ft (1:96) translated to 48.8in long overall, with a beam of 41.08ft or 5.13in. Some years ago, I built a 1960s FRAM 1 (Fleet Rehabilitation And Modernisation) version for a US client, so I had already developed a grp hull that I could use (with a slight modification of the hull bottom radar housing that needed to be smaller).

Since building the FRAM version from plans provided by The Floating Drydock, USA, they now supply an e-book reference for DD710 (DD692PB-CD) that gives just about everything and more a model builder could desire. No excuse now for not putting on everything that should be there. Individual drawings/photographs can be printed off and used when needed. Also of use is Sumrall's book, *Sumner-Gearing Class Destroyers* and Friedman's *US Destroyers*.

On one of my visits to the United States, Mike Wall, of

Below: USS *Gearing*: the finished model.

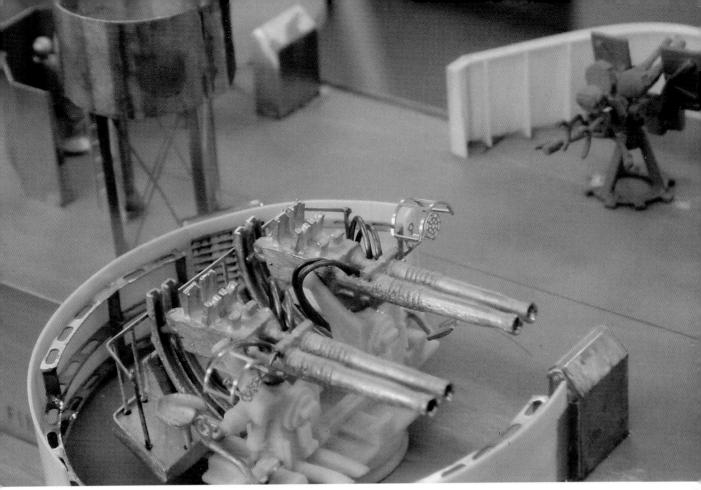

Above: Midships 40mm quad Bofors mounting with photo-etched Mk.51 director tub.

the American Marine Model Gallery, took me to Battleship Cove in Massachusetts to see the USS *Joseph P. Kennedy* DD850 (a FRAM 1) where I collated a lot of reference photographs of the smaller details.

The *Gearing* build follows my usual method of construction, namely, I build the model as a kit. During the course of construction the model is built up and taken apart continually. This also makes the important task of finish-painting the individual parts much easier.

The hulls that I produce have an inward return built into the sheerline to maintain this line accurately. It is a useful feature that saves a lot of time even though it makes the glass-fibre more expensive.

The hull was mounted on two brass supports with bolts and the nut fixed into the bottom of the open hull. Deck beams were then inserted, cambered, and a $^1/_{16}$in thick ply deck fitted. In the meantime, I am mentally constructing the model so I know where and how to 'break down' the superstructure as I build and re-assemble without leaving any visible signs. This also enables me to pick out all the new photo-etching that will be required, all the new parts to manufacture, rub-downs to initiate, paint to order, etc. Since the photo-etching takes quite a time, this task is done first. Also, I decided to add to the decks the visible anti-slip tread rub-downs that I have not done before. I tend to favour

rub-downs over decals, except on my own carrier-based aircraft in my range of fittings.

On the main deck there is an upstand all round just in from the deck edge forming a spurnwater with intermittent gutters which run over the deck edge. This was formed using litho plate to make an angle and the side fixed to the deck was faired in with Milliput to eliminate the edge.

The 01 level superstructure was outlined on the deck and an eggbox structure in balsa was quickly made. This was lined on the outside with 1mm ply and used litho plate was also added, being taken up above the 01 deck level to form the spurnwater. I started using litho plate some thirty years ago and have written about its use from time to time.

At this time, I needed to look at all my ship fittings now available on my site store and place the items necessary for the model in a separate box. Various new items were constructed and sent to my casters for duplication. At this point, I decide what might sell and put these items in my range.

The bridge 01 level was made similar to the 01 structure but the final litho plate was taken up beyond the 02 to form the open bridge, the deck of which was photo-etched. I always pay a lot of attention to open bridges as they attract most interest.

On the 10 thou. (0.010in) PE sheet, I included a lot of deck items such as various grilles, eyebolts, hoppers for spent

Above: Broadside view of hull after application of sprayed finishing coat.

40mm ammunition, depth-charge rails and storage racks, different types of ladders, Mk.51 director tubs and, most importantly, the hull side screens. The side screens have a rolled top and to achieve this I soldered on to the flat brass half a brass tube, cut down from the round with a slitting disc. A steady hand is required to get a straight line. I tried to curve over some 5 thou. (0.005in) copper sheet but the result was not good enough and too flimsy.

On the main 01 level there were two through-deck openings amidships. These were half-etched to achieve a rim around the square hole that left the surrounding plate at 5 thou. to match the thickness of the litho plate that met it. Other photo-etched items were pulled out of my range of fittings in various thickness of brass, namely the US Navy pattern stanchions, aerials, ladder rungs, and so on.

I always leave some watertight doors open, which give a better look to the model, and to this end I have now developed a small fret with six doors and frames that are available. On this model I used the cast metal ones I already have, and these were fine, but I felt photo-etched ones would be an improvement.

Other new fittings that had to be made were the re-

Below: Model seen from starboard quarter with most fittings loosely in place.

fuelling hoses, oil re-fuelling trunk, ship-to-shore cable reels, floodlamps, the funnel whistle and siren set and the funnels that were also used on the *Sumner* and *Fletcher*.

Some plastic sheet was used where I thought it was suitable but I am not a fan of this material. A sheet of brass can be bent and it will stay bent, whereas plastic needs to be held in place or it will deform. Also, the surface is less robust and any effort to correct faults or scratches will affect the look of the subsequent paint finish.

I tend to spray everything off the model; also any hand-finishing touches can be easily done. After spraying the hull in Measure 22 – navy blue 5N horizontally to the deck edge at its lowest point, and the remainder haze grey 5H, I hand-painted the deck 20B blue. Having the USN purple–blue colour chart makes it very easy to get the colours correct, but I am not a believer that transferring these colours directly on to a model will give the right appearance.

Since the viewer will be seeing the model as would an aircraft, and remembering that weather will quickly fade the dockyard look, I tend to lighten these colours considerably. I do not mean adding white which can change the tone, but looking at the lighter colours on the chart, i.e. for the deck 20B, use Humbrol 144; for hull grey 5H, use in equal quantities 127/144/130. Humbrol users will realise that this is a mixture of satin and matt. I try to do this as it gives a more

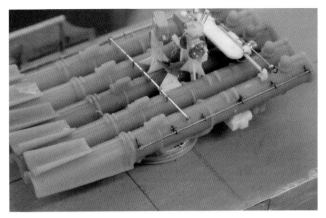

Above: Midships, showing quintuple torpedo tubes mounting.

forgiving finish whilst still matt in appearance; it resists finger marks and tends to take off the dead-flat look.

The reason I hand-paint the decks is that when fixing/gluing items to the painted deck during the assembly stage the slightest scratch or glinting glue-line can be touched in successfully. It will not be a total success to touch in with a paint brush on to a sprayed finish since the paint lies on differently and it could look as if a slightly different colour was used. Always mix up more than enough paint than the job needs and keep the surplus it in an air-tight jar.

On this particular model, before fixing the 01 assembly, I

Below: Starboard side of bridge with pilot house and Mk.51 director, pelorus, 12in signal lamp and voice tube.

Above: General view port side showing bridge.

Below: Close-up of 5in/38 twin D/P gun No.2.

applied the anti-slip treads where indicated on the drawing
and in the photographs, and I think the result is pleasing.
These treads, now in my fittings range, were usually black but
I decided that on a model this is too severe, so I had them
made in a dark blue, which on a lighter-than-20B deck looks,
in my opinion, more realistic.

I find building the model is the easiest part of the work.
The finishing part, spraying and painting, can enhance or
detract from the final result, so care is needed to ensure the
finished model is as good as possible.

At this point I would like to expand on paint finishes,
which is the most important part of the job. The following is
the sequence I used to get the Measure 22 combination. With
the model upside-down, spray the hull red: a mixture of
Humbrol 19 Gloss Brick Red and 70. Turning the model the
right way up and supported on the brass pillars, spray a wide
band of Humbrol 86 Coal Black. Put on Tamiya masking
tape the correct width to delineate the waterline, then spray
to complete the hull red. Put tape over the waterline tape and
newspaper attached down to the baseboard to cover the hull
red. This protects the waterline and hull red, so enabling the
upper hull to be sprayed.

Next spray the 5N Blue, a mixture of Humbrol 104 and
27. To finish, tape off a horizontal line from the sheerline

lowest point and covering the 5N Blue and waterline and hull
red, spray the rest of the hull.

On the open bridge in the relevant photographs is an
array of fittings including the Captain's chair, pelorus,
torpedo directors and the Mk.51 directors for the twin
40mm bofors, which sit to each side of the forward funnel.
On the starboard side are the port and starboard depth-

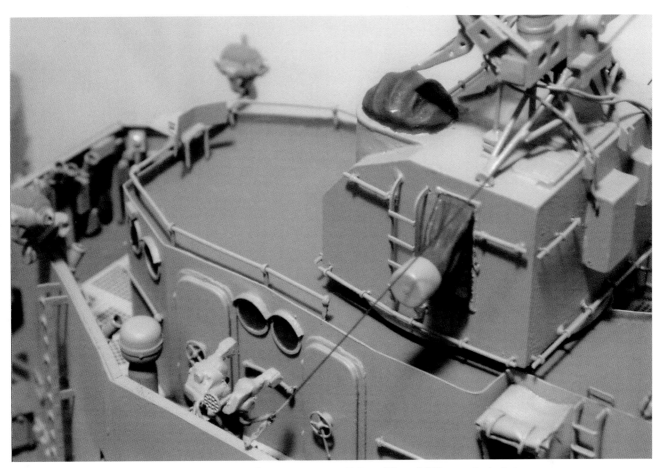

Above: Port view of pilot house showing Director Mk.37.

Below: View of 26ft motorised whaler.

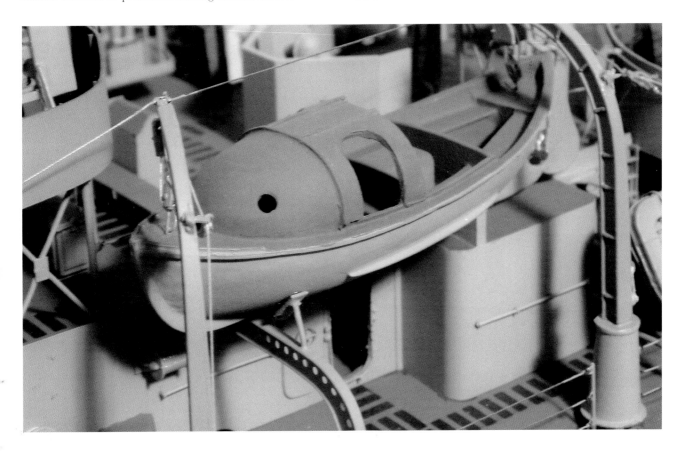

Above: Port view aft showing K guns and depth-charge storage racks with impulse lockers on the adjacent bulwark 01 level.

Above: Rear of aft funnel with platform having twin Oerlikons with Mk.14 sights and a Mk.51 searcher.

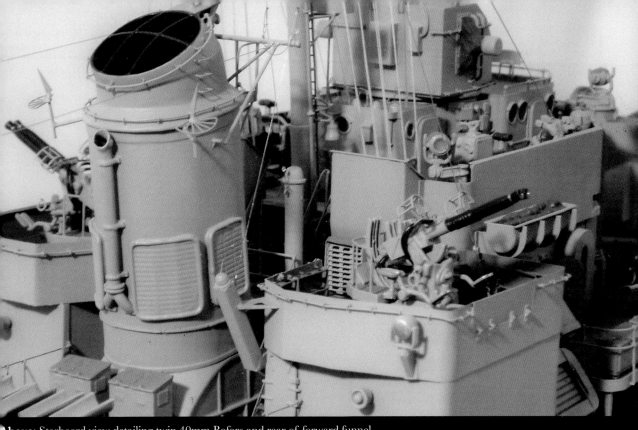

Above: Starboard view of bridge overall.

Above: Top of mainmast showing at the top the SC-4 radar and just below the SG radar. BK antennae are positioned at the ends of the crosstree. TBS is carried at the bottom.

Above: Front view of the rear funnel with a 36in searching forward. Just below the S/L is the 5in/38 D/P practice mount.

charge release handles. Atop the pilot-house is the Mk.37 director with Mk.12 and Mk.22 radars on top.

The mast carried SC-4 radar at the top and, just below it, an SG radar outfit. The mast itself was constructed with a brass tube lower section which slots into a larger brass tube set at the correct angle into the rear bridge structure. Into the lower section was fixed a length of tapered timber to which various pieces of equipment and ladders can be easily attached. The yardarm was drilled out and signal-line eye-bolts fitted before this was fixed to the mast.

During construction it is advisable to allow the mast to be dismantled easily since various items can be fixed at different stages. An example of this is the positioning of rigging eyes only becomes apparent when concentrating on the latter part of the build. Also, the whole assembly can be sprayed away from the model, knowing that the mast can be slotted into the fixed tube previously set at the correct angle (rake).

Amidships, between the funnels, are the 21in quintuple torpedo tube assembly and a 5in/38 twin practice loader. These loaders, and single loader machines, were carried on

all USN ships fitted with the 5in/38 guns, an idea not used on RN ships to my knowledge.

On the after funnel is a platform carrying a 36in search-light operated by two crew members, and adjacent are two 20mm Mk.24 twin Oerlikons. All the Oerlikons on later wartime ships were fitted with Mk.14 lead-computing rela-tive-rate gunsights. Adjacent to this platform is the 26ft motorised whaleboat carried on davits and also sitting on cradles mounted on the 01 level.

Behind the after funnel are the secondary steering posi-tion and a 40mm quadruple bofor set in tubs, port and starboard, as well as a twin Oerlikon. There is also a quadru-ple bofor at the aft end of the 01 level, and these were all controlled by the Mk.51 directors sited in tubs shown raised above the deck.

Each side of the 01 level at this point are three depth-charge storage racks taking six charges and the associated K guns. Stored on the bulkhead immediately behind are the spare arbors and the depth-charge impulse lockers. On the quarterdeck are two depth-charge stern rails and two extension racks carrying additional charges. Close by is a screened tub containing three twin Oerlikons and the ready-use lockers.

The only detail and fittings that are fixed to the individual model parts are the items that would be difficult to attach without adversely affecting the sprayed finish. Looking at the building photographs, it is obvious which parts are pre-fixed. All the guns are spray finished off the job and only fixed on the model at the end. The photo-etched depth-charge items are soldered on fixing pins that are easily located for final fixing.

The last tasks to be done are the rigging of the mast, signal lines, aerials and stanchions. I use a nylon invisible thread for the aerials and crochet cotton in various shades of colour for the rest. This type of cotton is quite sharp and clean to use.

I have developed 10 thou. (0.010in) photo-etched turn-buckles that I twist through 90 degrees in the central section only, which firms-up the item and makes a flat piece more acceptable.

At the end of the job, I unscrew the holding bolts and withdraw them from the hull (also removing the brass pillars that are, in effect, just spacers). Putting the model on one side, I can polish the pillars and spray on lacquer to protect the finish. The timber base of the case is drilled and the model remounted for display.

REFERENCES

The Floating Drydock :- www.floatingdrydock.com

Sumner/Gearing Class plan e-book, Adobe version DD692PB-A1.

Also *DD710 Class plans at 1:96 scale.*

Sumner-Gearing Destroyers by Robert F. Sumrall. ISBN 0-85177- 657-4.

US Destroyers by Norman Friedman. ISBN 0-85368-521-5.

USN Destroyers of WWII by John C. Reilly, Jr. ISBN 0-7137-1026-8.

Below: The finished model.

The *Mary Rose*

AN ARTIST'S VIEW

by Geoff Hunt RSMA

On 26 February 2007 I accepted an invitation from Rear-Admiral John Lippiett, Chief Executive of the Mary Rose Trust, to visit the museum and to view what remained of the ship and surviving artefacts. This turned out to be an intensive tour which lasted over two hours. At the end of that time John asked me if I would agree to paint a sizeable artist's impression of the ship, donating the painting, together with all its copyright interests, to the Trust. For some reason I said yes, not realising quite how many hours (hundreds, as it turned out) I was to devote to this project.

One of the things I explained was that I was very busy, so it would be some time before the *Mary Rose* came to the top of my schedule; but, inevitably, that time eventually came. After one further trip for a closer investigation of the ship's hull, when I was permitted inside the sealed, very wet environment which it occupied, I began work in October 2008. At the same time I was privileged to meet the Trust's principal Maritime Archaeologist, Christopher Dobbs, and their

Below: Preliminary colour sketch, *Mary Rose* at Spithead.

Above: Solid colour approximately indicates surviving piece of *Mary Rose*, ghosted area indicates artist's reconstruction.

Curator of Ordnance, Alexzandra Hildred. A little later I spent a day with Peter Marsden, writer of the Trust's academic volumes *Sealed by Time* and *Mary Rose: Your Noblest Shippe*. All three of these individuals were, of course, profoundly knowledgeable, but they also proved to be very approachable, helpful, and full of enthusiasm for their subject. In all these qualities they were exceeded only by John Lippiett himself, who might well be said to have assumed Admiral Sir George Carew's command, with great energy, after a gap of some 450 years.

The point of the exercise was to produce a new artist's impression, incorporating much information that had been learned since the only officially-endorsed painting, produced not long after the ship's raising in 1982. But, as it happened, my involvement was to coincide with the discovery of one new and crucially important piece of documentary evidence, one that was to change the generally-accepted impression of the ship's appearance which had prevailed for twenty years.

Having re-created the appearance of many historic sailing vessels, mostly belonging to the eighteenth and nineteenth centuries, I was familiar with the exercise of working from ship's plans and descriptions of mast and spar dimensions. But the *Mary Rose* was different; there were no original plans (it is unlikely that any were ever drawn), nor any rigging information for Tudor ships. All we had was the remains of the ship herself, consisting of about 40 per cent of the hull timbers, other remains such as scattered rigging blocks, and a very few contemporary drawings and paintings. The fragment of hull was all very well, but most of it consisted of the underwater hull, with not very much of the topsides. The challenge in producing a painting was that nearly all the things most visible on the ship – the upperworks, the masts and spars, the sails, the colouring – were all missing. Almost everything had to be determined by extrapolation from the surviving piece of hull, from some other fragments such as a small fighting top, by inference from known later practice in shipbuilding and rigging – and from that tiny piece of new documentary evidence which pointed me back to the one contemporary painting of the *Mary Rose* identified by name, that done for Henry VIII by his Ordnance Officer, Anthony Anthony.

By 1546 Anthony had catalogued and illustrated every ship in Henry's fleet, all drawn in the same artistically naive style. The general appearance of the *Mary Rose*, and the other Great Ships that he depicted, seems so exaggerated, so clumsy and top-heavy, so encrusted with guns, that much

Above: *Mary Rose*, portrayed in the Anthony Roll. *(The Pepys Library, Magdalene College, Cambridge)*

modern opinion has discounted these images altogether – especially since the recovery of the ship's hull. For we actually see a slim, apparently fine-lined hull, well-crafted, with relatively few gunports interrupting the smooth curves. Clearly such a hull, runs the reasoning, could never have supported the towering mass of 'castles' and rig evident on the Anthony drawing – and what about all those gunports? Hence received opinion about the *Mary Rose* was that the Anthony drawing was an irrelevance. The ship must have been a low-built craft, like the Elizabethan commands of Drake and Grenville, or like the later frigates, with just one upper deck above the weather deck.

All this changed with just a few words in a letter, found by Dr C. S. Knighton (co-editor of *The Anthony Roll* and co-writer of *Letters from the Mary Rose*) within the archives of Hatfield House in late December 2007. It is a report written by Henry VIII's master shipwright, James Baker, and the acting Surveyor of the Navy, Benjamin Gonson, addressed to His Majesty. Clearly someone, presumably the king himself, had been applying pressure to increase the armament of existing ships with yet more of the new heavy cannon. The weary-sounding professionals explain exactly why this is not possible in the case of certain ships, and to drive home their points they specify the location of the guns already aboard – and in the case of the *Mary Rose*, among other things, they say, '…and at the barbican head likewise forward over two culverins, and the decks over the same shooting likewise forward over two sakers'. What exactly did this mean? The barbican head was the front face of what we now call the sterncastle, the structure rising behind the mainmast, and the writer says there were two culverins located there, firing forwards. This accords perfectly with the archaeology, because one piece of that castle deck has survived, including part of the barbican head mentioned, and there, sure enough, was found a demi culverin, which is a very sizeable gun, facing forwards. But the writer goes on to describe another deck, as it were an upper castle deck, which mounted, above the two demi culverins, two smaller guns, known as sakers, also firing forwards. So the *Mary Rose* must have been two decks high abaft the mainmast. Would it be possible to reconstruct the true appearance of the ship, reconciling the recovered hull and known facts such as this with the Anthony drawing, which seems to show exactly this kind of piled-up superstructure?

Fortunately for me, a huge amount of work, representing many thousands of hours, had already been done by the archaeologists and surveyors of the Mary Rose Trust. This had resulted in a series of large-scale drawings of every part of the hull and decks that had been recovered, and it was upon these that I was able to base my reconstruction. Without these meticulous plans my own work could have been little more than a re-imagining of the Anthony drawing. As the work progressed on to the fine details I was able to make use of all the other archaeological work that had been done.

THE DRAWINGS

I began by re-drawing a plan of the surviving parts of the hull, at a more manageable size than the master scale drawings. Then I simply continued extrapolating from there, adding on upperworks and other missing areas, keeping credible deck-heights and so on, to correspond generally with the Anthony drawing, making due allowances for the naive style which shows a rather clumsy, ill-proportioned ship, in that respect very unlike the hull we actually had. I thought this exercise would be one that I would be forced to abandon at some point when it became obvious that it was clearly wrong, but to my surprise it all continued to work out; and the conviction started to grow upon me that Anthony, though he may have been a poor draughtsman, was not after all such an unreliable observer.

In my reconstruction the necessary decks were added, the height grew, but not unreasonably; the stern part of the ship seemed credible. But what about that crazy, towering, disproportionate forecastle? Artists of a slightly earlier period, leading up to the 1509 date in which the *Mary Rose* was laid down, often showed such a feature. They, and Anthony, may all of them have been wrong, of course, but why not give them the benefit of the doubt? Though the result looks so strange to our eye, they were portraying a particular kind of ship, the carrack, which in its military version was built to fight a particular kind of battle. These ships were armed with none, or very few, of the ship cannon of later times. Instead, they were crammed with soldiers armed with bows, stones, handguns, and great iron throwing darts. The objective was to get alongside an enemy ship, overwhelm the crew by raining down all these missiles, and then board. Obviously in this kind of fight it was a great advantage to be higher than your opponent; hence the high fore-

Below: First draft reconstruction drawing.

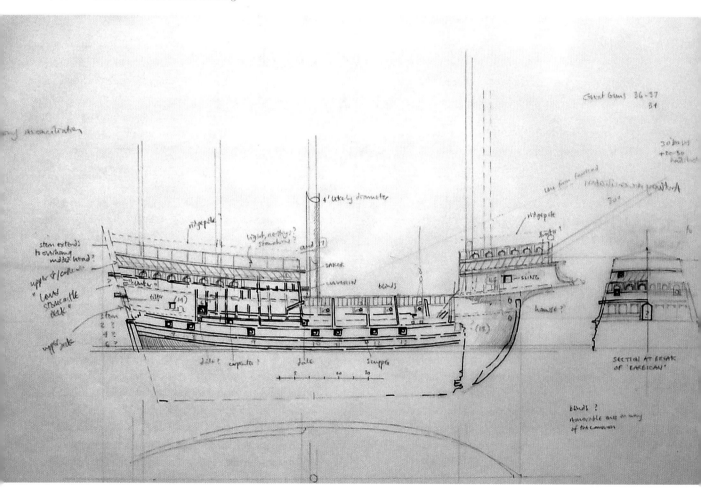

Above: A carrack, detail from 'Portuguese Squadron off a Rocky Coast'. *(© National Maritime Museum, BHC 0705)*

Right: *Mary Rose*, head on.

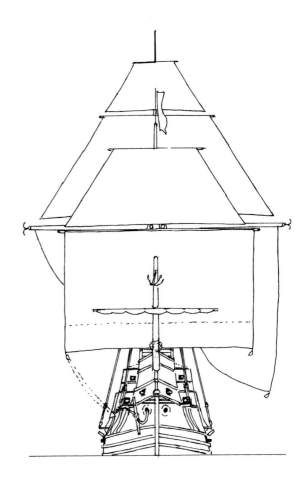

and stern-castles, which in a somewhat earlier period were often constructed and painted to look like castles on land. The *Mary Rose* was built in this age, the age of the carrack. She *was* a carrack, and one that appears to have been much esteemed for her fine qualities.

We know that in the 1530s, after many years' service, she was rebuilt. She was pierced for more gunports so that she could carry more of the new heavy ship cannon, probably the stern was remodelled from a round to a square transom and probably the masts were altered. But were her older carrack features much changed? Anthony seems to indicate not. In particular, the height of forecastle to which my interpretation of Anthony had led me – the highest part would have been 40 feet above the waterline – was this possible? From the side, it certainly looked incredible. But the situation was transformed when I drew a scale end elevation of the ship. Springing from the place where the forecastle meets the upper waist rail, which does survive and from which we know the width of the ship and the 'tumblehome' (the leaning-in of the sides) at that point, the forecastle is revealed as a narrow structure, perhaps only 10 feet wide or less at the top. The comparison with a light scaffolding tower springs to mind. Not only does this start to look possible, in comparison with the much wider bulk of the ship at the midships point, but also it clearly reveals that the four guns we encountered

above, the two culverins and two sakers firing forward from the barbican head, actually could have had a good field of fire forwards. Not dead ahead, but not far off the bow, and just the thing to deal with a very difficult type of opponent, the row-galley. In calm or in light airs, a galley could literally row rings around a helpless sailing-ship and pound it to pieces with a few heavy cannon – and the French had many of these galleys.

What about Anthony's guns? Why so many on what looks like three gun decks, like the *Victory*, when he, of all people, the ordnance expert, must have known that the *Mary Rose* had only two main gun decks carrying a total of no more than fifteen cannon per side? This is a case where his drawing style does tell against him for the ship, as he has drawn it, really is too stumpy, and he has drawn all the guns and gunports – the things that must have interested him the most – too large in proportion to the rest of the ship. The effect is that his ship seems fairly covered in guns. But if we carefully count all those guns, ranged along the broadside, we find that in fact he shows only seven guns on the upper gundeck, and seven is the number the recovered *Mary Rose* has. On the lower gundeck he shows a rather uneven double row of cannon, but they are located within the depth of the clearly-drawn three horizontal strengthening timbers, the wales, and in all there are only nine of them; and this nearly accords

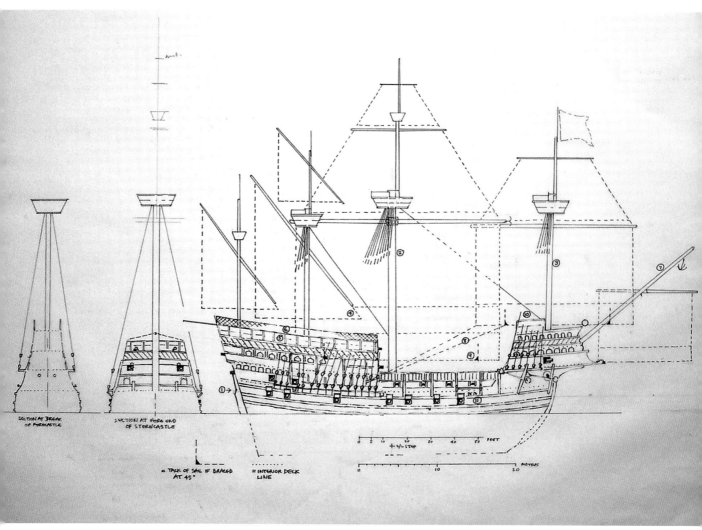

Above: Final draft reconstruction drawing.

with what we have recovered. Our section of hull has the three wales, and located there we find seven of those gunports; the lost bow part probably had an eighth. The gunports are not in fact regular; they are slightly different sizes, reflecting the different-sized guns they housed, and so exhibit at least some of the irregular up-and-down effect we see in the Anthony drawing.

By this time my plan reconstruction had progressed to the line drawing shown, together with a preliminary indication of the rig (the principal problems to address with this being the location of the foremast and the height of the mainmast) and I submitted this to the three experts noted above, Peter Marsden, Christopher Dobbs, and Alexzandra Hildred, together with my reasons for the conclusions I had reached. To my great relief their verdict was generally favourable. My *Mary Rose* did generally accord with the understanding of people who had devoted many years, in specialised areas of study, to this one ship.

THE PAINTING

Now the scale drawing had to be turned into a painting. I did not think it very useful, in this first picture at any rate, to create an impressionistic or compositionally dramatic image. What seemed to be required was a straightforward ship portrait, giving as much information as possible from the clearest viewpoint. With this in mind I sketched a simple composition, viewing the ship from forward of the beam. Like Bill Bishop, the artist responsible for that earlier artist's impression, I also made use of an old convention in marine art in which the same ship appears more than once in the picture. In this case I simply added part of a ship in the foreground so that the stern, not visible in the main view, could be seen. Nominally this anchored vessel is *Mary Rose*'s near-sister, the *Peter Pomegranate*; in fact it is a clone of the *Mary Rose* herself. The background was very simple, including a distant view of Southsea Castle, and another vessel, the sailing ship's mortal enemy, the rowing galley. Henry VIII had one of these in his fleet, the *Galley Subtile*, together with a number of vessels which could be sailed or rowed – as indeed smaller warships could be, even those as large as frigates, right up to the time of the Napoleonic Wars. That done, I painted my usual small colour sketch of the proposed final painting, also submitting this to the Trust.

The next stage was to draw the ship at the full size required for the painting (25 x 36 inches), scaling the sketch up to the required size and working over it in accurate detail. This I did by eye, using my long experience of working from plans and tracing, as it were, a transparent skeleton of the ship in three dimensions. The next stage would be to begin painting, except that late one evening I had second thoughts. This was to be such a significant painting, both for myself and the Mary Rose Trust, and I had already done so much research work on it – over one hundred hours by this time – that I thought I should, perhaps, draw the ship 'properly'. That meant a measured perspective drawing. I slept on this idea and came back to the studio in the morning, fresh and determined. There must be an easier way to draw a perspective view correctly, but the only way I know is the hard way. This involves preparing three scale drawings of the ship – plan, elevation, side – to a suitable size, and then deciding upon a viewpoint drawn to the same scale. From this viewpoint numberless lines are drawn and measurements made, from which a true and correct rendering of the subject can be derived. To begin with I picked a viewpoint 100 yards off

the *Mary Rose*'s starboard bow, but it soon became evident that this would be unsatisfactory. It was a true rendering, but that close to the ship the towering forecastle dominated the whole image. It seemed overwhelming – as no doubt it was intended to do in real life – but it was too much of a distraction for this purpose. So instead I chose a point 200 yards away – one cable's length – with an eye height 10 feet above sea level. As it turned out, this produced a result not much different from the drawing I had judged by eye, or indeed the original colour sketch, for which I was grateful; but it meant that I could forever sleep easy, feeling that I had done my job properly.

The painting itself proceeded smoothly, without major problems left to solve. The many smaller problems involved the rigging, which is all too evident and had to be painted rope by rope, but for which the evidence is absent or extremely sparse. For example, I am still mystified about how the fore course sail was handled on a wind, especially where its tacks were led. We will probably never be much wiser about such puzzles until someone builds a sailing reconstruction of a Tudor warship.

Regarding the ship's colouring and her flags, once again I generally followed Anthony's indications, together with some

Below: Perspective drawing: *Mary Rose* from 100 yards off starboard bow.

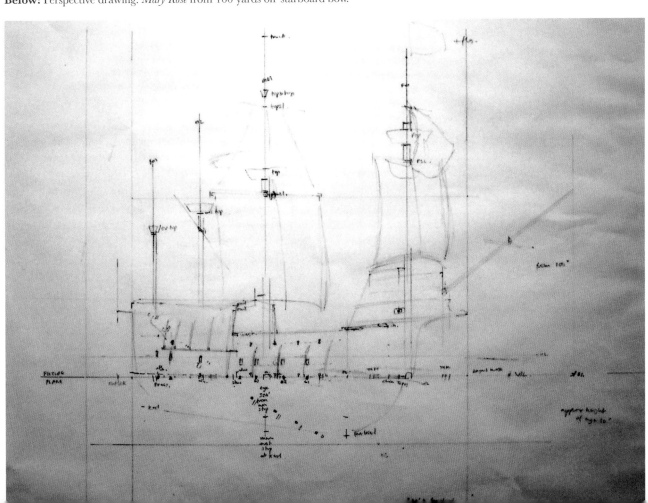

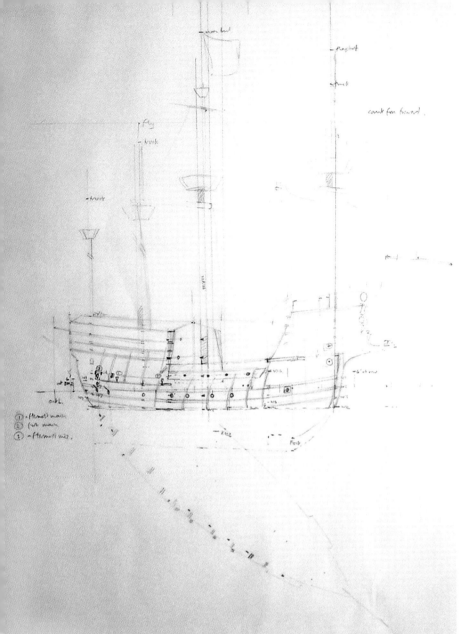

Above: Perspective drawing: *Mary Rose* from 200 yards off starboard bow.

ships, but then she was, like many warships since, a transitional type, an uncomfortable hybrid. Built as a carrack, of which she must class as the only surviving example, a long-vanished type which has left no descendants, she was rebuilt in an attempt to modernise her as a cannon-armed, broadside-firing ship, but apparently without cutting down her carrack fore- and aftercastles. No wonder she looks odd; if Anthony is to be believed, Henry VIII's other major warships looked much the same, and for the same reason. And perhaps it is little surprise that she overset and sank. It is surely no coincidence that within forty years of her loss, this type of ship had utterly vanished from the English fleet, and in its place was the Elizabethan galleon – low, fast, rakish and weatherly. The galleons fought their battles with cannon, and no one thought of manning them with hundreds of soldiers and archers: the broadside sailing warship had appeared, the pattern for the next 250 years. Some of those galleons were designed using drawn plans, by a master shipwright named Matthew Baker. He was the son of James Baker, Henry VIII's shipwright, he who had argued so determinedly against overloading old ships like the *Mary Rose* with yet more cannon which they could not bear.

I cannot close without a postscript. I completed the painting in January 2009 and shortly afterwards wrote essentially this same account of the painting's creation, thinking that all the loose ends were tied up. But four months later someone at the Trust emailed me another artist's impression of the ship which they had just found, one that I found astonishing in the light of what I had just done. It was completed by the Californian marine historian Raymond Aker back in 1981, and it accords with my own conclusions in almost every significant respect. Given that Raymond did not have access to the latest information which I benefitted from, it is a remarkable testament to his study of sixteenth-century naval architecture and to his analytical powers. I wish that I had seen this earlier – it might have saved me about fifty hours' work – and I much regret that I cannot contact him, for he died in 2003.

reference to another near-contemporary source, the paintings once at Cowdray House depicting Henry VIII's embarkation at Dover and his campaign in France (the paintings themselves were lost by fire in the eighteenth century, but accurate engravings of them survive). We know from documentary sources that in general Henry was very emphatic in stamping the Tudor brand upon the country and spared no expense on such heraldic things as flags and pennants, calling for very costly materials such as silk and real silver and gold thread. Presumably the *Mary Rose*, as a prestige flagship, would have had the best materials and most expensive colours lavished on her, at any rate whenever the King was due to inspect the fleet.

As to the final result, this *Mary Rose* still looks pretty odd to the modern eye, or to those of us more accustomed to the understandable and regular proportions of later sailing war-

The *Norman Court*

COMPOSITE TEA CLIPPER

by Robert A. Wilson FRSA

This fine British tea clipper was launched in July 1869 at the Glasgow shipyard of A. & J. Inglis. With a gross tonnage of 855, she was 197ft 4in long, with a beam of 33ft and depth of 20ft. She was of composite construction, the frames being of iron and the hull planking of wood. The total cost of the vessel, including stores and equipment came to £16,005. The mainmast truck was 139ft above the deck. The main yard was 74ft long, and the main skysail yard was 24ft long.

On her maiden voyage, she was commanded by Captain Andrew Shewan Snr. He was succeeded late in 1873 by his son, who remained in command until 1879. The ship's best performance over a week was 2,046 miles while crossing the Trades in the Indian Ocean in September 1874. During the seven days, her slowest 24 hour run was 271 miles and her highest was 319 miles. The best log reading was 15 knots. During this voyage, she raced the famous tea clipper *Sir*

Below: Port quarter view of the completed model ready to be set in the sea.

Above: Half model of the British tea clipper *Sir Lancelot*.

Lancelot. Sir Lancelot sailed from Shanghai on 18 July, whilst the *Norman Court* did not leave the Min River until 27 July. The two ships met on 29 July and kept close company until 6 August. They then separated and did not meet again until 25 August, by which time they were off the coast of Borneo. They did not meet again during that voyage; *Norman Court* anchored at the Downs on 17 November, whilst *Sir Lancelot* arrived two days later. In 1878 the *Norman Court* was reduced to barque rig by the removal of the square sail yards from the mizzen mast.

During the hard winter of 1878/79 the weather was especially bad in the English Channel, with frost, snow blizzards and easterly gales hampering homeward bound sailing ships. The upper reaches of the Thames were frozen hard. In January 1879 only two sailing ships managed to work up Channel without having to take on the services of steam tugs. They were the *Norman Court* and the magnificent Golden Fleece wool clipper *Mermerus*. At the end of that voyage, Captain Shewan handed over command to Captain Dunn. The *Norman Court* completed her last China Tea

Below: Hull of a model of a ship similar to the *Norman Court* ready to have the sheer cut.

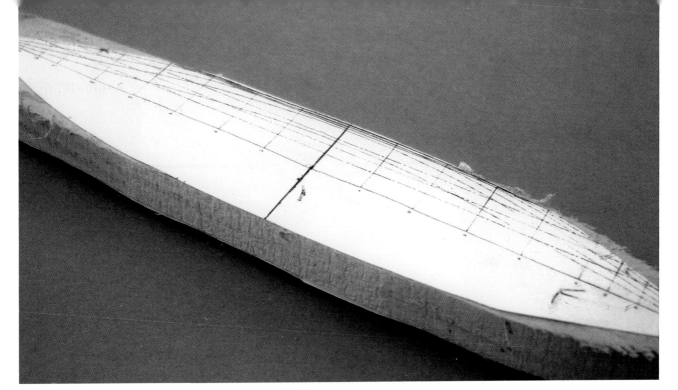

Above: Waterline template pasted to the bottom of the hull block.

voyage in 1880/81. By this time, the tea clippers had been driven off the route by steamers that were able to take advantage of the Suez Canal. Rather than accept lower freights in other trades the owners of *Norman Court* sold her to Baine & Johnston, who employed her in the Java sugar trade. On the sale of the ship, Captain Dunn handed her over to Captain McBride. She did not last long under her new owners. Leaving Queenstown on 29 March 1883 she was wrecked later that day in Cymmeran Bay, Anglesea, in a violent south-westerly gale. The Rhosneigr lifeboat made a valiant attempt to reach the wreck, but they were driven back to the beach by the ferocity of the weather. All the following day, the crew of twenty-two clung to the rigging of the stranded ship. The old steward and one able seaman died of cold and exposure before the lifeboat finally managed to reach them 25 hours after the stranding. The wreck was sold for the scrap value of her copper fastenings and sheathing. For a number of years, the iron frames were still visible at low tide. Her figurehead was removed and placed in a local garden.

Below: Forecastle and poop blocks, complete with scored deck planking, fitted on the hull.

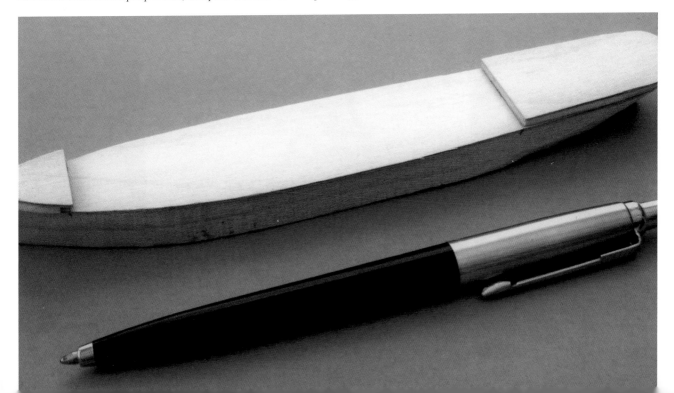

THE MODEL

I decided on a waterline model under full sail, built to a scale of 1in = 32ft (1:384), which gave it a length of just over 6in on the waterline. The plans were found on page 257 of *Fast Sailing Ships, Their Design and Construction, 1775–1875* (2nd edition, 1988) by David R. MacGregor, Conway Maritime Press, ISBN 0-85177-452-0.

A lines plan shows the shape of a ship's hull in plan, elevation and cross-sections; they are rarely available, but fortunately, with this ship, a lines plan was included in the set of plans in the above mentioned book. As this was to be a waterline model the shape of the hull when being carved was developed by reference to the upper part of the cross-sections shown on the body plan and the relevant lines on the half breadth plan for deck and waterline shape. As mentioned, a lines plan shows the shape of the whole hull. Just for interest I have included a photograph of a half model of the tea clipper *Sir Lancelot*, a ship very similar to the *Norman Court*, which gives a good indication of the shape of the hull above and below the waterline. If no lines plan is available, a builder of a full hull model is left to his own devices to develop the hull shape as best he can from such material as he can access.

A piece of wood was selected and cut and finished slightly larger that the overall dimensions of the hull. A spare profile of the hull was cut out and pasted to the side of the block aligned to the required waterline level. Using a small hobby bandsaw this was sawn along the line of the main deck, thus forming the sheer. With the sheer cut and finished, I got out a paper template to the shape of the main deck, as shown on the half breadth plan on the lines plan, and pasted it to the

top of the block. I cut the block to the shape of the deck. The after end is the first curve in from the level of the top of the poop deck, and at the forward end it is the line between the dotted line and the outer line showing the shape of the top of the forecastle. As its name implies the half breadth plan shows only half of the hull. It was a simple matter to fold the copy of the plan along the centreline and cut it out to obtain both sides of the deck.

The required waterline level was then selected on the half-breadth plan, at a level a little below the load waterline, thereby allowing for a certain amount of hull that would be under the moulded sea. A template was made in the same way as described above and pasted on the bottom of the block. It is important when doing this to make sure that the ends of the template align correctly with the deck template. This can be done by ruling a reference line across the lines

Below: Making the socket for the bowsprit.

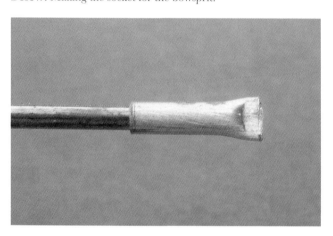

Below: Showing use of a template to obtain the correct height and angle of the bowsprit.

Above: Checking that the hull is a perfect fit in the recess in the sea before making a start on the planking.

plan copy and lining up the lower one with the plan pasted on top. [Note: an alternative way to do this is to mark the position of the fore perpendicular and after perpendicular on the block, and to mark these points on the templates, and align them accordingly. Editor]. The waterline I selected before cutting out the profile was the fourth one up from the bottom.

The shaping of the hull was done with a scalpel. At the bow it was simply a matter of tapering down the waterline with a slight inward curve. The same was true for the stern, but the inward curve was far greater. At this stage, it is only necessary to get a rough approximation to the final shape.

The main deck was then made from $^1/_{32}$in marine plywood, scored to represent the planking. The scoring may be done by hand, but it can be difficult to get identical and parallel plank widths. (For a number of years I have used a home-made deck scoring machine, but I have now built a new and improved version of this very useful device; a description of this device follows in the next article.) The scored deck sheet was cut to the shape of a template cut from a copy of the plan. In order to keep the deck clean, the template was pasted to the underside of the scribed deck piece. After cutting to shape, the underside of the deck piece was scraped clean and then glued to the top of the hull block. The raised

Below: Hull planked, painted and ready for deck details to be fitted.

Above: Example of deckhouse panels produced on a computer. These were not for *Norman Court*.

forecastle and poop were glued in position and the scored ¹⁄₃₂in plywood pieces of decking for these cut to shape, but not yet fitted. The poop deck had a thin brass template along the top, conforming to the shape of the poop deck. Another conforming to the shape of the main deck at the level of the counter's knuckle was glued underneath and the wood between the two filed away in order to obtain the shape of the counter. I find the use of brass templates essential in order to ensure a sharp knuckle. This process, together with illustrations, was described more fully in *Model Shipwright* 142.

Two vertical slots were cut, one in the bow and one in the stern, to take the stem and stern aluminium inserts. As the brass templates above and below the poop are very thin, the saw blade was not impeded in any way. The inserts were cut from thin aluminium sheet. The use of inserts ensures that the correct profiles of bow and stern are maintained.

The poop deck planking was fitted and the stern insert glued in position. A socket for the bowsprit was then made by sliding a short length of thin brass tube over the rod that will eventually be used for the bowsprit. The end was pinched with a pair of pliers. The top of the slot in the forecastle head was widened to take the bowsprit socket.

With the hull held down to a piece of smooth wood with two pieces of Plasticine, the bowsprit socket was placed in the slot at the correct angle and height. The angle was determined with a cardboard template, also held by two pieces of Plasticine. The rod in the socket will eventually be cut down to the required length but, at the moment, its extra length lies along the top of the angle template. Once I had the socket at the correct angle, I filled in the slot into which it fitted with

chemical metal and left it to dry. The bowsprit rod was then removed leaving the short socket embedded in the forecastle head. The aluminium stem and stern inserts were then cut and glued into position. In earlier models, I had used brass for the inserts so that I could solder the bowsprit socket directly to the top of the stem insert. This was not necessary this time as the socket is already fitted into the hull. An added advantage to using aluminium is that it is easier to cut and shape. The forecastle decking was glued on top.

The bulwarks were made from ¹⁄₆₄in marine plywood, glued into position with contact adhesive. The hull was then treated with chemical metal filler and gently rubbed down to a smooth finish using wet and dry carborundum paper. At this stage of construction, I had already made the sea from shaped Plasticine. I find it best to make sure that the model is a perfect fit in the sea before the hull is fully finished as the Plasticine could make a mess of the paintwork. A photograph shows how the two long bolts pass through the hull and the base. They are cut to the required length and the two holes beneath the base are also countersunk to take the fixing nuts. The bolt heads in the main deck will eventually be covered by numbers one and three hatches. In the illustration, the bevelled wood edging has been masked off to keep it clean while the sea was being painted, which was the next task after the model had been fitted perfectly in the space provided. The sea was made from Plasticine and painted using gloss enamel paints. Any white should be added while the main sea colour is still wet in order to make it run, thus giving a wet effect.

The *Norman Court* had a gold-coloured stripe along the

Above: Hull finished and ready for rigging.

outside of the hull at deck level. Rather than attempt to paint this on, I glued a length of thin brass wire, straightened by stretching slightly, round the hull at the required level.

A capping rail ran along the top of the forecastle deck, along the top of the bulwarks and along the top of the poop deck. It extended all round the ship. I made it from 24swg tinned copper wire. I bent the wire to the shape of the hull and beat it flat with a smooth-faced hammer, using a piece of flat steel plate as a small anvil. Flattening it caused some distortion, but this was easily corrected. It was spray-painted, first with matt primer and then with brown to represent the wood. It was glued along the top of the hull using a contact adhesive. The hull was planked with thin strips of self-adhesive labels, cut using the deck scoring device.

The hull could now be painted. I used artist's water-based colour for the black hull, applying it over the planking and over the brass wire. Being water-based, the paint dried in a few minutes and a second coat was applied in order to cover one or two places where the white paper planking was visible. Later, the paint was scraped off the brass wire thus forming the aforementioned gold stripe round the hull. The copper sheathing on the lower half of the hull was done with strips of thin self-adhesive copper sheet stuck on with one piece on each side.

The scroll work on the trail boards at the bow was formed from tightly twisted silver and gold wire. The self-adhesive copper sheet and the silver and gold wire were obtained from a hobby craft shop.

THE DECK MACHINERY

This consisted of winches and capstans turned from brass rod. The horizontal supports on the winches were pieces of fine copper wire. The whole assembly was glued on a base of thin white plasticard. I find it more convenient to leave the item on the plasticard strip until I have spray-painted it. Once dry, the strip may be cut off close to the winch and the cut white edges touched up with a spot of paint. The winch in one of the photographs does not appear to be of any great precision, but it is very small, only about 7mm long. It looks far better in real life simply because it is so small!

The deckhouse was faced with good quality paper on which I had printed the panels using the computer. In order to have a good surface on all four sides, the wood was cut across the grain from the end of a mahogany plank. This left the rougher end grain of the wood on the top and bottom surfaces where they aid the adhesive for fitting the roof of the house and the bonding to the deck. The fact that I used mahogany has no great significance. I have had the plank for some time and use it solely for deckhouses. Any similar hardwood would be just as good. For miniatures, I find that deckhouse panels are best made using the computer. I draw them out at 4ft = 1in and, after scanning them into the computer, open the file in a photo processing programme and colour them in using the Paint Bucket facility. They may then be printed on to matt photo paper to the required scale, cut out and stuck on the sides of the house.

The top of the house was formed from a piece of black plasticard with the corners rounded off. This was covered in a slightly smaller piece of scored 1/64in marine plywood.

The metal guard rails round the poop were made on a small winding frame. This is a piece of wood 80mm by

150mm and 6mm thick. Four lengths of threaded rod have been glued to the edge of the top surface with epoxy resin. The rails consist of 38swg tinned copper wire for the stanchions, wound around across the length of the wood using the threads for precise spacing. The horizontal bars, made of a wire of a slightly smaller diameter, should be wound on first and then the verticals wound at a right angle to them, again using the second pair of threaded rods for spacing. The ends of the wire can be made fast to pins in the ends of the wood. I then paint the whole network with a liquid soldering flux that has the consistency of water and quickly run a small soldering iron bit along each vertical in turn. This may have to be done several times to ensure that all the crossovers have been soldered. The completed rail lengths can then be cut off and spray painted with white matt primer paint. The wood capping on top of the poop rail was made using the same method as used for the capping rail round the hull. Again, it was thin copper wire bent to shape and flattened

Below: Showing hull with all fore-and-aft sails fitted and rigged.

with a hammer before being spray painted dark brown to simulate wood and glued on top of the wire rails. I have not shown a picture of the rail board, because the general idea is illustrated with a similar board used for making the shrouds and ratlines later. A rail frame, together with illustrations, was described more fully in *Model Shipwright* 144, page 48.

The plan shows the boats upside down on the skids. They were all made from thin plasticard sheet formed in a miniature vacuum box. The keels were fine copper wire glued on before spray painting. A miniature vacuum box was described in *Model Shipwright* 129.

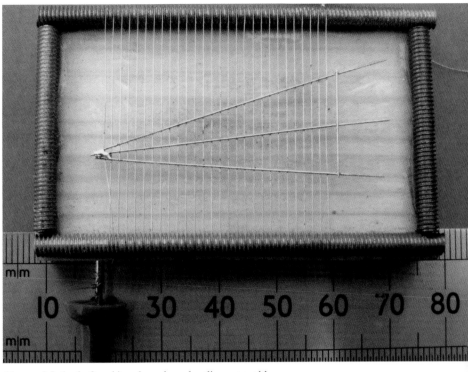

Above: Method of making shrouds and ratlines assembly.

MASTS AND YARDS

Although the *Norman Court* was a wooden vessel, all the masts and spars in the model were made from a combination of brass tube, brass, copper and silver steel rod. The tops of the lower masts and topmasts in way of the doublings were squared-off. To obtain this effect using metal tube, I soldered short lengths of square-section brass into them for the lower masts. The topmasts were solid rod, so I had to file out the square sections with a fine file. The various sections of the masts were soldered together using soft solder and then spray painted. As the lower masts were made from tube, they were glued over short metal stubs glued in the deck and bent to the correct rake of each mast. The bowsprit/jibboom was glued into the socket embedded earlier in the forecastle.

I prefer to set and rig all the fore-and-aft sails as soon as the masts are in position. Then the shrouds and backstays can be added. Note that the bowsprit and jibboom are not yet rigged at this stage. I have found that it is a mistake to rig that area too soon; however careful I am, I have often caught the end of the jibboom whilst working on the rigging. Being metal, it rarely comes to any harm, but its associated rigging is susceptible to damage. Consequently, I save that rigging until all the rest is complete.

The sails were made from white airmail paper that I had printed on both sides with fine lines to represent the seams. These lines consisted of an A4 sheet full of underlines typed on the computer. They should not be too prominent, so I printed them in light grey rather than black. The jibs and staysails were each made in two pieces so that the seams could run parallel to the after leeches, with the joint extending from the clew to the forward leech of the sail. The

spencer and spanker were each formed in one piece with the seams running down the after leeches. Each sail was edged with fine black enamelled wire. I applied a thin film of contact adhesive along the edge of the sail with a cocktail stick and placed the length of wire against it where it was gripped immediately by the adhesive. Each of the jibs and staysails was curved around a wooden dowel before fitting. The spencer and the spanker, being larger than the jibs and staysails, needed to be moulded into a wind-filled shape. The spanker reef points were added using a finely pointed hard pencil before shaping the sail. The sail was dampened and placed on the smooth surface of an ostrich egg and patted down until all the creases had gone. A large handkerchief was then placed over the sail and held tightly at the back of the egg while the sail was dried out using a small hobby heat gun. This is a very effective method of shaping a sail. Because it may shrink slightly, the sail should be made a bit larger than required and trimmed down after moulding. The wire edging was then added before the sail was glued to the booms with contact adhesive. If an ostrich egg is not to hand, a smooth plastic ball will suffice. The advantage of an egg, however, is in the choice of surface curves.

A similar, but smaller board to the one used for the guard rails, was used to make the shrouds and ratlines. The first three shrouds with the sheer pole soldered across them were made separately from the frame. They consisted of thin tinned copper wires, stretched slightly to straighten it, soldered together at the top and the sheer pole soldered across their lower ends. The frame was wound with ratline wire and the shroud assembly placed on top of it. The top junction of the three shrouds was painted with flux and touched with the soldering iron to make the initial joint. The lowest ratline was then painted with flux and the soldering iron run across it very quickly. Speed is essential; otherwise the sheer pole might become unsoldered. The whole piece was then painted with flux and the soldering iron run lightly up each shroud until all the ratlines were soldered on. Two more shrouds were then soldered between the first three. By that time, the whole assembly had become quite firm and the addition of the two extra shrouds was quite simple. After cutting from the frame, they were spray-painted with satin black before fitting to the model. The exact size of the shrouds and ratline assemblies was ascertained using a paper template held between the bulwarks and the mast top.

The rest of the rigging was fine black-enamelled copper wire. Each piece was stretched slightly to make it straight. It was picked up in the centre with a pair of tweezers, each end dipped in contact adhesive and placed in position on the model. Where a block was required at the junction of two wires, this was simulated by a small blob of white glue that had been mixed with a small amount of black water paint.

Once the fore-and-aft sails were set and rigged, I com-menced fitting and rigging the square sails, starting with the three lowest ones and working upwards, each sail being completely rigged before proceeding to the next. The final task was to rig the bowsprit and jibboom. The model was then lowered carefully into the sea and the securing nuts screwed on underneath the base. By tightening them slowly with a small box spanner, the model was pulled down into the sea to the required depth. The junction between sea and hull was given a wet look by filling it with liquid acrylic applied with a paint brush. Once it has dried clear, it gives a perfect wet looking junction.

By this time, I have normally completed the display case as well, so as soon as the model is in the sea, the case can be lowered over it.

The base of the model was made from 15mm chipboard edged with bevelled sapele wood. The junction between the Plasticine sea and the bevelled edging was covered with tightly twisted enamelled copper wire glued on with contact adhesive. The base quadrant was 18mm pine, veneered with steamed beech veneer. The display case was made from 3mm clear acrylic edged with steamed beech veneer. A piece of cardboard covered in green felt folded over and glued on the top was screwed underneath the model adding a very neat green felt edging beneath the base quadrant.

Below: Starboard bow view of model in its case.

Deck Scoring Device

DECK PLANKING SIMULATION

by Robert A. Wilson FRSA

I have been using a similar device to this for a number of years and have found it an indispensable aid for scoring decks to simulate planking on miniature ship models. Although it was very satisfactory, I decided to make a new and improved version based on what I had learned from using the original one.

The main baseboard was a piece of 15mm chipboard, measuring 19in x 12in (480mm x 300mm). A 2in strip of the 15mm chipboard was cut and nailed along the top of the main board. A piece of aluminium angle, 15mm x 5mm x 1mm, was glued along the lower edge using a contact adhesive. A third piece of chipboard was cut to the same width as the main board. A piece of aluminium angle, 40mm x 10mm x 1.5mm, was cut for the top edge of this board. Before fitting it, a 20mm strip of 0.8mm marine plywood was glued along the inside of the angle. The board at this stage of construction is shown in Photograph 1.

This was glued along the top edge of the board using contact adhesive. The marine plywood filler raises the lower edge of the aluminium, leaving a space for the workpiece to be clamped in place. After it had been glued on, I put three countersunk woodscrews along the top edge for added

strength. Along the lower edge, I drilled three holes, one at each end and one in the middle to take the workpiece clamping bolts. On completion, I found it necessary to add a third hole between the centre and the right-hand side one. This extra hole is not shown in the illustrations as it was added later.

A piece of T-section aluminium angle, 15mm x 15mm x 1.5mm, was placed along the top strip and the second large board pushed up close to it and secured in position with four thin nails. This was arranged so that the aluminium T-bar would slide easily back and forth in the groove formed by the aluminium-edged strip along the top of the main board and the second large board with the aluminium-edged top. I nailed the lower board in position because I noticed that if glue was used the different rates of shrinkage can cause the boards to 'bow'. The base of the device is now 30mm thick which may seem rather heavy. In the original one, I only used a single 15mm board and I found that the slight pressure exerted on the top of it whilst scoring planks, caused it to flex sufficiently to give inaccurate readings on the depth gauge if I was not careful. The double-thickness base eliminated that problem. The addition of a small amount of Vaseline to the

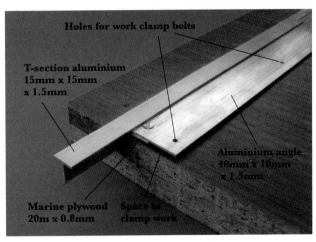

1. The prepared main baseboard.

2. The lower board has been fitted, leaving a groove for a length of T-section aluminium.

3. The main baseboard with all its fittings in place.

(labels in image 1: Thrust block, Threaded rod, Pusher bracket, Beam, Screw at an angle, Slot for slide, Work clamping bolts)

4. The Pusher Bracket glued and bolted to the five square nuts.

central leg of the T-bar made it move very smoothly from side to side.

A length of threaded rod the full width of the board was selected. Five square nuts were screwed on to it before fixing a small bearing at each end, each bearing secured by a hexagonal nut on each side of it. The square nuts will eventually take the pusher bracket. On the right-hand side, the threaded rod protruded sufficiently for a brass handle to be screwed tightly onto it.

Two pieces of wood were drilled to take the bearings, and cut down to a size that made the threaded rod stand about 12mm above the board. These bearing blocks were drilled vertically to enable them to be fastened to each end of the board with long wood screws. End bearings of the threaded rod were glued into the wooden blocks.

The Thrust Block to the left is for the depth gauge probe to push against when the device is in use. This must be cut to suit the height of the probe and its use will become clearer when the device is assembled. The Pusher Bracket is a strip of aluminium 25mm across. It was folded over and crushed into the shape shown in Photograph 4. Although it was drilled and had a nut and bolt through the middle, the open

ends were glued to the five evenly spaced square nuts with epoxy resin. It is essential that this bracket is firmly fixed to the nuts, hence the glue as well as the nut and bolt.

The basic principle of the device is that when the handle is rotated towards the operator, the Pusher Bracket moves the slide assembly (not yet made) along to the left. After each move the plank is scored manually. It is important that the handle should not be too loose; therefore it was fitted with a simple brake. This is shown in Photograph 5.

The brake bar was the earth pin from a mains plug. The opposite end was drilled to provide a fixing for the spring. The pin was screwed loosely to the side of the bearing block, whilst the spring was taken from the other end of it, over the handle shaft and screwed to the bearing block above the brake pivot. This provides a very effective brake that is not too severe.

The holes for the workpiece clamping bolts, see Photograph 3, were then drilled right through the baseboard. They must, of course, be countersunk. I used 6BA brass nuts and bolts for this purpose, and they were more than strong enough. Washers and nuts were fitted to the back of the board. When the workpiece is inserted under the space pro-

5. The brake, consisting of a brass bar and spring.

(labels in image 2: Spring, Handle shaft, Earth pin from mains plug, Pivot screw, Slot for slide assembly)

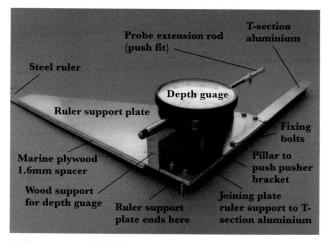

6. The completed Slide Assembly.

(labels in image 4: Probe extension rod (push fit), T-section aluminium, Steel ruler, Depth guage, Ruler support plate, Fixing bolts, Marine plywood 1.6mm spacer, Pillar to push pusher bracket, Wood support for depth guage, Ruler support plate ends here, Joining plate ruler support to T-section aluminium)

Work clamped in position for scoring

scoring hole

Pusher Bracket
(cut from aluminium)

Five square nuts

7. The device in use.

8. The completed device, viewed from the operating position.

vided, see Photograph 2, the nuts may be tightened on the back of the board using a 6BA box spanner.

The final part of the device is the slide assembly. The Ruler Support Plate is a triangular piece of aluminium butted up to the T-section slide bar with a joining Plate bolted across the top. It was bolted on with six countersunk nuts and bolts, with the nuts on top. This allowed for a smooth surface below the plate. A brass pillar was also bolted to this plate with a countersunk bolt underneath. The Pusher Bracket will bear on this when the device is in use and move the slide assembly along as the handle is rotated. A depth gauge with a 2in probe was fitted to a piece of wood that, in turn, was screwed to the top of the Ruler Support Plate next to the Joining Plate. A push-on brass extension was made for the probe to allow scoring a greater width of planking. Below the right-hand edge of the Ruler Support Plate, I glued an old steel ruler with a 1.6mm spacer in the form of two pieces of 0.8mm marine plywood glued together. When the slide assembly is in position, the flat end of the ruler should come almost to the Joining Plate. The purpose of the steel ruler is to provide a hard edge to score against as aluminium alone is too soft. The ruler edge is about 3mm clear of the aluminium plate. The completed Slide Assembly is shown in Photograph 6. The aluminium angle used in the construction was obtained from a Do-it-Yourself store, and aluminium sheet from engineering supply firms. Cutting aluminium neatly was done using a small hobby bandsaw. It is essential, of course, to wear protective goggles and a dust mask while doing this as it does produce a certain amount of aluminium dust. Despite my fears, I found it did not appear to blunt the saw blade. I did not force it through, but fed it in with a gentle pressure. The depth gauge was found at a car boot sale. The Thrust Block had to have an aluminium bracket fitted to extend it down in the way of the probe. Even if it had lined up with the probe, I would still have faced it in aluminium so that the probe has a relatively hard surface to push against.

To use the device, select the wood for the deck and smooth it off. Insert the top edge under the aluminium in the space provided beneath the aluminium strip along the top of the board. Clamp it firmly by tightening the nuts behind the board. Place the Slide Assembly in the slot and make sure the Pusher Bracket is to the right of the pillar and the end of the probe resting on the Thrust Block. Rotate the handle so that the Slide Assembly will begin to move to the left. The needle on the depth gauge will also begin to rotate in a clockwise direction. Press down lightly on the Ruler Support Plate and slightly to the right in order to keep the Pusher Bracket in contact with the pillar. Note the position of the indicator needle on the gauge and make the first score. Turn the handle until the needle has advanced to show the required plank width and make the second score, and so on until the required width of decking has been scored.

Photograph 7 shows the device in use with the Pusher Bracket touching the pillar attached to the Slider Assembly. Also visible under the board is a narrow strip of wood. This was to raise the top of the board, allowing the clamping nuts beneath to clear the surface when the device is not in use. In practice, I found the best position to use the device is to have the lower end resting on my knees and the upper end propped on the work bench. This makes it lie at a comfortable angle for scoring. In Photograph 8 the depth gauge's probe is already well in as the ruler is advanced along the workpiece. The extreme limit is when the right-hand end of the brass extension meets the steel probe tube. When this limit is reached, the extension is removed and the probe flies out giving a further 2in of travel. The maximum width of scoring that can be achieved on this particular device is 3.5in, or about 90mm.

Making something like this just for scoring decks may seem a bit excessive, but I find it absolutely essential, and it makes precision scoring of deck planking very easy. It may also be used for other purposes such as ruling parallel lines on paper.

Restoration of an Old Working Model Fifie

by Bruce Buchanan

In March 2005 my son Bruce telephoned to ask if I would like a model fifie. He informed me that a work colleague wanted to pass on the boat to any person who liked model boats and would look after it. Bruce said it was a plank-on-frame type of model and that it was at least forty years old. I told him I would be very pleased to have the model, and Bruce said he would arrange to obtain the model from Mr John Dunn from Anstruther, in Fife, Scotland. On 30 March my son phoned to say he had the model, and I collected it that evening. When I saw her I was overjoyed. She turned out to be about 100 years old; a vertically planked model of a

Left: Port side view of restored model.

sailing fifie, 38in in length and 14in on the beam. Sails and masts were in a plastic bag but I found them all present and correct. All the planks seams were open due to drying out, and I found out later that it was about thirty years since she last sailed on the water.

The boat was called *Girl Margaret*, registration KY741, and her home port was St Monance, Fife, but on her mainsail was the registration PD2853, indicating she came originally from Peterhead in the North East of Scotland. She had a large lead keel which looked like it had been fitted after the model had been built. This was confirmed in a telephone call to Mr Dunn who said his father had fitted the lead keel to make the vessel more stable in wind. He said, too, that his father was given the model by an aunt from Peterhead and that the boat had an internal water tank for ballast when built. He informed me that they sailed the boat at a boating pond at St Monance. She leaked a lot when first put in the pond but after a short time the planks swelled with the water and she became tight for the remainder of the sailing time.

The Buckie and Anstruther fisheries museums, when contacted, regretted that they had no record of a fifie PD2853. I telephoned Peterhead museum to ask if they had any records, and later a person from the Heritage phoned me saying they had no record but suggested I go to the central library in Aberdeen as they have some maritime almanacs and registers which may contain the information that I required. I then received an e-mail from museum curator Linda McGowan who said they had no record of PD2853 but this did not mean that a boat of this number did not exist as the museum did have gaps in their records. The lists are only of boats of 15 tons or over and if PD2853 was a Baldie (small fifie) she would not necessarily appear in these lists. Looking at the model and comparing her to old photographs she does have the lines of a Baldie. The modeller could also just have made up the number as I and other modellers have done in the past!

Baldie was the name give to the smaller decked fifies between 20ft and 30ft in length. The spars and sail were light enough for the crew to set by hand. It was after the invention of the steam capstan that larger fifies, up to over 70ft in length with heavy sails and yard, were introduced. There was no capstan fitted on the model, again making me think she was a Baldie. The boats were named after Giuseppe Garibaldi (1807–1882) the Italian political and military leader of the times when these boats were being built. Like the larger fifies the model had a dipping lug mainsail and a standing lug on the mizzen.

RESTORATION

Restoration commenced with returning the fifie to her proper lines by the removal of the lead keel, which was held

Above: This image shows her ancestral Viking lines.

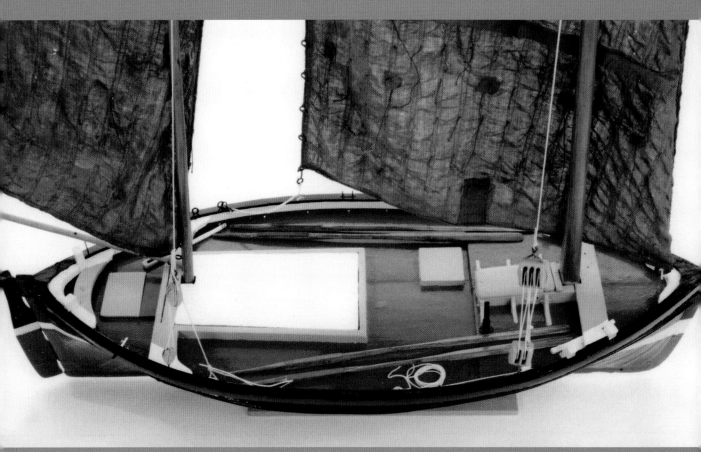

Above: Showing the deck layout. Note the position of the three hatches – fore, aft and fish hatch.

Above: The large oars or sweeps stowed on deck were used for manoeuvring the vessel in or out of harbour.

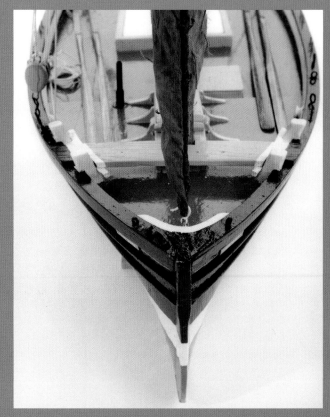

Above: Note sail attached to hook at vessel's stem.

Above: Their very fine lines made fifies fast in a good breeze.

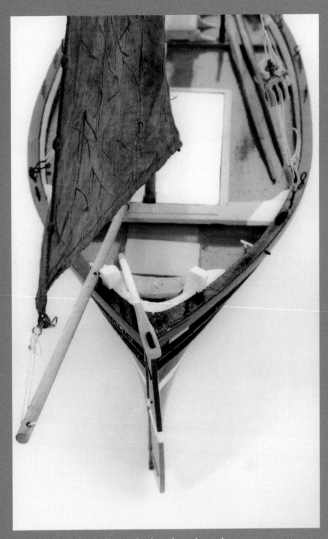

Above: Showing sail attached to the mizzen boom.

Below: The helmsman would stand in the open after hatch when steering the vessel.

Above: The very large blocks used for hauling up the main yard.

used a purpose-made filler to repair and fill the gaps in the planking. I found that there was not enough space for filling the gap between the wooden belts on the hull. I removed these belts and filled the upper hull gaps. The hull was then undercoated with four coats of white paint. The boat's bottom was painted with four coats of red Plasti-kote fast dry enamel paint. Then I applied two coats of Humbrol black enamel paint to the upper hull.

In June 2005 I floated the boat in Rosyth boating pond to test if she was watertight. I had her in the water for more than an hour and not a drop entered the hull.

The next job was to paint the deck. This was done with one coat of undercoat and two coats of Humbrol red enamel paint. The after hatch was missing and the fore hatch had fallen apart during the paint removing process. It appeared to have been made out of some type of card and this did not stand up to the paint remover. Two new removable hatches were made and fitted on the model. The fish room hatch was just repainted and refitted, as well as the fore-and-aft thwart. The boat had four oars though one was broken. This was repaired and the missing part replaced with a small piece of pine. The oars were sanded down ready to be varnished. After painting all the blocks, the rigging rope was replaced by new twine.

It was decided to change the model's name to *Fair Morn* and new name plates were made and fitted along with her original registration number. Her home port became Boddam, a small fishing village near Peterhead and the birth place of my mother. The yellow line was added around the upper hull.

A number of small holes in the sails were repaired using cuttings from a brown handkerchief. These were pasted over the holes with glue. The registration number was repainted on the mainsail. The rudder was repainted and fitted on the

on with wood screws and a few nails. I manage to remove the false keel without any damage to the model. After a talk with fellow model maker Jim McLaren on the best way to remove the paint without damage to the model, he suggested I spray Mr Muscle Oven Cleaner onto the model then place it in a large plastic bag, seal it, and leave overnight. This was done and next morning I removed it from the bag and set to work with an old washing-up brush. This worked well and before long I had removed most of the paint. I then used a scouring pad and water all over the model to make a smooth finish. A lot of the planks swelled with the water but most of them returned to their original size. I did have to nail a few mis-placed planks before they all dried out. When the model was originally built the plank seams were filled with what appeared to be putty and some of this had dropped out. I

Above: Upper part of sails. Note the vessel's registration number painted on the mainsail.

Above: The restored sailing fifie *Reaper* leaving Anstruther Harbour under sail. *(Scottish Fisheries Museum)*

model. New rowlocks were made and fitted. Only one of the originals had survived and I was able to get the size from this. Six eye screws on the top rail were missing but I was able to buy replacements.

On Friday, 15 July 2005 I transported the restored *Fair Morn* to Rosyth boating pond for her maiden sail. It was a nice dry sunny day in Alloa but when I reached Rosyth the wind had increased. I thought there was a bit too much wind for her as I had removed the lead outer keel and used lumps of lead as internal ballast. This would make the model less stable in a strong wind. She sailed very well until a strong gust caught her and she heeled right over putting her port rail under the water. I thought she was going to recover from this but I heard the lead ballast moving inside the hull and this made her capsize. The water entered through the fish hold hatch and she floundered. After removing sock and shoes and paddling, a successful rescue was carried out. The only damage sustained was a scrape to the red paint on the stem as she hit the bottom of the pond when she sank. A few of the

planks did swell a little because of the amount of water that had entered the hull, but all returned after a few hours drying in the sun.

If I sail her again I will have to choose a calmer day with very little wind but, as she looks so good as a static model, it would be a shame to damage the old girl.

A year after I completed work on the model I joined the crew of the restored sailing fifie *Reaper*. This vessel is owned and run by volunteers from the Scottish Fisheries Museum at Anstruther, Fife. She is a travelling museum and can be seen in fishing harbours in the summer months around the coasts of Scotland and England. Since sailing and working on *Reaper* I have learned how much knowledge and skill the builder of this model possessed in order to produce such a lifelike model of this type of fishing vessel, and of which I am now the proud owner.

Finally, my thanks to my daughter-in-law, Lisa Buchanan, a professional photographer, for kindly taking the photographs of my model.

HMS *Invincible* (1747-58)

ARCHAEOLOGY PROVIDES 250-YEAR-OLD TECHNICAL DETAILS

by John M. Bingeman, Government Licensee,
Invincible (1758) Historic Wreck Site

In the 1740s the French, as an emerging colonial power, conceived the idea of building a new design of 74-gun ship for their Navy. The second of these, designed by Pierre Morineau, was called *L'Invincible* and was launched on 21 October 1744 at Rochefort. Her service with the French Navy was short. Unfortunately for the French, she was captured by the British near Cape Finisterre after fighting a superior force under Admiral Lord Anson. While being towed back to Portsmouth, Anson sent his carpenter onboard to measure her, after commenting that she was 'a prodigious fine ship, and vastly large, I think she is longer than any ship in our Fleet and is quite new'. She was commissioned in the Royal Navy and frequently used as a flagship. On Sunday, 19 February 1758, while sailing as part of an expedition to oust the French from the Fortress of Louisbourg in Canada, she ran aground on the Horse Tail sandbank off Portsmouth and became a total loss. *Invincible*'s legacy was the introduction of 74-gun ships into the Royal Navy; they were to be the backbone of the Fleet with no less than sixteen present at the Battle of Trafalgar in 1805.

Invincible was re-discovered in 1979 by local fisherman Arthur Mack and became the twenty-second site to be designated by the Government as a historic wreck site. When excavating in the 1980s, artefacts were found lying within the port side of her hull. After their conservation in our laboratory, the Curator of Chatham Historic Dockyard Trust selected at least one of every type of artefact to form what we called 'The Representative Collection'. This article will consider a few of *Invincible*'s more unusual rigging artefacts. Some are on display at the Historic Dockyard; others will be found in their reserve collection.

THE *INVINCIBLE* ARTEFACTS

Invincible's Boatswain's Store was an 'Aladdin's cave' containing a whole range of different types of spare blocks, including replacement sheaves and pins. These are some of the finds.

The majority of the blocks recovered had their sizes marked on their respective shells using Arabic numerals up

1. Ten single-sheaved blocks sized from 21in to 5in. Shells were elm, sheaves and pins were lignum vitae. *(Peter Hales)*

XXVIII   XXIIII

5 cm

2. Topsail halyard 28in and 24in blocks. *(Peter Hales)*

to 9in, and then Roman numerals for the larger sizes. These sizes referred to the maximum dimension of the oval-shaped shells. Having said that, there were the following exceptions:

12in had 'J2'
18in had 'J8'
21in had '2J'

The 'J' represented '1' – a common eighteenth-century practice. Also, most blocks were marked with at least one broad arrow.

Four topsail halyard blocks (Photograph 2) were recovered. The block sheaves were rather thinner than one would have expected for such large blocks. Their respective sheave thicknesses were: 1¾in for the 24in and only 1½in for the 25in and 28in blocks. As before their shells were elm and the sheaves and pins were made of lignum vitae.

Fiddle blocks: their purpose was to control main sails when double blocks would have affected the air flow. Photograph 3 illustrates one of the seven sizes of fiddle blocks that ranged from 24in to 34in with intermediate sizes of 27, 28, 29, 32 and 33in. The largest had lignum vitae sheave diameters of 9in and 15in.

A 58in rack block (Photograph 4) would have been used as one of a pair lashed either side of the bowsprit. Its purpose was to provide leads for sheets (operating ropes) for

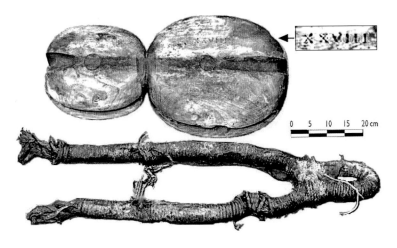

0 5 10 15 20 cm

3. A 'XXVIII' (28in) fiddle block with rope strop. *(Peter Hales)*

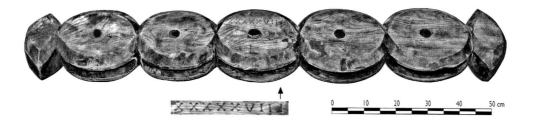

4. A 'XXXXXVIII' rack block, a solid elm shell houses five single blocks. *(Peter Hales)*

the spritsail(s) beneath the bowsprit – see illustration, No. 5.

Photograph 6 shows the one exception to the hundreds of rigging blocks from *Invincible* that all had sheaves and pins of lignum vitae. Lignum vitae is an extremely hard, oily wood from the Caribbean that came into use during the seventeenth century. This block appears to belong to an earlier, perhaps medieval, period. When recovered, it had a short length of rope through its eye.

Photograph 7 illustrates the severe wear that occurs to lignum vitae pins under constant use; these examples were recovered from *Invincible*'s Boatswain's Store. Subsequently, the firm of Walter Taylor in Bugle Street, Southampton, had the contract to supply the Admiralty with blocks and at

the height of this contract they were supplying up to 100,000 blocks a year. A third-rate alone was reputed to need 1,500 blocks.

Photograph 8 is an 8in Taylor block fitted with a pair of bronze coaks recovered from the *Pomone* (1811) wreck site off the The Needles, Isle of Wight. These bronze coaks were manufactured in two halves and secured together by four ferrous rivets. With the introduction of coaks, block pins were no longer made of lignum vitae but of iron.

This arrangement is a development from the *Invincible* 12¾in sheave, circa 1758, with a coak in one piece and attached on one side only with two rivets – see Photograph 9.

The coaks for smaller sized sheaves had three 'arms' rather than four. The Photograph 10 example was recovered without any trace of its lignum vitae wheel; its actual sheave size was not known.

Deadeyes (Photograph 11) were used with standing rigging to create a purchase when tensioning shrouds. A number of deadeyes had traces of metal bands in various states of corrosion. Sizes ranged from 3½in to 18in diameter and had similar size markings to rigging blocks; namely, those up to 9in had Arabic numerals and those of 10in and above had Roman numerals. Some had broad arrows; they were all made from elm except for one 8in deadeye made of beech.

Heart blocks (Photograph 12) were used for standing rigging in a similar way to deadeyes. The three depicted from left to right are:

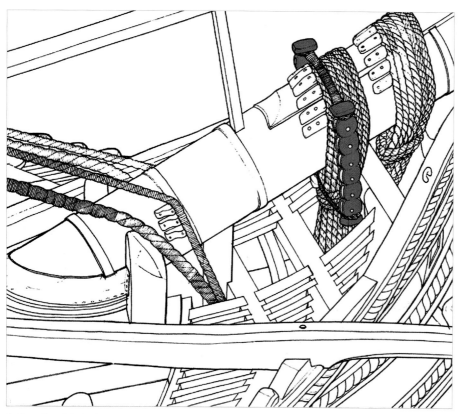

5. Jean Boudriot's drawing of a rack block in situ (see References). *Invincible* had five blocks rather than six.

6. Medieval-style block, length 278mm, width 128mm, depth 85mm. Sheave diameter 95 x 26mm thick. *(Geoff Lee, Conservation Officer, Chatham Historic Dockyard Trust)*

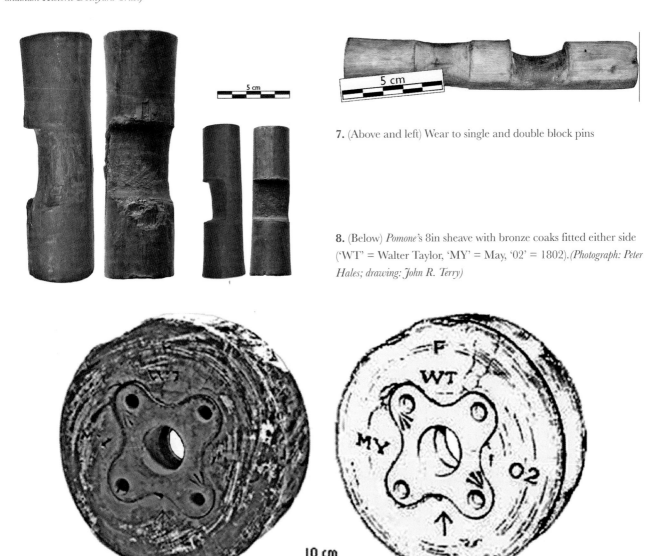

7. (Above and left) Wear to single and double block pins

8. (Below) *Pomone's* 8in sheave with bronze coaks fitted either side ('WT' = Walter Taylor, 'MY' = May, '02' = 1802).*(Photograph: Peter Hales; drawing: John R. Terry)*

9. *Invincible*'s lignum vitae 12¾in sheaves with bronze coak held in place by two iron rivets.

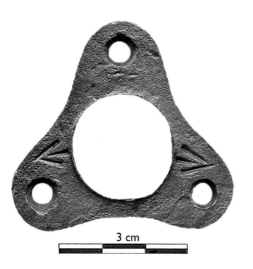

10. A bronze coak ex-*Pomone* (1811) – the centre hole showed considerable signs of wear.

14in plain style marked 'XIIII'
12in with a triangular hole
13in with four rope grooves at the base of the 'triangle'
8in not illustrated

The single elm euphroe or euvro block (Photograph 13) had a length of 710mm (28in) tapered from 120mm to 80mm. To secure a strop, it was grooved at either end and augmented by two pairs of small holes for a whipping. At right angles to the line of the strop, there are sixteen equally spaced 20mm diameter holes tapered towards the wider end. The purpose of the euphroe block was to be a centre point so that light ropes could be secured in a fan shape to suspend a quarterdeck awning. The arrangement is known as a crowfoot.

Clew garnet blocks (Photograph 14) were used with tackles to furl sails quickly by hoisting them upwards and inwards. The name came from their attachment to the lower corners of a square sail known as a 'clew'; the 'garnet' part is

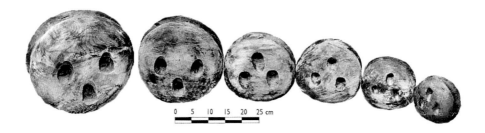

11. Six elm deadeyes from 14in to 5in diameter. *(Peter Hales)*

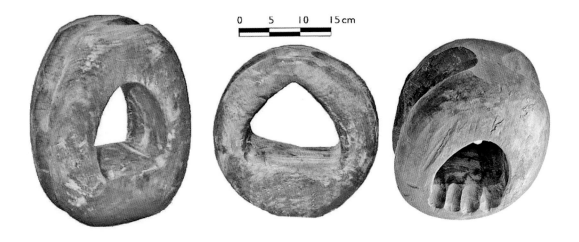

12. Three designs of elm heart blocks. *(left and centre: Peter Hales; right: Geoff Lee)*

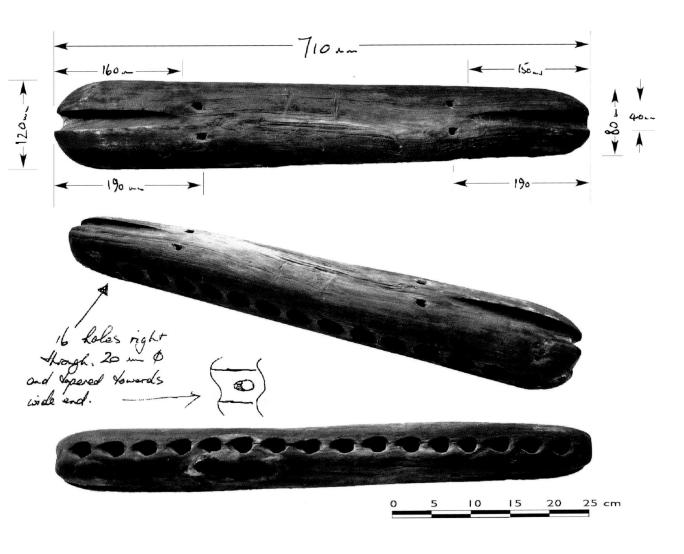

16 holes right through. 20 mm Ø and tapered towards wide end.

13. John Broomhead's measurements from his Diving Report. *(Geoff Lee, Conservation Officer, Chatham Historic Dockyard Trust)*

14. Clew garnet blocks. *(J. A. Hewes)*

more obscure but may be its resemblance to a pomegranate. The French for pomegranate was 'grenat', and this word was also used in medieval English becoming 'garnet'.

Like other blocks, clew-garnet shells were made from elm and their pin and sheave from lignum vitae.

The 15in clew block shown on the right hand of Photograph 14 is a different design with a 'mushroom' head. Although it stands 15in high, it is marked 'XVI' (16in). It is unknown whether this was intentional or an error. It is also stamped with a broad arrow.

In conclusion, I would like to say what a wonderful privilege it has been to have led the *Invincible* excavations. It has been a mammoth task not only running a Conservation Laboratory but complying with Government regulations, submitting annual reports, and responding to Government inspections ensuring that we complied with acceptable archaeological standards. All artefacts were declared to the 'Receiver of Wreck'.

Acknowledgement: Besides the photograph credits, I would like to acknowledge the work of John P. Bethell for enhancing the photographs including extra features such as the enlarged block sizes.

Editor's Note: This is just a small extract from John Bingeman's report to English Heritage concluding his twenty-nine years as Government Licensee of the Invincible (1758) Historic Wreck Site. The report entitled 'The First HMS *Invincible* (1747-58) – From the Licensee's Excavations (1980–1991)' is being published by Oxbow Books. Publication is expected in early 2010. Apart from more information on blocks, the report includes ropes (1in to 23in circumferences), ordnance, the army, navigation equipment, and domestic items.

Note

The illustration No. 5 taken from Boudriot, J., 1977, *Le Vaisseau de 74 Canons [The 74-gun Ship] en quatre tômes*, Collection Archéologiqie Naval Française, Paris, France, Vol.2, p18.

HMS *Teazer* (1801)

OR THE MISADVENTURES OF A NOVICE MODELLER IN THE WORLD OF LITERATURE

by John Thompson

Like a great many model shipbuilders, when I am not building model ships I am often to be found reading about the real thing and the era they occupied. I do not generally discriminate between fiction and non-fiction books in this regard and as long as they are imbibed with a certain saltiness then I am usually quite content.

One day my wife returned home from foraging in our local supermarket clutching a book, *Kydd*, which she had spotted and thought I might enjoy. If I am honest, I smiled at her with a gimlet glint in my eye as my wife's idea of suitable fiction and my own are usually, let us say, at odds.

And so I began to read about the adventures of Thomas Paine Kydd, a pressed wig-maker from Guildford, who found himself in the rough world of the foremast jacks aboard the 98-gun HMS *Duke William*. In a little over 24 hours I had read the entire book and was frantically searching to see if the author had produced any more in the series.

Fortunately he had produced eight books by this stage and I devoured them with a rapacity I hadn't felt since I first came across O'Brien.

In late March 2007, I contacted the author, Julian Stockwin, to tell him how much I had enjoyed his Kydd series of books. There were a number of email exchanges between us, following which, to my huge surprise and joy, I received in the post one morning, a piece of rope from HMS *Invincible* (captured from the French in 1747 and sunk off Selsey Bill in 1758) beautifully mounted and engraved. I was so touched by Julian's generosity to a complete stranger that I pondered

Below: Hull double planked and gunports and oar ports cut.

Above: Hull and waterline painted in typical Maltese colours.

how best I could return his kindness. The idea of building a model of HMS *Teazer* germinated. *Teazer* was a fictional brig-rigged sloop of war, built in Malta, circa 1801, and the first command of Thomas Paine Kydd.

WHERE TO BEGIN?

Whilst my intentions were noble, I began to get the feeling (as a novice modeller) that I had perhaps bitten off a little more than I could chew as there were no existing wooden model ship kits (*Teazer* being a composite vessel based on several real ships of the time), but to scratch build her would have taken up to two years or more and most likely would have been beyond my skills and ability. After some research to glean further details of her origins, I deduced (and Julian confirmed) that HMS *Teazer* was based loosely on the *Cruiser* class brig-rigged sloops in operation from 1797 onwards. The *Cruiser* class was, in fact, the most common type of vessel operated by the Royal Navy; they were the real workhorses – and the backbone – of the Navy.

I had decided to use the kit of HMS *Cruiser* (the name ship of the class) from a kit produced by Jotika which, in turn, had been well researched and drafted from the Admiralty plans still held at the National Maritime Museum in Greenwich. I decided that the *Cruiser* kit (to the scale of 1:64) would form

the basic structure of *Teazer*, and that I would scratch build the many differences that set her apart from the basic *Cruiser* class sloop. This allowed me to build a unique model, but within a more reasonable timeframe.

Above: Deck planking cut to scale lengths and marked to simulate caulking.

Above: False main gun deck marked up to facilitate laying three-step deck planking pattern.

Julian patiently answered all my initial questions and provided details from his own notes on her background, together with archive drawings and photographs. He also included the marine artist Geoff Hunt's research drawings and notes (a precursor to his painting which adorns the cover of the novel *Command*). I spent some time flagging up every reference to *Teazer* in Julian's books and also contacted Joseph Muscat, an authority on Maltese-built vessels, and Robert Squarebriggs in Canada, an experienced ship modeller and wood carver. They provided me with further invaluable detail and encouragement.

SECOND THOUGHTS!

Building such a model was going to present some challenges; for example, the difficulty of making the scratch-built elements blend in with a manufactured kit, notwithstanding my own very meagre set of woodworking skills. I realised, too, that Julian and his whole readership would have perfectly formed ideas about how she would have looked. It was only at this point that I (very much a novice modeller) began to realise the task and responsibility that I had undertaken.

UP AND RUNNING

Following the arrival of the kit, I checked the materials and plans for quality and made sure that all items were present. All such models begin with their basic structure, and the false keel and bulkheads form the backbone upon which everything else will sit. I started by preparing the basic skeleton of the ship in readiness for the hull planking.

THE MAIN GUN DECK

In considering *Teazer*'s main gun deck some modification to the standard *Cruiser* class layout would be necessary in order to accommodate Kydd's cabin. The ship's wheel would have to be moved forward and one of the several gratings aft removed. The opening in the deck in way of this after grating, and also that of the adjacent companionway hatch, would be planked over. The grating would not be relocated as there was not enough room on the deck. The companionway would be moved forward to just in front of the capstan, to provide access to the deck below. In addition, the rearmost gun and sweep ports would have to be boarded up and the bulwarks planked on the inside.

DECK LAYOUT

By looking at the deck plan (from bow to stern) the round hole furthest forward is for the foremast. Then there are two gratings, abaft which is the companionway. The second round hole is for the capstan shaft, then another grating. The third round hole is for the mainmast, followed by the aftermost grating. Finally there are the binnacle, ship's wheel and the transverse bulkhead to Kydd's cabin, and the upper aft deck.

This deck plan is a good example of the need to think ahead to see how the more individual details of *Teazer* will affect construction, and concomitantly what will have to be modified before items can be secured permanently in place.

GUNPORT PATTERNS

Fixing gunport patterns in place can be a fiddly task. First the gunport patterns have to be well soaked in water and then clamped into place on the hull frame assembly. When dry

they will have assumed the shape of the hull and it will be a more straightforward task to fix them in position later. (This pattern is a single strip showing the position of each gunport on the bulwarks).

THE HULL PLANKING

With most model ship kits the hull is planked in two layers, the first, in lime wood, providing a stable base for the second layer of planking in Walnut. The first layer was fastened using carpenter's glue and held in place with small nails (which were removed when the glue was dry). Later, when it came to applying and fastening the second layer of hull planking, thick cyano glue was used as the adhesive to avoid having any unsightly holes in the planking (i.e. no nails were needed this time). Occasionally some difficulty may arise when applying the first layer of planking. Despite bevelling the upper edge of each plank it is still difficult to eliminate the slight clinker effect, an inevitable side effect when

Above: Planked main gun deck.

working at this scale. However, this can be overcome by sanding and by applying wood filler to any hollows or inconsistencies in the hull surface.

THE GARBOARD STRAKE

The garboard strake is the first plank to be laid, positioned each side next to the keel. Hull planking begins from the bottom of the gunport strip downwards, and at the same time upwards from the garboard strake. It is vital when laying planks to lay two or three planks on one side, and then two or three planks similarly on the other side of the hull, or the keel may be forced out of alignment by the not inconsiderable strain exerted on it by the planks.

TAPERING

Each plank has to be tapered along its top edge before fitting. This is because the distance (girth) between the top of each bulkhead down to the keel is greater amidships than at the bow and stern. There are several ways of doing this but perhaps the most straightforward method is to offer up each plank to the hull and mark the overlap with the preceding plank and cut the taper before fitting. The taper usually begins about 8cm from the bow. With the first layer of hull planks in place *Teazer*'s lines become apparent, showing why this hull shape was so successful. These relatively small vessels had excellent sailing qualities and were tough, fast and very seaworthy. The Royal Navy deployed them all over the world and they were able to withstand the worst the

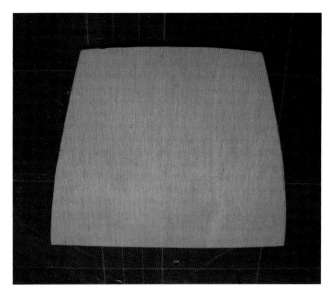

Above: False after upper deck.

weather (and the enemy) could throw at them. They were full-bodied (good for stability), but this did not lead to a sacrifice in speed as is shown by the run of the lines aft. In all, a nice combination of strength, stability and speed. The wide deck also made an ideal gun platform.

Sanding the hull after the first layer of planks has been fitted started with 240 grade wet-and-dry sandpaper and progressed through 400 grade and finally 600 grade. Running over the sanded surface of the hull with the fingertips will reveal any slight hollows or rises, which can be made good by applying some wood filler and/or sanding smooth.

With the first layer in place and sanded, work began on

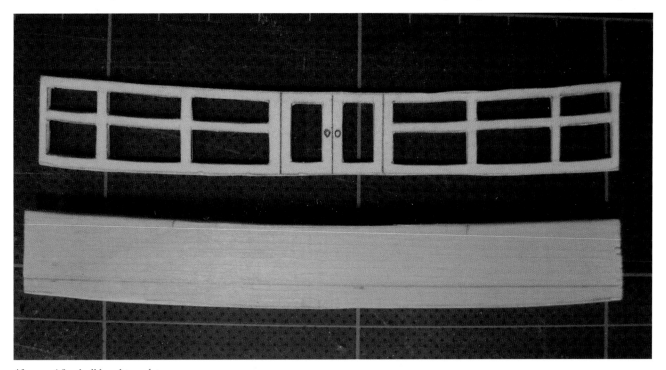

Above: After bulkhead template.

Above: After bulkhead painted and companionway hatch fitted.

fitting the second layer, this time using walnut. The original vessels were double planked on frames usually of English oak. These timbers were seasoned and then treated with a mixture of linseed oil and other (closely guarded) secret substances which varied from shipyard to shipyard. The end result of this treatment was to give the timbers quite a dark appearance, which I found could be well represented on a model by using walnut. After varnishing it had just the right colour.

The first plank was laid at the bottom of the main wale. This required a guide plank, made from scrap wood, to be fitted to indicate the line for the first plank. When fitting it I started where the sheer of the hull at the bow began to fold under itself. This, for a novice modeller, can be a difficult area to plank and it is important to ensure that the planks lie flat to the hull, and follow its natural curve. There was a pronounced curve to the planks at the bow where they were much higher than the position of the same plank amidships. This upwards curve becomes less and less pronounced as it approaches midships where it is more or less at the same level from bow to stern. On approaching this levelling off point it was necessary to start bevelling the planks at the bow.

THE STERN

The stern and stern counter were planked using the same method as for the hull planks to fasten to their outer edges. The opening for the rudder stock was formed in the stern counter ready to receive the stern post and rudder stock at a later stage.

With the second layer of planking in place the hull was given its final sanding. This left it in a very smooth and somewhat slippery state, to such an extent that once or twice it almost flew out of my grasp as it was being handled.

BULKHEADS

It is at this stage that the protruding bulkhead tabs on the inside of the gunport patterns had to be snapped off. There are several ways to do this but the best way, I found, was to grip the tab with a pair of pliers and just snap it off.

THE MAIN WALE

The main wale was made up of three 3mm x 1mm planks which were laid around the hull after measuring their height from the keel on the ship plan. The most difficult part of this

Above: Stern gallery glazed, curtained and decoration fitted.

process was to get them at exactly the same height on each side of the hull. The wales were then sanded and painted matt black along with the stem.

Whilst I had the paint pots out, I went on to paint in the gunport decoration. In this respect, I was fortunate to have the considerable knowledge of Joseph Muscat, an authority on Maltese-built vessels, who confirmed that a broad white band with a narrow black stripe at each side was entirely accurate and consistent for Maltese vessels of her type and time. This painting required a lot of masking off, for which I used a special type of masking tape used by graphic artists. I also gave each broad stripe four coats of white paint, sanding between each coat. Care had to be taken when plotting the run of each stripe to ensure that they matched up (aligned) correctly on each side of the hull where they met at the stem.

When *Teazer* was first placed into Kydd's command, she was painted with 'white stuff' below the waterline (usually a lead-based paint). It was not until she returned to home waters that her hull below the waterline was copper plated. After checking with Julian, he decided that the model should look as she did when Kydd first saw her, and so I painted her hull below the waterline off-white.

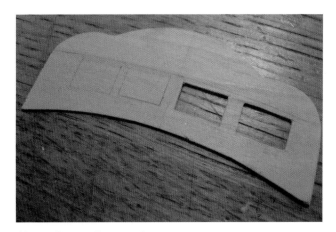

Above: Stern gallery template.

DECK PLANKING

Working at this scale (1:64), the deck planks were cut into 8.5cm lengths which broadly correlate to deck planks about 20ft long. This was more or less a standard length used for most vessels. To cover the model's main gun deck involved the cutting of 190 planks. The deck planking was also caulked, i.e. the gaps between the planks tightly filled with oakum, unpicked rope fibres which were then tarred. To simulate this on a model each plank edge was coloured with a black pen or pencil. I had carried out some trial and error experiments previously to find a pen which gave just the right result without the ink bleeding into the plank. If it did, then sanding would give them an unwanted dirty appearance; unwanted because of the many references to decks being holystoned to a pristine, neat and bright condition.

I laid the deck planks on the three-step principle. This meant that every fourth plank butt lay on the same deck beam. In order to keep this pattern consistent, I marked up the false main gun deck with coloured guide lines.

CAPSTAN

Because the companionway had been moved forward to accommodate Kydd's cabin, the lie of the capstan was not quite right since it sat slightly too far forward for my liking. The original capstan shaft hole in the false main gun deck was filled in and a new one cut slightly further back, so that it

lay equidistant between the companionway and the grating just behind it.

The deck planks were fastened individually using carpenter's glue, sparingly applied with a toothpick (perhaps a modeller's most valuable tool). The planks were laid starting at the centreline of the deck, running from fore to aft and working out to the bulwarks. Once all the deck planks were in place they were sanded and given four coats of matt polyurethane varnish.

BULWARKS

The inside of the bulwarks was planked. This can be quite a tricky job, as all the gunports and oar (sweep) ports have to be cut back and access from the deck side of the bulwarks is quite restricted.

To finish off, the inside of the bulwarks was given a light coat of red ochre paint, followed by one or more coats of

Below: Stern gallery in place and with nameboard.

Above: Components of quarter gallery.

Above: Quarter gallery painted and in place.

matt polyurethane varnish. The trick to getting a nice crisp line from the lowest bulwark plank (the one that lies next to the deck) is to paint it red ochre before gluing it to the bulwarks, thus also keeping the deck clear of any involuntary splashes of paint.

CABIN ROOF / UPPER DECK AFT

Construction of the roof to Kydd's cabin (which also formed the upper deck aft or pseudo poop deck) came next. First a card template was made to get its exact size and shape. This was transferred on to a piece of 1mm plywood, cut out and planked, in much the same way as the main gun deck. Brackets were glued along the inside of the bulwarks to support the cabin roof at the level of the top of the bulwarks.

Another card template was made for the bulkhead that would fill the transverse space between the main gun deck and the roof of the cabin, and include the entrance to the cabin from the main gun deck. This was transferred on to a piece of 0.5cm plywood, which was cut out and shaped to the deck's camber. This bulkhead would be fitted with the companionway style access doors and panelling. These were sketched on a piece of 200gm card. Panelling recesses were cut out with a scalpel and the card glued on to the plywood bulkhead.

When I originally questioned Julian about the make-up of *Teazer*, I raised the issue of how Kydd managed to get into his cabin as the clearance between the main gun deck and the cabin roof was only about 4.5ft (the height of the gun port bulwarks), requiring him to bend double to ease himself inside.

Once inside there was no problem as Julian had mentioned in his books that there were several steps down from the main gun deck, and therefore the headroom was more like 5.5ft to 6ft. I suggested that a companionway style sliding

hatch cover would solve the problem and Julian agreed.

Originally I intended to site the companionway doors on the starboard side of the bulkhead. It became apparent, however, that this was not entirely practical as they would be obstructed by the aftermost starboard gun. So I placed them centrally in the bulkhead, which would bring Kydd out immediately behind the ship's wheel. This was a reasonable arrangement for vessels of this time as indeed Nelson's first command, HMS *Badger* was formulated in the same way. After being given two coats of red ochre, two dressmaker pins were inserted for the door handles, together with four bespoke iron door hinges. Access to the cabin was improved by fitting a companionway style sliding cover on the cabin top in way of the doors.

When the aft upper deck and cabin bulkhead were in place, this part of the construction was completed by drilling the catheads with the four holes ready to receive the cathead rope work, cutting the slots into the bulwarks to receive the catheads, and fixing them in place. Finally the head rails were positioned and glued into place.

THE STERN

A card template was made of the stern gallery to obtain its size and shape. This was transferred on to thin 1mm plywood and cut out. The general design and positions of the stern lights were plotted, transferred on to the plywood, and the window recesses cut out. The window frames were made from surplus deck planks, which were split into 0.5mm x 0.5mm strips. A cardboard template was made that fitted perfectly into the stern light window recess and the shape of the template was traced around on to the sticky side of a piece of masking tape. Pieces of the 0.5mm square strips of wood were placed on to the masking tape, following the outline of the template, and the frame cross members were

Above: Deck furniture, including elm tree pumps, companionway, fore and main bitts, capstan, ship's wheel, and gratings.

put into place. Once I was satisfied with the alignment of everything, thin cyano glue was applied liberally all over the frame. When the glue was dry, the frame was cut from the masking tape with a scalpel and given a light coat of white paint. It was then glazed with thin clear plastic. A set of curtains was made for the windows from coloured paper.

The stern gallery was painted French Blue, which, despite its name, was a colour often used by the Royal Navy, particularly for stern galleries.

The decorative carved work was more problematic as I had no idea as to how it looked. I did some research on decorative carved work and found that after 1776 the Navy had reduced opulent ornamentation as it was too costly to build, maintain and repair. I contacted John Wright at Jotika (the company that produced the Cruiser kit) and he mentioned that their model for HM Yacht *Chatham* had pre-cast decorative carved work that might be suitable. In fact it was

Above: Deck furniture temporarily placed in position.

Above: Guns in place and with simplified rigging.

Above: Channels, pinrails, and ladders in place.

ideal for *Teazer* and the two angelic heralds can be seen at each side of the stern lights.

Between each window was a very simple decorative motif, and similarly just below the stern plate decorative carved work. All that was left was the nameplate.

The location for *Teazer*'s name was just under the bottom of the stern gallery. It was made from two 3mm planks glued together and cut to shape, then painted black. *Teazer*'s name was painted in a sans serif font in yellow ochre.

STERN QUARTER GALLERIES

The scratch-building construction of the stern gallery was a very challenging task, particularly for someone of limited experience such as myself, and took quite a bit of time to achieve. Next came possibly the most difficult feature of the model (for me at least): scratch-building the quarter galleries.

Here I have to express my eternal gratitude to Robert Squarebriggs, a skilled modeller and wood carver from Canada. He provided several sketches of the constructional steps and parts involved in the preparation of the quarter galleries. Whilst I had an idea of how to go about it, his drawings made the process entirely clear and, more importantly,

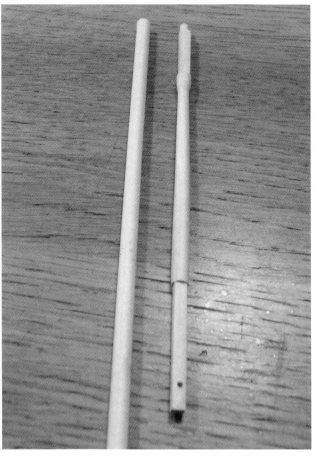

Right: Shaping a topmast.

Below: Masts and yards.

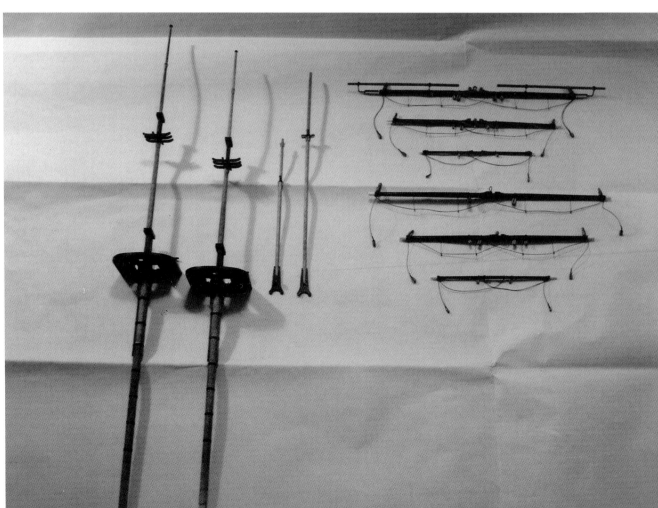

Above: Anchors.

gave me real confidence to tackle this crucial part of the construction. Each quarter gallery had about seventeen separate components, and all had to be made from scratch. Each gallery was constructed as a unit and then fixed to the hull.

Below: Quarter davits and boats.

Each part had to be individually shaped to the sheer of the hull, which required much cutting, carving, offering up to the hull and measuring, then repeating the process until the part was just the right shape and size. The windows were glazed and the French Blue and the Gold colour scheme adopted for the stern was applied.

At this stage, while the deck was clear of cannons, bitts, water pumps and so on, the positions of the two brass pedestals, which would support the finished model, were marked. Two holes were drilled in the keel to take the large screws that pass through the pedestals to secure *Teazer* to the baseboard.

RUDDER

First the gudgeons and pintles were put in place. This required much measuring and dry fitting to ensure that the rudder lay at the correct height. The rudder straps were fitted which strengthened the assembly. These were nailed in place, the nails being cut down to a length of about 1.5mm. It was crucial during this process to ensure their

Above: Flag locker.

DECK GRATINGS

These were made by first assembling the hatch coamings, which were brushed with watered down PVA glue and lined with 2mm walnut coamings. The dimensions for each grating were taken from its opening in the main gun deck and the coamings bevelled around their circumference and mitred at the corners. A piece of coarse sandpaper was then placed on the deck (coarse side up) and the grating sanded in situ to the camber of the deck. This is a job that takes time, and has to be repeated for each of the four hatches on the main deck. After receiving a coat of matt polyurethane varnish and they are ready to be glued into place.

Next to be made were the elm tree water pumps. This

correct alignment on rudder blade and hull. When everything was in place the waterline was painted in on the rudder to correspond with the waterline of the hull. The rudder moved quite freely; it was not glued or fixed permanently in place.

needed patience as the pumps were fragile and fiddly to make. The seven parts of each pump had to be glued almost simultaneously.

BITTS AND PIECES

The fore, riding and mainmast bitts were made up, painted red ochre, and fixing pins were glued into the bottom of each post to secure them to the main gun deck. This was essential as they take a fair amount of strain when all the rigging has been belayed to them.

The capstan was assembled from fourteen separate parts. The footstrips, which gave the seamen purchase when raising the anchor, were glued in place on the main deck around the capstan, which was painted red ochre, followed by a coat of varnish.

The ship's wheel was prepared, but with a slight modification. The *Cruiser* class vessels (having a single deck running fore and aft) had the tiller ropes rigged above deck, running from the wheel via blocks to the bulwarks in a zigzag arrange-

Above: Standing rigging.

Above: Figurehead.

ment until they were fastened to the tiller. This could not be done on *Teazer* due to the presence of Kydd's cabin, which obstructed the run of the ropes. I opted to put two small cowlings under the ship's wheel which show the ropes running through the main gun deck, where they then travel aft along the deckhead of the lower deck to the tiller, which lay just under the floor of Kydd's cabin. This was a common tiller configuration for those vessels that did not have an unobstructed fore and aft single main deck.

The binnacle, which I had to scratch build, housed two compasses (larboard and starboard) with a lanthorn space in between. The three binnacle windows were glazed.

The crew's companionway hatch, made up from no less than thirty separate parts, was assembled and stained with a walnut dye. Dressmaker pins were used to represent door handles. The brass handle on the sliding cover was made from a piece of 1mm wire, bent into shape.

ARMAMENT

Each cannon was made up from twenty-two separate parts (excluding rigging), so for *Teazer* this equated to 352 parts in total. To assist in their assembly I made a small jig out of scrap wood to ensure that all the gun carriages were the same height and consistent in shape. The gun barrels were made from brass and each part was painted before assembly. The trunnions were locked in position with caps nailed to the carriage (using nails cut down to 1mm in length) yet allowing the barrels to move freely up and down. Each barrel muzzle was painted red ochre.

Originally I fully rigged the first cannon with gun haul tackles and rear training tackles, but at this scale it did not look very good. There was just too much cramped into too small a space. The 2mm blocks utilised looked out of scale. Using 1mm blocks was not really an option. Not only would I have to make the ninety-six blocks, together with their ringbolts of correct scale size, but even if I had the ability to do

Below: Deck furniture fitted in place, also shot garlands.

so, the additional work would have seriously upset my very tight time schedule, and that was unacceptable.

COMPROMISES

Model ships generally include a number of compromises. What usually sufficed was to create an impression of the object and usually the eye and mind fill in the blanks. Therefore I decided to rig only the breeching, the main restraining rope that runs around the cascabel. This simplified the gun rigging, but did not detract too much in terms of appearance. When all the guns were secured in place, the rest of the deck furniture was permanently fixed into position.

Before starting work on the masts, there were still several

Below: Another view of the standing and running rigging.

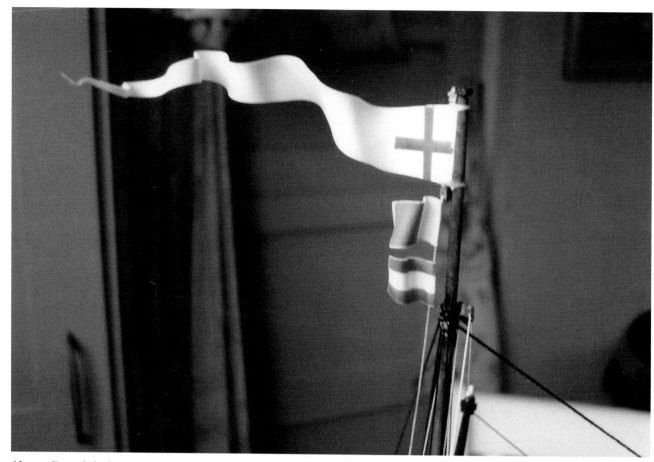

Above: Commissioning pennant and signal flags which indicate 'attack the enemy' were taken from an original signal book owned by Julian Stockwin.

jobs to be done. These included painting, drilling and fixing over sixty eyelets (representing ringbolts) on deck for the gun restraining tackles, around the foot of each mast for the running rigging, inside bulwarks and to the outside of the hull and channels. In addition there were several cleats to paint and fix to the bulwarks, two sets of ladders to be assembled and paint, ten timberheads to be made, painted and fixed in position. The entry port steps on each side of the hull with their attendant side ropes to be made and fitted. The ship's wheel tiller rope cowlings, which protect the tiller rope from chafing where it runs beneath the main gun deck and along the deckhead below, had to be completed. The pin rails inside the bulwarks to be made, glued and pinned in position, and fitted with belaying pins. The hawse hole bolsters, cathead support brackets and side fenders would also have to be made, painted and fixed in place. Although these were all small tasks in themselves and time consuming, they had to be done at this stage while access was still available.

CHANNELS

Prior to fitting the masts, some preparatory work had to be undertaken: making and fixing the channels, deadeyes and chainplates. The channels were painted black and fixed with several ringbolts (eyelets) to take the running rigging (of which more later). In addition, several nails were sunk into them to strengthen their bond to the hull as they would be under very great strain later when the shrouds had been rigged. The deadeyes were secured in position by chainplates made from brass, assembled in four sections, painted black, and nailed to the hull. Positioning the chainplates was important as they had to follow the run of each respective shroud. To do this a temporary mast dowel was placed into position in its footing and the location of the fighting top marked on the dowel. Then a shroud rope was fastened at this height, run down to its respective deadeye and the angle marked on the hull under the channel. This was repeated for each shroud and backstay. The chainplates were then fixed into position, following the marked angle on the hull.

MASTS AND YARDS

The masts on the *Cruiser* class were very robust for vessels of this size and could carry a tremendous press of sail. In general, the foremast and the mainmast were identical in shape and construction but the mainmast was slightly higher.

For the model all the spars and masts were made from length of dowel shaped as needed. Some modellers make masts in multiple sections, effectively beginning a new section each time the mast shape or dimensions change. These sections are then pinned together at a later stage. I do not like this method, preferring to work the mast as a single full-length piece, shaping each section as required. This made a stronger mast than one made up of several pieces, but an error means starting a new one from scratch, instead of simply replacing the damaged section.

For *Teazer*, I give some details of how the shape and dimensions of her mainmast changes along its length below. This is a typical example of the way a mast shape changes.

LOWER MAST

This is a uniform 8mm diameter for the first 252mm; however, the mast cheeks have to be marked on each side of the mast and the mast filed flat on each side from 170mm to 252mm to accommodate them. The mast, from 252mm to 291mm, is then filed from a round shape into a square shape with 6mm sides. Then from 291mm to 295mm the mast is filed from a square section back to a round section (to take the mast cap) and its diameter is gradually reduced from 6mm to about 4mm.

MAIN TOPMAST

This is made from 6mm diameter dowel and for its first 44mm is filed to a square section with 4mm wide sides. From 44mm it returns to its original round 6mm diameter section and tapers gradually over the next 98mm to a diameter of 4mm. At the end of this taper the mast flares out over the next 9mm to its original diameter of 6mm to form the hound. Then, for the next 27mm, it is filed to a 4mm square section. Finally the main topmast is completed by filing its last 4mm from a square section back to a round section and reducing the diameter to 3mm to take the topmast cap.

MAIN TOPGALLANT MAST

This is made from 4mm diameter dowel. For the first 34mm it is filed to a 3mm sided square section. From 34mm it returns to its original 4mm diameter round section and tapers gradually to a diameter of 3mm over the next 60mm. Then, over the next 7mm, it flares out to its original diameter of 4mm to form the topgallant hound. Then for the final 52mm it tapers from 3mm to 2mm where it is crowned with the mainmast cap. (This was sometimes called the 'cheese'; there have been reported accounts of seamen using real cheese, which was so old that it had hardened into something as solid as wood, as mast caps.)

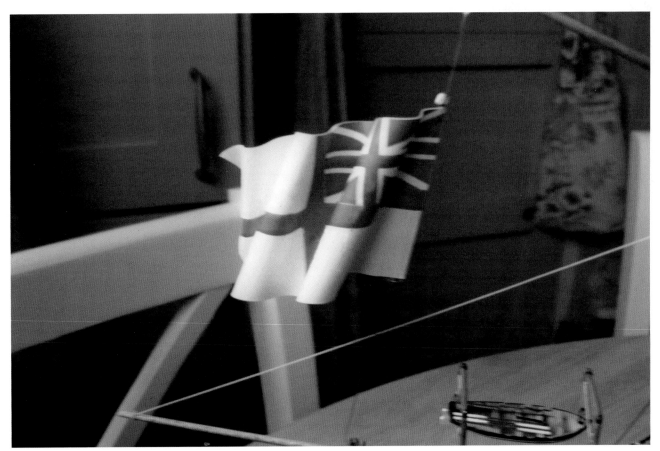

Above: Largest British ensign.

THE BOWSPRIT (AND JIBBOOM)

This was made in two parts. The lower one, 8mm diameter and 212mm long, was untapered over its whole length. The foot of the bowsprit had to be shaped to fit the angle of the deck and to fit precisely under the foremast bitts. The jibboom was smaller (4mm diameter and 150mm long) and tapered from 4mm to 2mm throughout its length. It was given a slight flare at the end (which may just be visible in one of the photographs). It was joined to the bowsprit with a cap where the dolphin striker was also fixed. The cap was fitted at 90 degrees to the keel and then bevelled at its top and bottom edges to run at the same angle as the bowsprit. This can be quite a tricky job, and requires care during the cutting and shaping processes. The bowsprit was also fitted with a saddle upon which the jibboom rested (and to which it was lashed) and also the bees of the foretopmast preventer stay. The dowel was then coated with walnut wood stain and varnished.

It was at this stage that the various rigging blocks were also fastened to the masts and spars as required.

The bowsprit required two closed heart blocks and four small deadeyes. Where the blocks were located on the mast or spar, it would also be necessary to make a small cleat from a 5mm piece of walnut to keep the block/deadeye in place.

In *Teazer*'s case I had also carved the cleats to look a little more authentic and fastened to the cleats ready for the bowsprit gammoning, which would be fitted later. The mainmast preventer stays still had to be rigged, but, again, not until later. The bowsprit had been dry fitted to give some idea of its large size and dimensions when compared to the rest of the sloop.

To complete the bowsprit it would be necessary to fashion the spiritsail yard. This was made from a piece of 4mm diameter dowel, which had to be tapered from its centre to 2mm at each end. This was painted black with the exception of its outer ends which were painted white (to indicate the ends of the yard at night). The spiritsail yard was fixed with five single blocks, cleats for the sling, and the pendant braces at each end. Finally, the footropes were added. These run from each end of the yard, crossing each other in the centre of the yard, and were fixed behind two cleats. It was important to get both footropes equal and to allow them to hang naturally from the yard.

Below: Stern view of model.

Above: Model seen from ahead.

FOREMAST

This was prepared in much the same way as the mainmast, though its overall height was a little less. A piece of dowel was cut to the correct length and one (the upper) end was squared off to form a tenon to fit into the foremast cap. The mast was then stained with walnut dye and the squared end painted black. Next the two sides of the mast were planed flat in readiness to have the cheeks fitted in position. The foremast bibs, which were first painted black, were fitted on top of the cheeks. Black cartridge paper was used to simulate the mast bands. This was cut to 2mm wide lengths and glued into position around the mast. The mast was then coated with a matt polyurethane varnish.

FIGHTING TOPS

With the lower section of the foremast complete its fighting top was prepared. The first job was to make the crosstrees and trestletrees. These are the support timbers which fasten to the foremast and upon which the fighting top will rest. Care has to be taken to ensue that they sit on the mast at the correct angle and are aligned correctly. The fighting top was glued together in two sections (the floor and the outer rim in which the topmast deadeyes sit) and braces made from 1.5mm x 1.5mm walnut fitted around its inner circumference. The top was then fixed to the crosstrees and trestletrees and the shroud bolsters shaped and fixed into position on each side of the foremast. Four eyelets were sunk into the after part of the top (where part of the foretopmast and topgallant mast rigging will later be belayed) and on the

Below: Overhead view of completed model as seen from port bow.

underside of the top (they are fixed into the crosstrees); four single 3mm blocks were fixed into position ready to receive the spritsail yard braces at a later stage.

An after rail was fitted on the top, made from 1.5mm x 1.5mm walnut, and the whole top was then painted black and ready to be fixed to the foremast.

FORETOPMAST

This was a much trickier mast to prepare as it required some very precise shaping. First, a piece of 6mm diameter dowel was squared off to a width of 4mm and a 1.5mm hole drilled through about 10mm from the lower end to take the fid. The fid was made from a toothpick which was carved down to a diameter of 1.5mm and shaped at each end. Next the mast was tapered gradually from 6mm diameter down to 4mm diameter, and then flared back out to 6mm diameter to form the hound (upon which the mast's crosstrees would rest). This required careful planing and carving, together with constant measuring with calipers to ensure that the mast was being tapered uniformly. When this was done and the hound was shaped, the mast's diameter was reduced to 4mm, and squared off at the end to form a small tenon for the mast cap. The greater part of this mast was stained with walnut dye, with the exceptions of the top and bottom which were painted black. The mast was then fixed into place through the foremast cap and the fid pushed into place.

FORETOPGALLANT MAST

This was made from 4mm diameter dowel and was almost identical to the foretopmast. A 0.7mm hole was drilled just under the mast hound to take the foretopgallant yard hoist when rigging at a later stage. The mast cap was made from a thin slice of 4mm dowel, which was glued into position and painted black.

A DIVERSION

To make a short break from working on the masts, I decided to assemble one of *Teazer*'s boats. The boat carried a kedge anchor, for which I made a rope cheese (flat coil), and also made two boat hooks and four oars. For aesthetic reasons, I shipped the rudder (normally done only when the boat was in use). The boat will be hung off the after upper deck on quarter davits. A second boat will be made later to be fitted on the opposite quarter. While I was at it, I fashioned a galley chimney for the main gun deck and lined it with walnut coamings. I decided also to install a ship's light (lanthorn) from the stern gallery and painted it gold and French Blue to echo the stern gallery colours.

THE YARDS

The foremast had four (five if each stunsail yard was counted separately). The yards were: fore yard, stunsail yards (starboard and larboard), fore topsail yard and foretopgallant yard.

The first yard (and possibly the most complex of all) to be prepared was the large fore yard. This was made from a piece of 6mm diameter dowel 270mm long. First the exact centre of the yard was marked and then, working from this point, the central section of the yard was marked off then carved to an octagonal shape. After this, the yard was tapered from 6mm down to 3mm at each end, using a small plane, followed by sandpaper to smooth off any rough edges, and calipers to ensure that each side of the yard was tapering uniformly. Cleats were fixed on each side of the yard (fore and aft) near the outer edges of the yard, eventually to be the tying-off point for the pendant braces and footropes. Larger cleats were also positioned near the octagonal centre part of the yard for the sling. Once this was done, the whole yard was painted black, except for a short length at each end which was painted white, and followed by several coats of matt polyurethane varnish. Next the numerous blocks were fastened to the yard ready to accommodate the rigging later on. The fore yard had two large 7mm single blocks on its upper edge on each side of the sling, with two more 7mm single blocks on its lower edge, position just outside the sling blocks. The octagonal section was completed with two single 5mm blocks on its lower edge.

Out near the end of the yard a 7mm block and a 5mm block were fastened one on top of the other (imitating a sister block) on the upper edge of each side of the yard. Finally pendant braces were fastened at each end of the yard.

THE STUNSAIL YARDS

These were made from pieces of 3mm dowel, each about 125mm long with a gradual taper from 3mm at one end down to 2mm at the other end. The yards were held in place by iron support brackets. These were fixed in the centre of the fore yard and at each end of the yard. They were quite difficult to align, and had to be held so that each stunsail yard lay just forward of and slightly above the fore yard (rather than directly above it). To help in their alignment, I placed the stunsail yard in its iron support brackets before I glued the brackets into place on the fore yard. When this was done, the footrope stirrups were fitted. These were made from 0.5mm wire and painted black. Each stirrup was fixed into a 0.5mm hole drilled into the yard, and black thread was tied around the yard to simulate the stirrup ties. Then the footrope was threaded through the stirrups and tied off.

TOPSAIL YARD AND FORETOPGALLANT YARD

These were made in much the same way as the fore yard (but without stunsail yards and brackets) and have their own collection of blocks, stirrups and footropes to be attached. The foretopsail yard also had an octagonal central section like the fore yard, but not the foretopgallant yard, and tapers from its centre to each end.

This completed the yards for the foremast. The work was then repeated for the yards on the mainmast, however, this mast carried a crossjack yard, which did not have a sail (course) nor stunsail yards.

DRIVER BOOM AND GAFF BOOM

With the mainmast yards finished, that left just the driver and gaff booms to be made. These were hung from the mainmast (on a brig-rigged sloop) and project directly aft over the taffrail. They were made from pieces of 4mm dowel, which tapered at the outboard end to 3mm for the driver boom and 2mm for the driver gaff. The booms were fitted into gaff jaws, which required careful fitting. They were secured to the mast with the open end of the jaws closed with thread carrying a number of beads (which acted as rollers); this would be done later. The booms, which were fitted with a variety of blocks, eyelets and cleats, were stained with walnut wood dye with the gaff jaws painted black.

One of the photographs shows all *Teazer*'s masts and yards (with the exception of the bowsprit and spritsail yard). From top to bottom they are: fore yard, foretopsail yard, foretopgallant yard, crossjack yard, main topsail yard, main topgallant yard. On the left of the yards are the gaff and driver booms. On their left the foremast and mainmast.

With all the yards completed, the fore and main masts were glued in place.

ANCHORS

The four bower anchors are made with the stocks in two halves lengthwise glued to the shank of the cast metal anchor just below its top. The ends of the stock were rounded off to prevent the stock snagging and tearing the vessel's copper sheathing when being raised or lowered. The anchor ring was made from 1mm brass wire bent around a piece of 8mm dowel and the ring snipped off and put through a hole drilled just below the end of the shank. The ring was then fitted with 'puddening' formed by winding 0.5mm thread round the entire circumference. To finish off the anchor the iron bands on the stock were made from black cartridge paper cut into 2mm wide strips and glued in place. The anchors were painted black and then given several coats of matt polyurethane varnish. The anchors will be placed on the hull and the hawse fastened much later in the construction.

THE FIGUREHEAD

Given that my carving ability was very minimal, I asked my friend Clayton Johnson, a highly skilled ship modeller and wood carver, to produce the ship's figurehead and I provided him with several preliminary sketches of what I had in mind. He carved *Teazer*'s own 'Lady Teazing' using scalpel blades (no power tools) from Swiss pearwood. When she arrived she was painted and her position plotted on the stem. This required grooves to be cut in the stem and a groove cut in the figurehead's back.

The upper and lower bow railings, bow cheeks and the bow gratings were fitted to complete the bow assembly.

HAMMOCK CRANES

I found this to be a difficult part of the construction. First I found a source from which I was able to obtain the exact size of the U-shaped hammock cranes I needed. Next, their positions were marked on the main bulwark rail (ten each side) and small slits cut in the rail into which the cranes were glued. Great care was taken to ensure that each crane was perfectly vertical and aligned correctly. Then some hammock netting was purchased. This ran through the cranes to keep the hammocks in place when stowed. This had (at this scale) an incredibly fine mesh, and was very small, fragile and hard to work with when fitting in place. I tried a number of different ways of fastening the netting to the cranes, which were largely unsuccessful. Eventually after much trial and error I settled on threading the main crane tensioning rope through the netting eyes along its entire length.

RIGGING

The shrouds were made from 1mm thread and in adjacent pairs. The first two shrouds were to larboard and were slung around the foremast fighting top cap. Each one was fitted with a deadeye at the end and then measured to ensure that they both sat at the same height above the channels. For this purpose a couple of pieces of wire were used to link the lower and upper deadeyes to get the positioning correct. When this was done the two deadeyes were linked together with a lanyard.

The same process was then carried out to starboard, all the time checking that the foremast had not been pulled out of alignment. This process was repeated for all the lower shrouds on the mainmast. Due to the earlier measuring when fitting the chainplates, all the shrouds and their chainplates lay at the correct angle. When all the lower shrouds were in place the ratlines were rigged.

Above: HMS *Teazer* model in its case on display in Ivybridge Library, Devon.

FUTTOCKS

A 1mm brass wire was fastened across the lower shrouds just below the mast bibs to form the fixing point for the futtock shrouds (and catharpins). Then 0.75mm threads were fastened to this wire and pushed up through the fighting top where they were fastened around a deadeye. This process was repeated for all the futtock shrouds for both the fore and main masts on both larboard and starboard sides.

CATHARPINS

The catharpins were ropes which fastened across the base of each futtock shroud from larboard to starboard and kept the

shrouds and the futtock shrouds correctly tensioned to ensure that they were stable for climbing and generally added to their integrity. There were three ropes to fasten for each catharpin fore, middle and after, and these were repeated for both masts.

UPPER SHROUDS

The upper shrouds were positioned in much the same way as the lower shrouds, being slung in adjacent pairs and fastened to a deadeye secured to its lower deadeye in the fighting top with a lanyard. The upper shrouds also had futtock shrouds of a sort, but these were not really for climbing up as they had no ratlines but were threaded through the crosstrees to the topgallant mast hound to add strength and integrity to the topgallant mast.

With these finally in place, the shrouds for the fore and main masts were complete and the shrouds (or rather the ratlines) in general, have at last count, required a total of 1,125 clove hitches.

Teazer had now been fastened to her pedestals and baseboard. This was because the standing and running rigging could be rather delicate and would not stand any rough handling required to drive 5in screws through the baseboard and up through the keel.

STANDING RIGGING

As with most forms of rigging this started at the fore end of the vessel in the centre of the deck, and progressed aft and outboard, beginning with the lowest element of the rigging and working up the masts, fixing and rigging each yard in turn. This ensured that (for the most part) anything fixed in place was not going to get in the way of other rigging that might need to be fixed later.

Before the yards were secured, the standing rigging was fixed in place, beginning with the fore and main stays and preventer stays, before moving on to the larboard and starboard fore and main backstays.

The fore and main stays and preventer stays were linked by means of two closed heart blocks lashed together and fastened to the bowsprit. The lashing allowed them to act as a sort of crude shock absorber and let the stays and masts 'work' when the vessel was sailing. The fore and main stays were (with the exception of the hawse) the thickest ropes in the ship's rigging. Each had a 'mouse' which was a length of rope wound around the stay near to the mast until it was wedge-shaped. Each stay had a loop at one end through which the stay was threaded and secured into place when the

Above: The Princess Royal inspects the model of HMS *Teazer* with Julian Stockwin in the Ivybridge Library during a visit to the town.

loop hit the mouse. This formation prevented chafing of the stay ropes when the masts were 'working'.

Next came the backstays. These were rigged to the channels with deadeyes and lanyards, much like shrouds but without the ratlines. With the standing rigging in place the yards were fitted followed by the running rigging.

THE YARDS

Although much could be said about the fixing of yards, I will confine it to the main points of interest. In full-size practice the yards were suspended by their rigging and fittings. On a model ship, however, some modification may be required. Each yard had a 1mm hole drilled at its centre, with a corresponding hole drilled on the centreline of each mast at the approximate height that the yard would be hung. A short length of 1mm wire was fixed into and through this hole, and the free end put into the hole in the mast to secure, with a spot of glue, the yard in its correct location. This also gave each yard a certain amount of stability and permitted it to be properly squared off.

The foremast main yard was suspended by a sling which was fixed around the top of the foremast cap and lashed with a lanyard. There was also a series of heavy blocks suspended around the mast cap which were rigged to the yard and belayed to the foremast bitts. These were used for raising and lowering the yard. The main fore yard was also lashed around the foremast which was belayed by means of various blocks and cleats. The topmast yard had its own arrangement of blocks and rigging to get it into place. The fore topmast yard halliard was belayed to the pinrails running by way of trucks fixed to the foremast backstays.

Of special interest were the parrels (shaped like the letter B) and beads used to lash the fore top yard to the topmast, and to make raising and lowering it smoother. They were difficult and frustrating to get into position. The beads were so small (100 of them would not take up more space than a current UK 1p coin – approx 20mm diameter). They had to be threaded on to a 0.25mm thread already fixed in place on the yard and around the fore topmast. First a parrel, then a bead, then a parrel, then a bead, and so on. Once this procedure had gone from the larboard side of the yard, around the back of the mast to the starboard side of the yard, it had to be repeated, threading back through the other hole in the parrel back to the starting point, where it was secured. This, too, was another difficult and frustrating job, exacerbated by the presence of rigging and other obstacles.

To complete the foremast yards, the topgallant yard was fixed into place; its rigging was simple, being hung from a hoist which passed through a hole in the topgallant mast just below the hound, and belayed to the fighting top and also the main deck below.

The entire process was then repeated for the mainmast yards.

The driver and gaff booms were quite tricky to get right as they require several lines to be fixed simultaneously. The gaff boom was quite straightforward and was fixed by its gaff jaws to the mainmast. The gaff boom was then secured both larboard and starboard by various blocks down to deck cleats on the upper aft deck, and I made a couple of rope cheeses (coils) to finish them off. The driver gaff was far trickier, and was attached to the mainmast by beads. However, there was a sling underneath the mainmast fighting top with large blocks to hold it in position and rigging from the end of the driver gaff by way of the mainmast cap, which eventually was belayed to a cleat fixed on the mainmast at deck level. The sling and the driver gaff rope had to be rigged simultaneously to get its height on the mainmast and the angle of the driver gaff just right.

Finally, the spritsail yard was attached and the rigging for the bowsprit, such as the bobstays which were rigged to deadeyes and lashed together with lanyards, were completed, along with the rigging to the boomkins, and any other small items of rigging left over.

As a small diversion to rigging the yards, I made several shot garlands, complete with 6pdr cannon balls. These were placed around the gratings. I also fashioned an after deck rail (a sort of pseudo quarterdeck rail) as I decided that it would not do to have Kydd's companionway hatch unprotected.

I did a little experimenting with flags. I asked Julian if he wanted *Teazer* to fly any signal flags in addition to the commissioning pennant and ensign. He replied and as a result I made a mock-up of the two signals which would fly from the mainmast ('attack the enemy'). These were taken from an actual Navy signal book of the age, which Julian was very fortunate to posses.

While I was fitting the last parts of the running rigging, I decided to make and fit a flag locker to go on the upper aft deck. In addition, I fitted the binnacle I had made earlier.

FITTING THE SAIL-HANDLING RIGGING

With the standing and running rigging for masts and spars completed, the running rigging that directly affected the sails was fitted. This turned out to be the trickiest part of all the rigging for a number of reasons. To begin with, access on the model became more and more restricted. Secondly, more often than not, two elements of rigging had to be tightened at the same time, the brace pendants for instance, to ensure a mast or yard was not pulled out of alignment. Thirdly, belaying the rigging to the pinrails became progressively more of a challenge to gain access. Finally, despite having exercised great care, when all this rigging had been completed, one or two hitherto taut lines would be seen to be slack or sagging.

The only remedy is to remove them and rig new lines. Of special note were the clew, sheet and tack lines, which were a particular challenge as three lines had to be rigged simultaneously on each side of the model to get them aligned correctly. The true complexity of rigging now became apparent, even for such a small and simple vessel as a brig-rigged sloop. All in all, the rigging had required about 250m of thread.

With all of the rigging in place, the four anchors were installed, two of which were lashed to their cables. Note that the cables were fed around the riding bitts and are laid along the deck until they disappear down the foremost grating into the cable tier.

DAVITS
The quarter davits were fashioned from two pieces of 4mm dowel which were carved, shaped and joined at an angle of about 100 degrees. A cleat was fastened to each as a belaying point, and a pin was fixed to the bottom of each to be sunk into the hull for extra strength. The ship's second boat was constructed, and I installed the quarter davits and boats on to the model.

FLAGS
I made all the flags from paper using Microsoft's Paint program; nothing else was really needed and perfectly acceptable results can be achieved. As well as *Teazer*'s original commissioning pennant, I made up the signal flags in accordance with Julian's wishes, and gave them a windswept appearance which was something I always wanted to see when viewing a model ship.

It will be seen that all the flags are flying aft. This would not be the case if the ship was under sail, when they would be flying forwards. However, as she was under bare poles and because the ensign would foul the driver and gaff boom rigging, I decided that it was acceptable to have her flags flying astern. Each Royal Navy ship carried a number of ensigns of different sizes, from 9ft to monsters of over 30ft. I decided (with Julian's concurrence) to fly *Teazer*'s largest battle ensign. On a ship of her size this would have been around 18ft. I made it from paper and gave it a windswept appearance.

To finish off, I placed several water storage barrels on the deck for the crew.

COMPLETION
All that I now had to do was prepare *Teazer*'s nameplate with a few details about her dimensions, armament, crew and captain, and check over the whole model, touching up and finishing off as necessary, and ensuring that she was clean and whole.

CONCLUSIONS
I would estimate, conservatively, that *Teazer* required between 750 and 850 hours to build. It was a very pleasant experience as I had never scratch-built anything before, and I have learned a lot (and made a lot of mistakes) during this project.

It required much research, and although based on a kit, I soon found that I had to scratch build many of the items and construction details I needed (a little over 50 per cent of the overall model). The other pleasing aspect of the model is that she is entirely unique and this, for me, makes the model a bit more special.

Acknowledgments: I cannot finish without some words of thanks; firstly to Bob Squarebriggs, Joseph Muscat and Clayton Johnson for their encouragement, knowledge, technical skill and generosity. Finally, I would like to thank my wife Barbara for stoically being a modelling widow for the duration of this project, Julian (for allowing me to badger him for information) and especially Kathy Stockwin who was a constant source of encouragement and good humour throughout.

Restoring a Model of an Unnamed Brig

by David Mills

Recently I was asked if I would undertake the restoration of a model which had been mouldering in a barn for some years. It had been the retirement project of a former commodore of the Orient Line, who went to sea under sail, but the model suffered an accident and he abandoned it. As a great deal of work had already been undertaken, it would have been a shame to allow its decline to continue; so I agreed.

The model arrived in the condition shown below. Only the two course yards were complete. The jibboom and

Below: Model as received.

spanker gaff were broken and the rigging was mostly in dis-array. The hull was stained, the bottom of the sternpost was missing, the cabin top hopelessly split and the decks dirty and sprinkled with bat droppings to say nothing of the broken or missing skylights and other parts.

Its overall length was approximately 41in, so I reckoned the scale to be ¼in=1ft (1:48). It had no name but appeared to be a model of a typical brig built at the end of the nine-teenth century. The source of the plans used by the commodore was unknown.

THE RESTORATION

I began by dismantling the rigging, masts, spars and all deck fittings except for the main pinrail, which was held too firmly in place, and by carefully labelling each part. Then I made a jig to hold the hull upside down, so that I could remove the old varnish with varnish remover and white spirit. It all came off quite easily, including the stains. Every strake ran the full length of the hull and had been secured with brass screws to each frame. In the course of rubbing down, several of the screw heads became visible, so I obscured them with a blob of brownish paint. The hull strakes and the decks were of obeche, but the stem, keel, sternpost and rudder were of iroko. Fortunately, I found a small piece of this wood with

which I was able to replace the missing part of the sternpost; it also matched up well. The lowest gudgeon and pintles were missing and were replaced with new ones made of brass to match the others. Originally the rudder and rudder post were of one piece of wood to which a small tiller was fixed and controlled from the wheel. The whole hull and rudder were given four coats of satin varnish with a gentle rub down between the last two coats, and the figurehead (a 'harpy'?) painted white.

Next, I made a case for the model, based on the lines by Donald McNarry in *Model Shipwright* 85 (page 37), with the baseboard of 6mm MDF and the plinth of 15mm rounded moulding, strengthening the mitres with splines. They were veneered with West African mahogany with mahogany feet added to the corners of the plinth, both were then varnished and rubbed down to give a fine finish, and the plinth was then set aside. Mahogany chocks, finished and varnished, were screwed to two convenient frames of the hull and with bolts put through holes drilled through the keel, chocks and baseboard; the hull was secured with washers and nuts. The baseboard was then covered temporarily with soft paper and then with two pieces of MDF, meeting at the centreline, and held in place by duct tape along the edges and centre joint.

The decks were thoroughly scrubbed using an artist's well-worn nylon bristle paintbrush and a little water and

Below: As received. Broken jibboom, cathead and ugly nut on capstan.

Above: Model as received showing bat droppings by broken doors and split cabin top.

Above: Showing poor state of deck amidships.

detergent. This removed all the dirt and bat droppings, leaving the decks looking fresh and clean. The next job was to make a new cabin top. The original one had come off quite easily, as had most of the glued parts which I wanted to separate. This surprised me as Cascamite glue had been used, which I thought was a strong and lasting glue. Subsequently, I learned that it has to be squeezed out to produce a firm joint, the glue itself not being that strong. I made up the decking from strips of obeche, with narrow lengths of thin black plasticard between each to represent the caulking, glued to a piece of thin plywood as a base. The margin covers of this deck were made from West African mahogany, which matched well with existing material. The original cabin top had no edge moulding, which made it look rather stark. So I added a rounded edge of edging boards. The skylights were repaired and added to as necessary and the lids cleaned and firmly shut so that they could not be opened once the model was in its case. Similarly, the wheel was disconnected from the rudder.

The deckhouse was refurbished and secured back in place, complete with repaired skylights, the doors securely shut. The boats, thought possibly to have been made by another hand, were cleaned, overhauled, and then set up on repaired skids, being duly fitted with chocks and gripes. Two anchors were carved from boxwood and fitted with flukes made from plasticard and stocks from brass rod. These were duly fitted, one hanging from a cathead and the other, with its stock released and lying along the shank, stowed on deck. The capstan, complete with pawls to prevent it running back, had a rather inappropriate nut on top. I covered with filler, which was rounded off and painted to simulate a brass cover plate. A windlass was fitted just abaft the break of the forecastle. After cleaning and some adjustment, this turned when the rocker arm was operated.

MASTS AND RIGGING

The bowsprit standing rigging had been set up, and a brass dolphin striker, chain bobstays, martingales, and bowsprit guys fitted. With the original jibboom broken, I made a new one and all I had to do was reset everything in place with the

Above: Port quarter view showing layout of brig's deck.

original deadeyes. I decided that the standing rigging was either of tarred hemp or wire for which I used 0.75mm black rigging cord. I used this to rig inner and outer jibboom guys after I had replaced the broken starboard cathead and whisker boom.

The masts were re-stepped and the shrouds fitted. I found it easier to get the lanyard taut by reeving them first through the deadeyes set up in a jig as shown. The shroud then passed through the lubber's hole, where necessary, around the mast and back down, being kept taut by hanging one or more

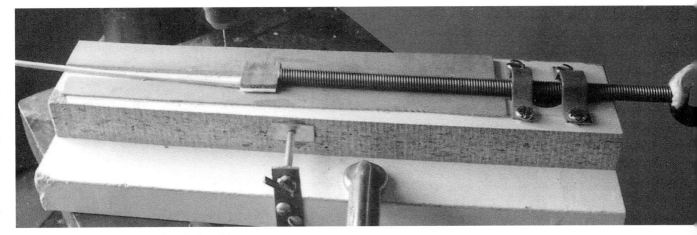

Above: Jig for preparing strips for block making.

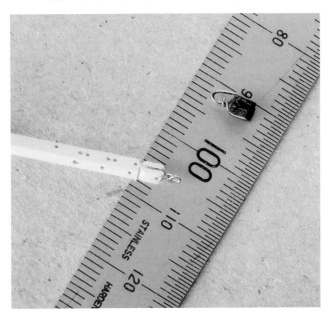

Above: Jig for setting up lanyards.

Left: One complete double block and one single about to be cut off.

Above: Jig for forming rope coils.

crocodile clips on the end until a seizing was made with fine black cotton to form a bight around the mast. The ratlines were set up using a notched card behind the shrouds, as described by John York in *Model Shipwright* 139 (page 46). I deferred fitting the backstays until the running rigging was complete, so that there was more room to work at the after side of the mast.

I worked out the dimensions of the spars from Harold Underhill's books using the size of the existing course yards as the basis, and made the yards from well seasoned Parana pine. I tried, with moderate success, to simulate the standard of existing ironwork fittings using thin brass sheet, copper wire and paste solder. These were painted satin black to match the repainting required on the existing ironwork. I crossed the yards on the foremast first, working downwards and starting with the royal yard. For the running rigging I used 0.5mm natural rigging cord dyed grey. Here again I found Underhill's books an invaluable guide as to the appropriate leads and belaying points (pins). I ended up with a few spare belaying points (pins), for which I was glad as I would have been hard put to replicate these as they were turned to a nice shape with a collar at the shank. At each belaying pin the rope was led around the lower part of the pin and tied off

with a half-hitch around the top and secured with a spot of glue. There was no sign of a bumkin, so I led the main braces to the pinrail around the foremast. The sheets were made from fine brass chain of about 45 links per inch (obtained from the Floating Dockyard Company) and which I blackened using Carr's Metal Black. When all the running rigging was in place I made small coils of rope to hang on the belaying pin of the appropriate cord. I used a jig to do this, covered with Sellotape first so that the coils would not stick to it after being given a stiffening coat of diluted Seccotine.

I have evolved a method of making blocks based in the use of a jig (shown in one of the photographs). For this model I prepared strips of boxwood 1.6mm x 2.6mm (the side of the block) 10cm long. Holding a strip with the wider side against the guide, I drill 0.6mm diameter holes along the centreline at a spacing produced by every third and fourth turn of the screw after drilling the first hole. When I had drilled about a dozen pairs of holes I turned the stick through 90 degrees, adjusted the centring slightly, and wound on one more turn. Holes were now drilled at every fourth reverse turn so that the sets of holes were the pitch of the screw out of step. I then began by removing the surplus wood at one end by cutting through the top hole on the wider face and with a small tri-

Above: The finished model.

angular file I made a shallow groove between the top and the next hole down on both sides. The top was rounded off and a deeper groove made with the small triangular file along the edge with the sheave holes. I threaded a length of 28swg Constantan wire through the next hole down and round and the remains of the top hole, pressing it down close to the sides, making one tight twist at the top, chopping off one end and forming a hook with the other. (Constantan is a resistance wire and stiff enough not to distort when set up in the rigging.) Before finally forming the block, I threaded a length of iron wire through the sheave hole and then cut off the block at the next hole with a knife using a file to produce some rounding. It was at this stage I found I could get a better shape both to the block to be cut off and the next by having a pair of holes instead of a single hole. I repeated the process until I had a 'bracelet' of blocks which I dipped into some brown stain. I used iron wire because if it was dropped it could be found easily by using a magnet. For double and treble blocks I started with strips 2.5mm and 3.3mm deep respectively, the lateral displacement required for the sheave holes being obtained by a couple of turns of the small screw set perpendicular to the main screw. To attach a standing end to a block I drilled a 0.6mm hole just inside the wire at the tail of the block. The jig was rather crude but I am sure someone with better facilities than I have could produce a better one.

Finally, the case was finished off using acrylic sheet and frame made from veneered fabricated angle strips and with one end panel removable so that the model on its baseboard could slide into place. I countersunk the fixing screws in this end panel so that their heads were hidden by mahogany wax filler.

REFERENCES

Plank-on-Frame Models and *Masting and rigging, the Clipper Ship and Ocean Carrier* by Harold A. Underhill (Brown, Son & Feerguson, Glasgow)

The Floating Drydock Company: www.floatingdrydock.com

Carr's Metal Black

Finescale, Clapton in Gordano, Bristol BS20 7SD

Above: The model fitted into its case.

Making Treenails

A TOOL FOR THEIR PRODUCTION

by John Dodd

I first started to make treenails in 1971 after I read Volume 1 of *Plank-on-Frame Models* by Harold A. Underhill. He advocated using them to fasten together every piece of timber and not to rely solely on adhesives.

I know that adhesives have improved a great deal since the book was first published in 1958, but I still continue to make and use treenails to fasten every fitting and timber. Not just for added strength, but also to improve the appearance of a wooden model.

Until recently I used the usual set up of a drawplate and well-dried split bamboo for the nails. The best grips to use for pulling the bamboo through the drawplate are jeweller's draw tongs, as shown in one of the photographs. The chequered marking on the tongs grips the material better, and I found the curved end of the handle makes pulling easier.

Quite by chance, a few months ago, I found a maker of small machine tools in the USA by the name of Vanda-lay

Above: Treenail maker.

Above: Hollow brass mandrel with a cutter head fitted. The brass guide head is behind.

Industries and saw that they have a treenail maker (trennel maker) amongst other small machine tools. I made contact and after reading their instructions for using it bought one. They also make various other fittings that make good use of any Dremel drill, plus what looks to be a suitably sized sander for model work. Their e-mail address is: vandalay1 @verizon.net and the contact there is Larry.

After I bought the treenail maker I recalled reading a brief mention of it in Brian King's book *Workshop Practice for Ship Modellers*. There is an incomplete mention of the trennel maker on page 103. There also seems to be a printers' error as the commentary says 'Trennel Maker. This is a device used in a drilling machine to convert…' and nothing further, but the illustration in the book is clear.

I bought the complete set of the trennel maker, which comprises a well-machined aluminium table that holds the

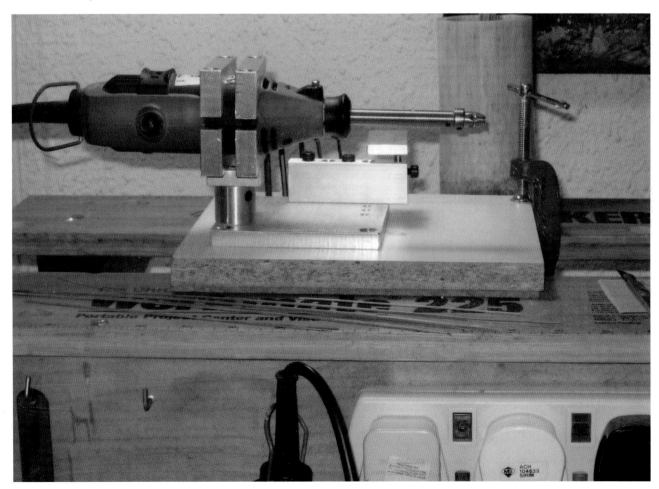

Above: Ready for use.

Above: Examples of machine-made treenails.

Above: Usual drawplate and jeweller's draw tongs.

can think of would be for the maker to stamp the cutters with a number to indicate size. To use the equipment set the drill speed to 15,000 to 20,000 revs.

A piece of stripped bamboo about ³⁄₆₄in roughly square is then inserted into the open end of the brass guide head and it is then slowly inserted into the cutter head. The total length of nail that can be made this way is about 2.5in long, but the work is fast. Avoid having any piece of bamboo with a part of the hard node in it, and use only sections of material between the nodes.

I have two cautions to add. The bamboo being fed into the guide must be held firmly or the cutter head will grip the material and spin it at high speed burning and cutting the fingers holding it. Secondly, any temptation to press the bamboo into the cutter too fast will result in breaking a tooth on the cutter. Replacement cutter heads are available but are quite costly.

I have never found making treenails by hand to be all that tedious and usually it is a task that I give myself early on at the start of a model. I select a day when I do not feel like concentrating to any great extent and I am happy to sit thinking of something else while steadily pulling the bamboo through. It is a peaceful and quiet task, quieter than making machine-made treenails.

Dremel firmly in place with two machined aluminium brackets. The cutting part is an extended hollow brass bar which screws on to the Dremel head and on to which fits either of the two hardened steel cutters that come with the set, plus a brass guide head that fits tightly on the outer end. The cutters produce treenails 0.025in or 0.030in thick.

I screwed the machined plate on to a 1in thick piece of pressed board but this needs to be held firmly to the bench with a small G clamp because I found the vibration and movement impossible to control without it being held down firmly.

The parts fasten together with set screws and the hex wrenches to tighten them are provided. One improvement I

The photographs are not of my small workshop, but as I live in the tropics I have a Black & Decker Workmate that I use on my verandah in the cool of the mornings just to make small components. When it becomes hotter in the afternoons I then go to my workshop and enjoy the benefit of air-conditioning and more worktop space.

By the way, I have found an excellent source of drawplates in the USA from Byrnes Model Machines. I bought one to replace my old jeweller's drawplate and found it to be much better, maybe because it is sharper, but certainly it is larger and can be held firmly in a vice. They also sell some excellent machine tools for model makers that might be of interest to other *Shipwright* readers.

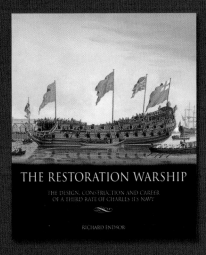
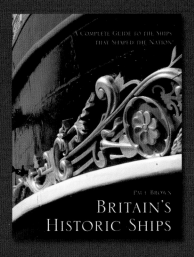

Ships of the Wilkes Expedition

ANTARCTIC EXPLORATION 1838-42

by Rorke Bryan

The decline of Arctic whale stocks and blockades during the American War of Independence and the War of 1812 caused serious damage to the economies of the prosperous towns along the New England coast from Connecticut to Maine. Sealing in the southern hemisphere provided some relief following the discovery of valuable fur seal colonies in the South Shetland Islands in 1819, but these were virtually wiped out in three years during the resulting 'Seal Rush'. The loss of this profitable 'skinning trade' put great pressure on ship owners and the United States Government to find new

seal colonies in Antarctica and the South Pacific. In 1829, three prominent New England ship-owners, Edmund Fanning, Benjamin Pendleton and Nathaniel Palmer,[1] mounted a 'scientific' expedition with the brigs *Annawan* and *Seraph*, and the schooner *Penguin*. The ships briefly visited Elephant Island and the South Shetlands before seeking other 'seal islands' in the South Pacific without much success. The expedition included James Eights, the first American scientist to visit Antarctica, though very little time was devoted to science. The expedition also included one Jeremiah

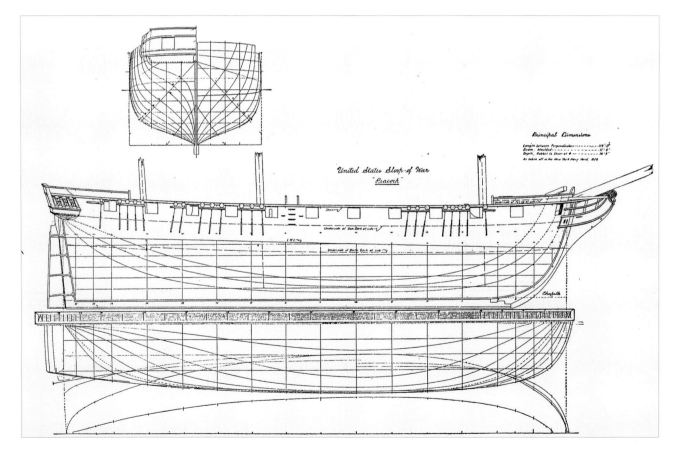

Above: Lines of the sloop-of-war USS Peacock, designed by William Doughty. Originally built in 1813, she was completely rebuilt in 1828. *(Courtesy of the Smithsonian Institution, MNAH/Transportation)*

Reynolds, a special agent of the United States Navy Department, to collect information relevant to maritime operations in the Pacific Ocean. Reynolds was a lobbyist who had been a thorn in the side of the government throughout the 1820s. He was also an ardent disciple of an extraordinary but fashionable theory usually known as 'Symmes' Hole', proposed by John Cleves Symmes who believed that the 'earth is hollow and habitable within', consisting of solid concentric spheres and open at both the north and south poles.[2]

The expedition diminished Reynolds' enthusiasm for 'Symmes' Hole' but whetted his determination to arrange a serious government scientific expedition to Antarctica and the South Pacific. He pursued this goal tirelessly from 1831, acquiring powerful enemies and leaving a trail of political intrigue, bruised egos and professional jealousies.[3] There was strong support from the shipping lobby, as far too many American ships searching for whales and seals were winding up on uncharted reefs in the South Pacific and more than a few sailors were being killed by 'Feejee' islanders. There was strong opposition, however, particularly from the Secretary of the Navy, who felt that there were many more urgent priorities for a cash-strapped government. Nevertheless, by April 1838 the United States Exploring Expedition appeared at last to be an imminent reality and a commander had been appointed.

Charles Wilkes was a lieutenant in the US Navy, appointed after command had been refused by a succession of senior officers, wary of such a political minefield. Although he was not a scientist, and was very junior for such a significant command, Wilkes was a very talented mathematician who had been appointed as head of the Navy's Depot of Charts and Instruments in 1834. In 1836 he had been sent to buy navigational and scientific instruments for the possible expedition from the best European manufacturers. Despite not having commanded of a ship for fourteen years, on his return he was appointed to command the brig USS *Porpoise* on a survey of the notorious, but valuable fishing ground of Georges Bank, a perennial bone of contention between New England and Nova Scotia. His reputation was enhanced when the logistically complex survey was completed very efficiently within two months.[4] Nevertheless, his appointment was only secured by the personal intervention of Martin Van Buren, the new President.

Above: Rig of USS *Peacock*. (Drawn by H.I. Chapelle, 1925)

The expedition was already contentious and Wilkes' fractious personality did nothing to help. He was immediately at loggerheads with the twenty-seven scientists already appointed who were not particularly impressed with the instruments he had purchased in Europe for $19,000 (equivalent to a present-day value of about $650,000). These included no less than twenty-nine chronometers, but not a single microscope for the scientists. As a result, Wilkes decided that civilian scientists were quite unnecessary for the expedition.

THE SHIPS

The issue of the ships for the expedition was also unresolved. A large frigate, the USS *Macedonian*, had already been assigned as flagship and, in preparation, had been fitted with a hot water heating system. This was not the *Macedonian* captured from the Royal Navy during the 1812 war by Stephen Decatur of the USS *United States*, but a new replacement designed by Samuel Humphreys and launched in 1836. She was 50m (164ft) long, 12.5m (45ft) beam and drew 5.49m (18ft) and registered 1325t, which Wilkes felt was much too large for exploration in uncharted, ice-ridden coastal waters. Within a month he managed to get four more suitable ships assigned to the expedition: the sloops-of-war USS *Vincennes* and *Peacock*, the brig USS *Porpoise*, which he had commanded

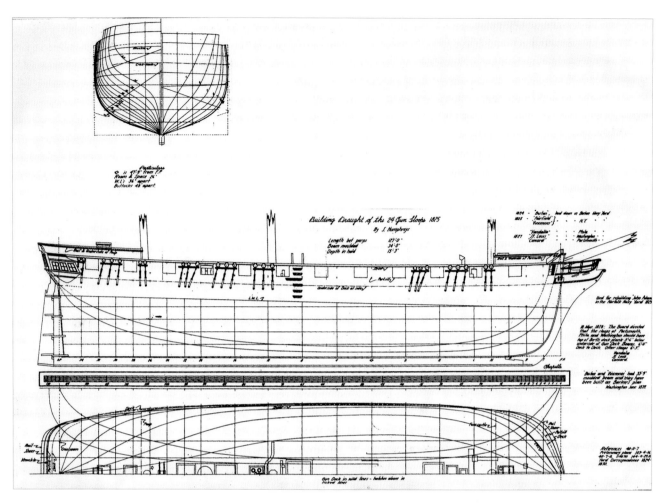

Above: Lines of USS *Vincennes*, commanded by Lieutenant Charles Wilkes. *(Courtesy of the Smithsonian Institution, MNAH/Transportation)*

on the Georges Bank survey, and the store ship USS *Relief*. Wilkes did not record the criteria he employed to select these

Above: Proposed spar draught and sail plan for USS *Vincennes*, as drawn by Samuel Humphreys, Chief Designer of the Navy, 1830. *(Courtesy of the Smithsonian Institute, NMAH/Transportation)*

ships but it appears, as well as size and draught, priority was given to speed and passage-making capability. *Vincennes*, *Peacock* and *Porpoise* were all well-regarded in the Navy as fine, swift, well-designed ships, and the store ship *Relief* was newly-built. As the expedition was due to leave in a few months, there was little time for extensive re-fitting and no particular modifications were made to increase the suitability of the ships for ice navigation.

Peacock was a well-known and successful ship, whose design strongly influenced ship-sloop design in the US Navy for the next three decades, but she had a somewhat curious history. The original *Peacock* was one of six 'ship-sloops' commissioned by Congress in 1813, and designed by William Doughty.[5] Impressed by the very fast Baltimore Clippers, Doughty designed three sloops (*Ontario*, *Erie* and *Argus*) on the same principles, with a lot of drag to the keel, drawing nearly twice as much aft as forward.[6] These ships were successful but the extreme drag made them difficult to handle. The other three (*Peacock*, *Wasp* and *Frolic*) were very similar apart from the addition of quarter galleries, but had less than half the drag to the keel and less sheer, though *Peacock* was slightly sharper with a bit more sheer and forward rake than the other two.[7] Built by Adam and Noah Brown in New York, she was 509 tons and measured 35.97 m (117ft 11in) length, 9.63m (31ft 6in) beam, and 4.98m (16ft 4in) draught. She had a single gun deck, carried twenty-two 32lb carronades and two long 12lb guns, and had a complement of 140 officers and crew. With a low, flush-decked hull and sharp ends but a full mid-section, she was a weatherly, sta-

Below: Model of Charles Wilkes' sloop-of-war USS *Vincennes*, by Arthur Henning, showing the light spar deck and foc'sle installed for the US Exploring Expedition. *(Courtesy of the Smithsonian Institute, NMAH/Transportation)*

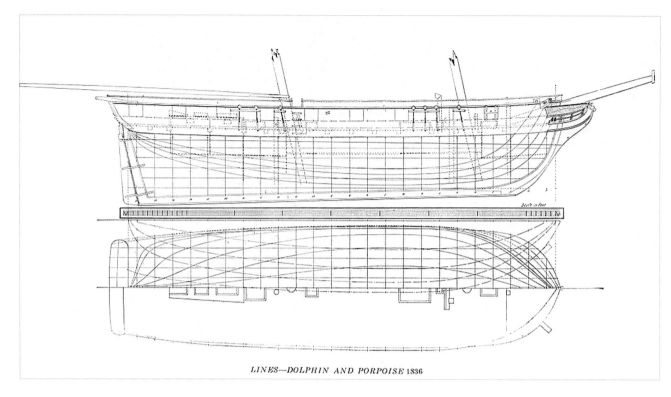

LINES—DOLPHIN AND PORPOISE 1836

Above: Lines of the hermaphrodite brig USS *Porpoise* designed by Samuel Humphreys and used by Charles Wilkes on the Georges Bank survey. (Courtesy of the Smithsonian Institution, NMAH/Transportation)

ble ship and could fit adequate stores for long voyages, but her main claim to fame was that she was very fast.

She was a ship-rigged three-master which carried topgallants and royals on all three masts and in a fresh breeze just off the beam could reach almost 15 knots.[8] Catesby Jones, her first commander, preferred her rigged as a barque. He claimed that the main and mizzen masts were too close together making the mizzen square sails useless as they could not be braced round sufficiently.[9] She was faster than all her sister-ships and was frequently able to outsail larger ships in strong winds, including Decatur's *United States*.

During her first cruise, *Peacock* captured the 18-gun British brig *Epervier* and $120,000 in a fierce battle off Florida, which earned the commander a gold medal from Congress. Over the next decade, *Peacock* made several Mediterranean cruises, and in 1824 rounded Cape Horn to spend two years cruising along the South American coast. This voyage was terminated when she received severe hull damage in a collision with a sperm whale.

On her return to New York in 1827, *Peacock* was decommissioned and broken up, but was immediately re-built for a surveying expedition to the Pacific in 1828. A few bits of the original ship, including some berth deck knees and parts of the capstan, were incorporated in what was really a completely new ship, though it was still classified by the Navy as the original. This was a strategy to circumvent the need for a new authorization from Congress. The new ship had al-

most exactly the same dimensions, it had an elliptical stern and the hull was sharper forward, with less sheer and rake, less deadrise and less drag in the keel. Burden was increased to 650 tons and there were now only ten guns: eight long 24pdr and two long 9pdr. Although she was only ten years old when assigned to the expedition, the intervening years had treated her harshly. She had been aground on a coral reef in the Arabian Gulf for 60 hours, escaping only by heaving her heavy guns overboard. Her extremely resistant live oak bottom was intact, but her upper works were in poor condition, and little work had been done since her return to the United States, apart from the addition of a light spar deck to accommodate her complement of 130 men.

The *Vincennes* was also a young ship; the second of ten new sloops-of-war to be laid down in 1825, she was commissioned in 1826 from the New York Navy yard at a cost of $115,889.[10] The sloops were designed by Samuel Humphreys, Chief Designer of the Navy, and though they were not flyers like *Peacock*, they were fine seaworthy ships and were popular in the Navy. Chapelle[11] described her and her sister-ships as essentially enlarged *Peacocks* with round or elliptical sterns (introduced by Doughty on USS *Brandywine*[12]) and false galleries. However, *Vincennes*' lines are somewhat fuller at both the stem and stern, though her sheer was identical to *Peacock*'s. She was 700 tons burden and measured 38.72m (127ft) length, 10.29m (33ft 9in) breadth, and 5.03m (16ft 6in) draught and originally carried twenty-four 24lb guns. Like *Peacock*, she was three-masted and ship-rigged fore: 42.5m (136ft); main: 45.12m (148ft); mizzen: 36.9m (118ft 6in), carried topgallants and royals and a spencer and could set a total of about 1680m² of sail. She was a good sailer, particularly with the wind abeam, and actually beat *Peacock* in light winds in the Pacific, but in strong winds with topgallants and royals she tended to bury herself and actually sailed best with just topsails and courses. As the main and mizzen masts were exactly the same distance apart as on *Peacock*, she presumably had the same difficulty in bracing the mizzen square sails. Her great merit was the 'great facility with which she performs all maneuvers and the capacity to carry a great deal of sail without strain'[13] and Wilkes later claimed that she could 'do everything but talk'.[14]

Immediately after commissioning, *Vincennes* departed on a four-year voyage round Cape Horn and through the Pacific, to become the first American ship to complete a circumnavigation. On her return to New York in 1830, she was re-fitted and then again sailed round the world between 1833 and 1836. She was re-fitted again for the Wilkes expedition. A light spar deck and foc'sle were added to provide better protection for the crew and additional accommodation. Her original complement was 80, but for the expedition this was expanded to 190. To accommodate the remaining scientists, a new 10.98 m (36ft) long after cabin was constructed, well-equipped with drafting tables, a library and a conference room.

Porpoise, the gun-brig employed by Wilkes on the Georges Bank survey, was one of two brigantines built in 1836 which were almost replicas of three schooners built to Humphreys' design in 1831, and subsequently converted to hermaphrodite brigs. They were influenced by developing ideas on clipper lines, and, intended for suppression of the slave trade, were fast but rather tender ships. *Porpoise* and her sister ship *Dolphin* were the same length as the originals at 26.82m (88ft), but had slightly broader beam: 7.62m (25ft) and draught: 3.35m (11ft).[15] *Porpoise* registered 230 tons and carried two long 9lb guns and eight 24lb carronades. She could set a lot of sail (around 732m²) on her tall masts (28.7m and 31.1m high) and was regarded as one of the fastest sailers in the Navy. With a lot of drag to the keel, she was very responsive to the helm, but with a spanker boom nearly 16m (52ft) long she must have been a real handful in the Southern Ocean. After she had been altered for exploration in the Arctic she was called a 'horrible rolling' brig and a 'man-killer' but Canney suggests that the modifications may have changed her seaworthiness.[16] Following experience on the Georges Bank survey, for the expedition a foc'sle, light spar poop and poop cabin were added to house the large complement of sixty-five men.[17]

Relief was the only ship built specifically for the expedition, launched as the first commissioned store ship in the US Navy at the Philadelphia Navy Yard in 1836. She was also designed

Above: Model of USS *Porpoise* built by William Brown showing the light spar deck and focs'le installed for the US Exploring Expedition. *(Courtesy of the Smithsonian Institution, NMAH/Transportation)*

by Humphreys like a bluff-bowed merchant ship with the capacity (468 tons) of a trans-Atlantic packet.[18] She was 33.23m (109ft) in length, 9.15m (30ft) beam and 3.66m (12ft) depth of hold and was pierced for sixteen small guns, though she actually carried only six 18pdr and two 12pdr.[19] She was also a three-masted full-rigged ship, but the main innovation was the capacity to set spencer trysails on both the mainmast and foremast on gaffs which did not interfere with lowering the yards. This allowed her to be worked to windward in strong winds under the spencers and the spanker, functioning as a three-masted schooner. She was a very comfortable ship with a stern cabin, but despite the innovative trysails, she proved to be a slow sailer and eventually would try Wilkes' not very abundant patience to breaking point.

The expedition was meant to depart in the early summer, but Wilkes faced a chaotic situation, with preparations far from complete and hindered by what he regarded as the obstructive lethargy of the Norfolk Navy Yard (although there was a new Secretary of the Navy, the opposition to the expedition continued). He had to find commanders for all the

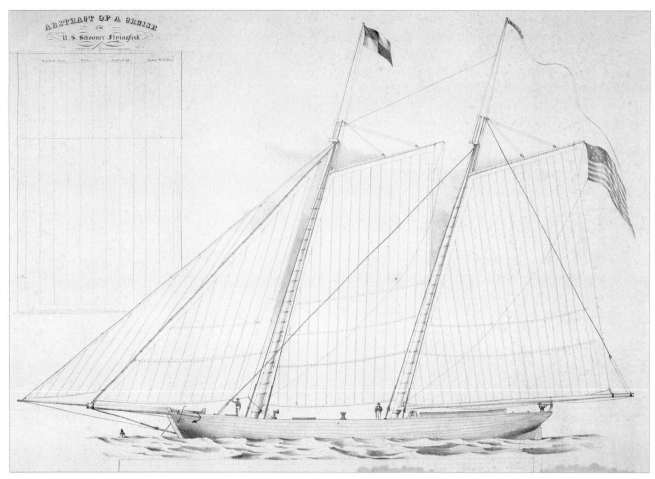

Above: Lithograph of USS *Flying Fish*, formerly the New York pilot schooner *Independence*. *(Courtesy of the Peabody Essex Museum, Salem Massachusetts)*

other ships (preferably ones who did not out-rank him), and he also, very reasonably, insisted on the addition of two tenders for inshore activities. This role was filled by two former New York pilot boats, the 96-ton *Flying Fish* (formerly *Independence*) and the 110-ton *Sea Gull* (formerly *New Jersey*). *Flying Fish* measured 26.06m (85ft 6in) in length and 6.86m (22ft 6in) in beam. Both were two-masted schooners, with the strongly raked tall masts characteristic of fast pilot boats and equipped with tillers rather than steering wheels. Wilkes had the masts and sails reduced to make them more manageable in the rough waters off Cape Horn (though, even then, *Flying Fish*'s mainmast measured 30.8m (101ft). It says much for Wilkes's logistic ability that the modifications to the two schooners were completed in three days. With Wilkes in command of *Vincennes*, the commanders appointed to *Peacock*, *Porpoise*, *Relief*, *Flying Fish* and *Sea Gull* were Lieutenants Hudson, Ringgold and Long, and Passed Midshipmen, Reid and Knox.

THE EXPEDITION

By 18 August 1838 the squadron was, at last, ready to depart from Hampton Roads, with an overall complement of 83 of-

ficers, 342 enlisted men, 7 civilian scientists, 2 draughtsmen, an instrument maker, a taxidermist and an interpreter. Wilkes's orders for the ambitious voyage called for coastal surveying off Patagonia and Tierra del Fuego and southward thrusts into the Weddell and Bellingshausen Seas from a base near Cape Horn, surveying in the Society and 'Feejee' Islands, before assembling at Sydney for further exploration of the coast of Antarctica, a voyage northwards to the coasts of Washington, Oregon and California, and finally back to the United States via Japan and the Philippines. Although Wilkes had accomplished logistic miracles, he was 'well aware that we were anything but well-equipped for such a cruise', and set off with the 'feeling…of one doomed to destruction'.[20]

The journey south towards Rio de Janeiro was comparatively uneventful, but *Peacock* started to leak through poorly caulked seams as soon as she put to sea, requiring a diversion to Madeira. Her condition was so bad that twenty-five days later Wilkes and Hudson sent a long letter from Madeira to the Secretary of the Navy, complaining of rusty, worn-out pumps, with bands in fragments, and leaking through the rotten waterways, upper decks and the eyes of the combings, with water 'running by bucketfuls down the apron to the store-room'. Links in the chain cables were rusted solid, and both fore and main masts had started and worked considerably at sea. In one of many complaints Wilkes said that 'the *Peacock* has been fitted out [as far as the Navy Yard was concerned] with less regard to safety and convenience than any vessel I have had anything to do with'.[21] The defects required prolonged repairs in Rio de Janeiro, where, amongst other work, 46cm (18ft) had to be cut off the top of the mizzen mast to remove a defect which 'appeared to have been filled with rope yarn and putty, and painted over'. Even after the repairs, Wilkes found *Peacock* to be 'wholly unseaworthy with respect to such a cruise'.

Due to the delays for repairs, most of the ships did not reach their rendezvous and proposed base at Orange Harbour until 17 February 1839, (the slow *Relief* had been sent ahead). Orange Harbour is a small bay on Hardy Peninsula (55°31'S, 68°00'W), 61km from Cape Horn. It was too late in the summer to accomplish much exploration, but Wilkes set out for the South Shetlands on *Porpoise* accompanied by *Sea Gull* on a rather futile trip which only reached 63°10'S. The attempt to reach land was foiled by thick ice, fog and gales, which coated both ships with ice, making life miserable for the poorly clad crews, particularly on *Sea Gull* whose deck was swept by waves every few minutes. By 5 March the situation for *Sea Gull*, with frozen sails and rigging, and 'foresheets the size of a sloop-of-war's cable'[22] was intolerable and the ships turned north. In the meantime, *Peacock* and *Flying Fish*, sent to the southwest had fared somewhat better, though the ships were separated within 24 hours, and *Flying Fish* was damaged by heavy seas which smashed both boats, injured several crewmen and half filled the cabin with water. Despite this, *Flying Fish* reached 70ºS, 101º 11'W, short of Cook's furthest south on his circumnavigation on HMS *Resolution* in 1774, but only about 180km from the Thurston Peninsula. *Peacock* was less successful, reaching only 68º08'S, 97º58'W, and losing the captain of her maintop. However, at least she had now been rendered watertight for the first time by ice frozen to the outside of the hull, which Hudson described as 'the Antarctic caulker'.[23]

Back at Orange Harbour, men from the *Vincennes* had been surveying in a 35ft cutter. This nearly ended in disaster in a severe gale when *Vincennes* dragged her anchors. *Relief*, detached to bring the scientists to the west coast and through the Straits of Magellan, was delayed by headwinds and, while

Below: USS *Sea Gull* and USS *Porpoise* during the first approaches to Antarctica by Wilkes' ships in March 1839. *(Courtesy of the Alfred T. Agate Collection, U.S. Navy Naval Historical Centre, Washington, D.C.)*

attempting to shelter near Isla Noir in the same storm, progressively lost all her four anchors and missed grounding on the notorious reefs known as the 'Western Furies' reefs by only half a ship's length, by 'splendid seamanship and rare good fortune'.[24] Lieutenant Long actually conned the ship through a speaking trumpet, standing on the fore yard. As *Relief* was now helpless without anchors, Long headed for the winter rendezvous at Valparaiso, where a boat was sent in, and an anchor borrowed from Captain Locke of HMS *Fly*.[25]

Wilkes waited in vain for *Relief* to return to Orange Harbour until 15 April; then he also sailed for Valparaiso, leaving *Flying Fish* and *Sea Gull* to follow. *Flying Fish* arrived on 19 May but *Sea Gull* disappeared with all eighteen hands, having last been sighted in bad weather just off False Cape Horn.

The loss of the *Sea Gull* was the final blow of the expedition's initial Antarctic season. Virtually nothing had been achieved at the expense of significant damage to ships and more loss of life than during the combined voyages of James Cook with HMS *Resolution* and *Adventure*, and Thaddeus Bellingshausen, with *Mirnyi* and *Vostok*. Morale had also been badly undermined by Wilkes' persistent intolerant micromanagement, excessive secrecy and capricious treatment of his ships' commanders. Philbrick described Wilkes' interpersonal skills as 'next to non-existent', resulting in his nickname of 'the Stormy Petrel'.[26] He was obsessed with minor disciplinary matters (such as bringing the *Vincennes* close abeam *Flying Fox* to check the cleanliness of the crew through a telescope), seeing them as indicators of a 'mutinous cabal'.[27] Wilkes was also quick to blame others when his plans miscarried, notably Long who he blamed for the failure of *Relief*'s

mission (and the loss of *Sea Gull*) rather than crediting him with the near-miraculous survival of the ship off Isla Noir. Wilkes solved the 'problem' by sending Long and *Relief* back to the United States from Valparaiso. Wilkes was already thoroughly detested by most expedition personnel, but questions were now being raised about his seamanship and judgment. Leaving Valparaiso, *Vincennes* twice fouled *Peacock*, and also a Danish ship, which William Reynolds[28] attributed to the commander's 'mismanagement and obstinacy'.[29] Not surprisingly, deserters began to drift away from the expedition in increasing numbers.

The expedition was now expected to cross the Pacific, to survey and carry out scientific work in the Navigator's Group, the Society Islands and Fiji, before proceeding to Sydney. Wilkes interpreted his orders to give priority to surveying while providing very limited opportunities for scientists, though his own unscientific descriptions fill many pages of his *Narrative*. Wilkes enlivened affairs by promoting himself and William Hudson to the rank of Captain, which the Navy had pointedly failed to do before the departure from Hampton Roads. The voyage was marked by many more incidents of Wilkes' erratic behaviour and questionable seamanship, notably at Pago Pago, in Samoa, where *Vincennes* narrowly avoided becoming a total loss on a reef.

The remaining ships reached Sydney by the end of November 1839, with little time to prepare for a second encounter with Antarctica. Many of those who visited the ships in Sydney commented on the inadequate preparations, including lack of ice saws, watertight bulkheads, special clothing and antiscorbutics. Wilkes did note that the 'means for protecting ourselves in the ships for winter quarters were anything but sufficient' and tried to improve matters by installing heaters to keep temperatures between decks up to 10°C (50°F).[30] Fuel was limited, however, and space could only be found for seven month's fuel and twelve month's food by using the boats for storage. All the ships were re-caulked, and *Flying Fish* had new Kauri pine masts fitted, which were slightly shorter and wider than the originals. The biggest concern was again *Peacock*. On 21 December the ship's carpenter complained that 'the sheer-streak is quite rotten in many places as well

Above: Wilkes' supply ship USS *Relief*, in the 'Western Furies' off Isla Noir at the western outlet of the Strait of Magellan, March 1839. *(Courtesy of the Alfred T. Agate Collection, U.S. Naval Historical Centre, Washington, D.C.)*

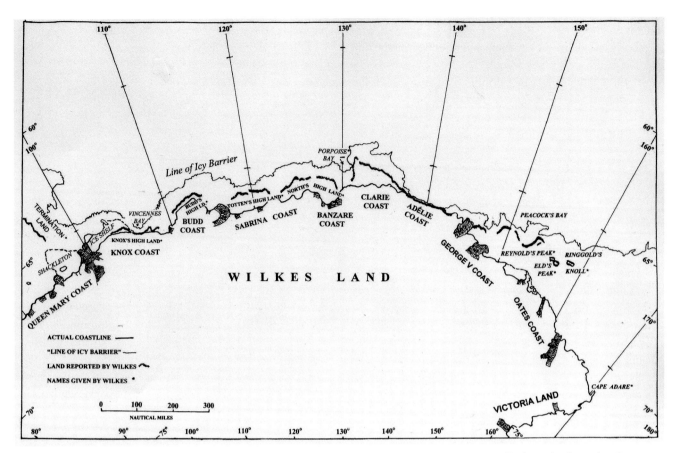

Above: Sightings of land along the coast of Wilkes Land, reported by Charles Wilkes in January, 1840. (Redrawn by the author from a map by K.J. Bertrand, 1971[41])

as gun and berth deck waterways…the gun and spar decks are quite worn and leaky. Stanchions supporting the bulwark on the spar deck are very much decayed and apart from 3 or 4 are unsafe and not able to support the rail and boats attached'.[31] Proper repairs would have taken two months and would entail her missing the Antarctic cruise. Wilkes decided that 'the credit of the Expedition and the country' required *Peacock*'s participation and on 26 December all four ships left Sydney, though thanks to continuing desertions, *Flying Fish* was now critically short of crew.

Wilkes intended to sail in company, but the ships were soon separated in gales and bad visibility, *Vincennes* and *Porpoise* missed a planned rendezvous, at Macquarie Island and the non-existent Emerald Island, but continued south until blocked by pack ice at 64°11'S, 164°30'E. *Peacock* reached an ice barrier at 65°45'S, 158°E on 15 January and next day was joined by *Porpoise*, and later, *Vincennes*. *Flying Fish* reached the ice barrier on 21 January but did not meet the other ships, and by 5 February, severely battered by gales, leaking badly with her cabin awash, and with insufficient fit crew to reduce sail, retreated north to the planned rendezvous at the Bay of Islands, New Zealand.

The events of 16 January and the following few days are critical to the expedition's place in Antarctic history. On 16

January, Midshipmen William Reynolds and Henry Eld sighted what they believed to be three distinct peaks from *Peacock*'s cross trees. 'Captain' Hudson was not convinced (though he did not bother to come on deck) and no entry was made in *Peacock*'s log book. Lieutenant Ringgold on *Porpoise* was also convinced that he saw land the same day. All the ships cruised westward separately along the ice barrier and several other sightings of land were made in clear weather on 19 January from *Peacock* and *Vincennes*, and again on the 23rd from *Peacock*. Attention was soon distracted from the discovery of land. In trying to get closer in a large bay, *Peacock*'s rudder was badly damaged by a collision with ice. Unable to steer, the ship now drifted towards the ice barrier, repeatedly colliding with ice, and eventually struck stern to. The spanker boom and stern boat were crushed, and the bulwarks, with rotten knees and stanchions were torn away from the taffrail to the gangway. Many spars were damaged, but the mizzen top just missed the towering ice barrier. By superb seamanship, Hudson managed to set the sails, and bouncing off ice floes like a billiard ball, drove *Peacock* through the ice and out of the bay.[32]. *Peacock* managed to escape the ice, but was severely damaged, leaking badly with part of the keel torn off, and her stem ground back nearly to the plank ends. The carpenters managed to rig a jury rudder, but it hung by only two pintles. Hudson had no option but to abandon the cruise and head back to Sydney. Subsequent underwater examination showed that the cutwater had been ground back to within 1.5in of the plank ends, and another hour or so of grinding by ice would have caused the whole stem to burst open.

While *Peacock* was fighting for survival, *Vincennes* and *Porpoise* cruised separately westwards along the ice barrier. On 30 January *Porpoise* sighted two strange ships at 64°50'S, 135°27'W, which turned out to be Commandant d'Urville's corvettes *L'Astrolabe* and *La Zelée*. Through a misunderstanding that managed to offend both parties, no direct contact was made.[33] *Porpoise* continued westward for another two weeks to 100° E, without finding any break in the barrier, but collecting rock samples from ice bergs, before heading off to the northeast. *Vincennes*, cruising westward as close to the barrier as possible, also found no gaps, but several sightings of land were made during brief intervals of clear weather between the recurrent gales. Finally, on 21 February at 61°34'S, 100°49'E, faced by deteriorating weather, and with more that thirty crew members sick, Wilkes belatedly responded to the demands of the doctors and turned north, reaching Sydney, four days after *Porpoise*.

THE CONTROVERSY

During the journey to Sydney, Wilkes assembled the observations taken along the ice barrier into a draft map. In Sydney, sightings from *Porpoise* and *Peacock* were added to provide a comprehensive record of the ice barrier over 65° of longitude. Controversially, Wilkes also added other reputed sightings to the draft map. Then, in direct contravention of instructions from the Secretary of the Navy, he sent a copy of the draft map to Hobart, for James Clark Ross, then on his way south with his own expedition with the bomb ketches HMS *Erebus* and HMS *Terror*. This generosity was most atypical of Wilkes and appears to have been motivated by a desire to bolster his claim to have sighted the Antarctic continent before Dumont d'Urville, who had sighted and landed on Terre Adélie on 19 January. To support this claim he also had to revive the previously ignored sighting from *Peacock* by Reynolds and Eld on 16 January, which were not reported in the ship's log.

Wilkes' career was endlessly controversial: his seamanship was questionable, he was an appallingly bad leader, and he was disturbingly willing to change his stories retroactively and to claim personal credit for the achievements of others (in a letter to his wife, he claimed that 'it was through my wisdom and perseverance that we have achieved so much in such a short time'[34]). He was unquestionably a skilful and meticulous surveyor, so it is ironic that it was the draft map sent to Ross with his claims about the coast of 'Wilkes Land' that turned him into a figure of scorn and generated a century of controversy. On 6 March 1841 Ross's ships sailed over the position of Wilkes' coastline, finding no bottom at 600 fathoms.[35] Consequently, Ross questioned all of Wilkes' observations, and publicly censured Wilkes for his claims and particularly for including reported but unconfirmed sightings on his chart. Wilkes' charts, observations and claims have been subjected to intense scrutiny, beginning with his court martial, held shortly after the expedition's return. His observations of longitude have actually turned out to be extraordinarily accurate, particularly as many were taken on a ship in stormy, ice-strewn waters. His observations of latitude, however, were very inaccurate, and the distances to the various peaks sighted greatly underestimated, so that the coastline shown on Wilkes' chart is well out to sea.[36] The reason for the error is now believed to have been some combination of miraging and the frequent exceptional visibility in Antarctica during fine weather. It is ironic that Wilkes' most vociferous detractors, James Clarke Ross and Douglas Mawson, both later made similar errors in reporting the non-existent Parry Mountains and MacRobertson Land, respectively.

After leaving Antarctica, the expedition continued for another two years, carrying out extensive exploration throughout the Pacific, By the end of the 140,000km voyage, 280 Pacific islands had been surveyed, some 1,300km of coastline in the northwest United States had been mapped, 180 charts had been drawn and 400 zoological specimens and 200 new species had been collected.[37] The collections provided the foundation of what became the Smithsonian Institution, and the expedition eventually generated twenty-two volumes of scientific results. The importance of the expedition in Antarctic exploration is based entirely on the observations along 2,400km of the coast of East Antarctica in early 1840. Wilkes' deficiencies as a person and a leader are clear, and were thoroughly aired in the court martial which took place shortly after the return of the expedition. He was cleared of all charges except illegal punishment and received only a public reprimand, but his reputation and that of the expedition in the United States were significantly damaged. For many years, the charges and Ross's scornful dismissal of his claims overshadowed a major achievement in Antarctic exploration, carried out in thoroughly unsuitable ships with recalcitrant crews, along one of Antarctica's stormiest and least accessible coasts. Wilkes was also amongst the first to recognize the evidence of the continental nature of Antarctica. Though his reputation was tarnished, his career was not impaired as he was promoted to Commander in 1843 and to Rear Admiral in 1866. Despite Ross's scorn, he was also awarded the Gold Medal of the Royal Geographical Society. His subsequent career was not without incident, most notably in 1861 when, as commander of the sloop-of-war *San Jacinto* cruising off Cuba, he intercepted the British packet *Trent*, and arrested two passengers, Confederate commissioners James Mason and John Slidell.[38] Though this initiative turned Wilkes into a hero in Washington, it nearly brought Britain into the American Civil War on the side of the Confederacy. He died in Washington in 1877.

Wilkes returned from the Exploring Expedition with only three of the original six ships. *Peacock* was wrecked while attempting to cross the bar of the Columbia River in July, 1841, although all the crew survived. When the expedition arrived in Singapore, *Flying Fish* was found to be 'much weakened in the frames' and was sold to a British resident for $3,700.[39] She ended her days as the *Spec* smuggling opium into China.[40] *Vincennes* had a long and eventful career, including trips to Japan, transportation of Ecuadorean revolutionaries, involvement in Ringgold's survey of the China Sea, suppression of the slave trade along the African coast and service in the Civil War, before being auctioned off in Boston in 1867. *Relief* continued in naval service until 1883 while *Porpoise* disappeared during a severe typhoon somewhere between Taiwan and China in 1854.

REFERENCES AND NOTES

1 In the United States, Nathaniel Palmer, from Stonington, Connecticut, was long believed to have discovered the Antarctic continent on board his 44-ton sloop *Hero*, though in fact he arrived ten months after Edward Bransfield of the Royal Navy on the brig *Williams* and Thaddeuw Bellingshausen of the Imperial Russian Navy with *Mirnyi* and *Vostok*.

2 Stanton, W., *The Great United States Exploring Expedition of 1838-1842* (University of California Press, Berkeley and Los Angeles, 1975).

3 Philbrick, N., *Sea of Glory* (Viking Penguin Books, New York, 2003). President Andrew Jackson and the Secretary of the Navy, Mahlon Dickerson, feuded about the proposed expedition for years and Dickerson did everything in his power to prevent it.

4 *Ibid.*

5 These were designed following Samuel Humphreys', Chief Designer of the US Navy, principle of being able to either outshoot or outrun their opposition. They were some 8m (26ft) longer than brig sloops of the Royal Navy, and could mount more guns to a broadside.

6 Chapelle, H.I., *The History of the American Sailing Navy: the Ships and their Development*, (Norton & Co., New York, 1949).

7 Canney, D.L., *Sailing Warships of the U.S. Navy* (Chatham Publishing, London, 2001).

8 *Ibid.*

9 *Ibid.*

10 *Ibid.*

11 Chapelle, *op cit.*

12 Anon, *The American Neptune*, 25, 1995, p.255.

13 Canney, *op cit.*

14 Philbrick, *op cit.*

15 Chapelle, *op cit.*

16 Canney, *op cit.*

17 Wilkes, C., *Narrative of the United States Exploring Expedition*, (Philadelphia, 1844).

18 Lundeberg, P.K., and Wegner, D.M., 'Not for Conquest but Discovery: Rediscovering the Ships of the Wilkes expedition', *The American Neptune*, 49(3), 1989, pp.151-167.

19 Chapelle, H.I., *op cit.*

20 Wilkes, *op cit.*

21 Wilkes, *op cit.*

22 Wilkes, *op cit.*

23 Stanton, *op cit.*

24 Bradford,G., 'On a lee shore', *The American Neptune*, 12(4), 1952, pp.282-287.

25 *Ibid.*

26 Philbrick, *op cit.*

27 Stanton, *op cit.*

28 William Reynolds, a Passed Midshipman on *Vincennes*, kept a private journal throughout the expedition. He had earlier been an ardent admirer of Wilkes' but swiftly became one of his most prominent detractors.

29 Stanton, *op cit.*

30 Wilkes, *op cit.*

31 Wilkes, *op cit.* Appendix XXI

32 William Hudson was very widely respected as a seaman and commander, being regarded as one of the most skillful in the US Navy.

33 D'Urville's ships sighted the Antarctic mainland at Terre Adélie on 19 January 1840, but due to contrary winds, could not land for several days. As *Porpoise* approached the French ships, d'Urville realised that she was sailing much faster and added sail so that his ships could match her speed. Wilkes interpreted this as a snub and desire to avoid meeting.

34 Philbrick, *op cit.*

35 Gurney, A., *The Race to the White Continent*, (Norton, New York, London, 2000).

36 Bertrand, *Americans in Antarctica, 1775-1948*, (American Geographical Society, New York, 1971).

37 Philbrick, *op cit.*

38 Viola, H.J. and Margolis, C., (Eds.), *Magnificent Voyagers: The U.S. Exploring Expedition, 1838-1842*, (Smithsonian Institution, Washington, D.C, 1985).

39 Wilkes, *op cit.*

40 Gurney, *op cit.*

41 Bertrand, K.J., *op cit.*

Atlantic Transport Line

THE *MINNE* CLASS OF BAKER'S CELEBRATED PASSENGER SERVICE

by Jonathan Kinghorn

The Atlantic Transport Line (ATL) was founded by the dynamic Baltimore businessman Bernard N. Baker in 1881. Although remembered as a passenger service it was always principally a freight carrier. It was American owned but avoided the high costs of operating from the United States by establishing its base in England and using British built, registered, and manned ships. The line's business in London was managed by its agents, Hooper, Murrell, & Williams, who restructured as Williams, Torrey & Field in 1886. Baker fought tirelessly to have American navigation laws updated so he could transfer his fleet to the American flag, but he was never able to achieve this.

The Line's first steamers were small single-screw ships built in various yards in the north east of England and the London area. They were named after English counties beginning with 'S' but after the business restructured in 1886 American place names beginning with 'M' were used. With *Minnesota* in 1887 the Line developed a strong preference for vessels built by Harland & Wolff, Belfast, and most of its later ships were typical Queen's Island coffin ships – long, thin, and very square in section. By 1890 the line was ordering nothing but twin-screw vessels, each with a single funnel and four masts.

Shipping live cattle was a very important part of the business. Steers travelled in pens on the uppermost cargo deck in the forward part of the ships, with a large open hatch for ventilation. The line sought stable ships for the benefit of the cattle even though it was widely thought that livestock

Above: Launched as the *Swansea* in 1887, this steamer was renamed *Maine* soon after and was loaned for use as a hospital ship during the Boer War.

Above: Cattle steamer, from an article in *Scribner's Magazine*, November 1891.

helped steady a ship as they braced themselves against her rolling. Large numbers of horses and mules were carried and the Line developed an excellent reputation for handling thoroughbreds and exotic creatures. Several large collections of zoo animals were shipped and Barnum & Bailey's Circus routinely contracted with the Line when taking its amazing menagerie overseas.

Passengers were occasionally carried but it was only with the introduction of a line running directly from New York to London in 1892 that they became an important part of the business. Baker had spotted a niche market for comfortable first-class passage at modest cost on vessels that were not quite ocean greyhounds. Service was excellent, and the steadiness of ATL steamers appealed so much to passengers who were bad sailors that 'Steady as a Rock' became the motto of the Line. In addition, because the ATL ran from metropolis to metropolis passengers did not have to bother with a train journey from Liverpool or Southampton and could simply hop into a taxi to reach their hotels in town.

Only a few passengers were carried. They had full run of the ship from stem to stern and going down to see the animals was part of the fun. Food was abundant; homely rather than fancy, but good. A later brochure noted nostalgically that the 'ships and service appealed to persons who appreciated a restful ocean voyage in an atmosphere of well regulated social life amidst unexcelled attributes of personal comfort'. ATL steamers left London and New York every Saturday and aimed to arrive 'the second Monday out'; a fleet of four steamers was required to maintain this service. By the time the United States went to war with Spain in 1898 the ATL had successfully established as itself a passenger line.

The war revealed that there were not enough American registered ships to serve as military transports, and Baker was asked to sell seven of his ten steamers to the United States Government for $4,000,000. Fortunately, he was able to buy five new ships from the Wilson & Furness-Leyland Line almost immediately. These ships had been designed to compete with the ATL and were ideally suited to Baker's needs. One of them, *Mohegan*, was wrecked on the Lizard with the loss of 106 lives. The others, well managed and comfortably run, were an immediate success.

The war highlighted the fact that the ATL was, from a legal perspective, effectively a British operation; hence the Atlantic Transport Company of West Virginia was incorporated in 1898 as a holding company to assert American ownership of the line's foreign assets. Besides introducing a new company flag, one of its first acts was to order a new generation of steamers for the North Atlantic. The celebrated *Minne* class, undoubtedly the best-known of all Atlantic Transport Liners, were much like the Wilson & Furness-Leyland Line steamers, only significantly larger. An ATL brochure later boasted, 'No ship ever had a more devoted following than these', and they were described by the *New York Times* as: 'Probably the most popular single-class ships in Atlantic shipping history'. Four were ordered from Harland & Wolff, and two more from American yards.

These 13,400-ton ships were 600ft long and could carry 250 first-class passengers. *Minneapolis* and *Minnehaha* were delivered in 1900 and *Minnetonka* followed in 1902. Passengers were accommodated in the superstructure, where the best state rooms and suites were located on the promenade deck. The library and smoking room were on the boat deck above and the dining saloon was forward on the deck below. These ships had black hulls, white superstructures, light brown deck fittings, milk chocolate brown masts and brownish-red funnels with black tops. Below the waterline they were presumably given Harland & Wolff's usual red anti-fouling paint.

As built, the first two Minnes had elaborate awning frames over the houses on their boat decks, and their saloon deck bulkheads, promenade decks, and steering gear houses were painted light brown below the handrails. In early 1902 they were among the first transatlantic steamers fitted for wireless telegraphy, and by mid-1911 each had separate shacks for the wireless equipment and operators constructed above the smoking room at the after end of the boat deck. The most conspicuous alterations to the first three *Minnes* were made in 1907, however, when the senior officer's accommodation was moved to a new structure behind the

Above: Lady passengers negotiating hazards near *Minnetonka*'s stern during a game of shuffleboard, *c.*1903. *(Chauncey Walden)*

wheelhouse to create space below for additional luxury suites. (Presumably this was when most of the awning frames were removed.) *Minnewaska*, whose debut was delayed until 1909 by an economic downturn, needed none of these updates and offered more passenger accommodation than her sisters, and many other improvements. By 1910 these ships sported a band of funnel red along their sides between the superstructure and the hull, and the light brown below the handrails seems to have disappeared.

Bernard N. Baker built the ATL into a significant operation but he lacked the capital to keep up with the quickening race to build ever bigger and faster ships for the North Atlantic. In 1899 he negotiated the sale of the line to his principal British competitor but pulled out of the deal when approached by Clement A. Griscom about merging instead into his International Navigation Company (American and Red Star Lines). To cut a long story very short, in 1900 Baker agreed to merge the line into what became J. P. Morgan's gigantic Trust, the International Mercantile

Marine Company (IMM). Baker retired from the shipping business when the IMM was formally established in October 1902 and reportedly lost much of his fortune in the debacle. The IMM sold the two *Minne* class ships under construction in the United States and delayed ordering *Minnewaska*, but the ATL sailed on much as before – only less profitably.

In April 1910 *Minnehaha* managed to run aground on the Scilly Isles. Nobody was hurt in the incident but much of her cargo was thrown overboard in an attempt to lighten her forward so she could be towed off. At first she was considered likely to be a total loss but after three weeks she came free and she returned to service in October. The Line's reserve steamer *Mesaba* took over *Minnehaha*'s duties while she was out of commission, and was later one of the ships that gave *Titanic* detailed ice reports on the day she sank. *Minneapolis* was one of several steamers to respond to distress calls from the burning emigrant steamer *Volturno* in October 1913, lowering all of her boats in heavy seas and participating in the rescue of survivors.

Above: A morning ritual at sea – washing the decks, *Minnetonka*, c.1903. *(Chauncey Waulden)*

Above: The 1891 *Mississippi* was one of the ships sold for use as military transports in 1898. She was renamed *Buford* and is seen here in remodelled form deporting undesirable aliens to Soviet Russia in 1920. In 1924 she emerged from retirement to take a leading role in Buster Keaton's movie *The Navigator*. *(Library of Congress)*

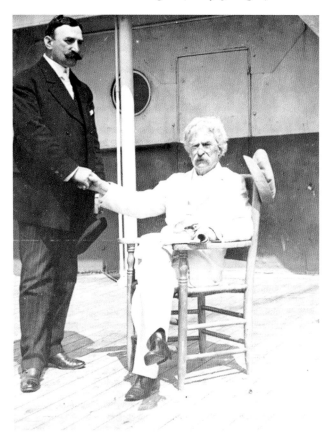

Above: Mark Twain on board *Minnetonka*, 1907. *(Ian Newson)*

In 1913 *Minnekahda*, the first of a new generation of triple screw *Minnes*, was ordered but the outbreak of The First World War changed everything. Work on *Minnekahda* stopped abruptly and only resumed in 1917 so she could be completed (without most of her intended superstructure) as a military transport. Three of the *Minnes* served as transports from very early in the war and each in turn was lost to enemy action. *Minneapolis* was torpedoed on 23 March 1916 when 195 miles from Malta. *Minnewaska* supported the landings at Gallipoli and struck a mine off Crete on 29 November 1916. *Minnetonka* survived until 30 January 1918, when she encountered two submarines 40 miles off Malta. *Minnehaha* remained with the ATL steadily working the London–New York line and continued to sail as a freighter after her passenger service was given up. She became a well-known carrier of munitions and survived a fire-bomb attack in 1915 only to be torpedoed in September 1917.

Most of the Line's freighters survived the war but all of the *Minnes* had gone, and measured in tonnage, the company had lost as much as 75 per cent of its carrying capacity. Although the first two *Minne* replacements were ordered in 1919 their construction was delayed and the United States Shipping Board did not authorize the London–New York service until 1923. These ships were much larger and more opulent than their pre-war namesakes, but their cargo

Above: The aft deck of *Minnewaska, c.*1911. *(Ian Newson)*

ATLANTIC TRANSPORT

Above: A postcard of *Minnewaska* by Charles Dixon.

capacity proved too great and first-class passenger traffic too scarce. The second pair of ships was never ordered, and the IMM turned its attention instead to the new tourist third-class market, for which *Minnekahda* was finally returned to the ATL in 1925. The Line was not able to offer a balanced weekly service again until 1927; and then only with first-class steamers sailing one week and tourist class the next.

Meanwhile, the IMM was working to restructure itself as an exclusively American operation. The prestigious White Star Line was sold in 1927 and the other British-flagged lines were sold or systematically scaled down and liquidated. This process had begun even before the Wall Street Crash and by 1931 the few remaining ATL ships had been laid up or transferred to the Red Star Line. One by one they were sold, mostly for scrap, and while the holding company survived until at least 1936 the ATL had effectively ceased to exist. It was the victim of crippling wartime losses and dreadful post-war trading conditions, but ironically its demise was ultimately brought about by the government-inspired revival of the American mercantile marine for which Bernard N. Baker had fought so long and hard. The destruction of the Line was instigated by Baker's former right-hand man, P. A. S. Franklin, president of the IMM from 1916. It was a sad end to a story that had begun so promisingly fifty years earlier.

Minnewaska (1909)

CONSTRUCTION OF A 1:1200 SCALE MODEL

by John Bowen

Model Shipwright 20 included an article, with plan, for the construction of a 1:1200 scale model of the ATL *Minnewaska* of 1909. For the interest of readers, an amended version of that article is included here.

The *Minnewaska* was built for the Atlantic Transport Line's (ATL) North Atlantic service in 1909 by Harland & Wolff, Belfast. She became a troop transport in 1915, but struck a floating mine the following year when in Suda Bay. Badly damaged, she was beached nearby, but nothing was done to her, and ultimately she was sold to an Italian shipbreaking company.

Minnewaska's main details were:

Length bp: 600ft 0in (182.6m)
Breadth: 65ft 6in (19.8m)
Gross tonnage: 14,327
Machinery: quadruple expansion engines, twin screw
Speed: 16 knots
Passengers (as built): 340 first class

MODELLING NOTES

Minnewaska is a large ship with an impressive profile, but she is not a difficult subject to model. The hull is flush decked, so the hull block can be cut to the level and sheer of the Shelter

Above: *Minnewaska* as built. Seen here lying in the Thames at Tilbury in May 1909.

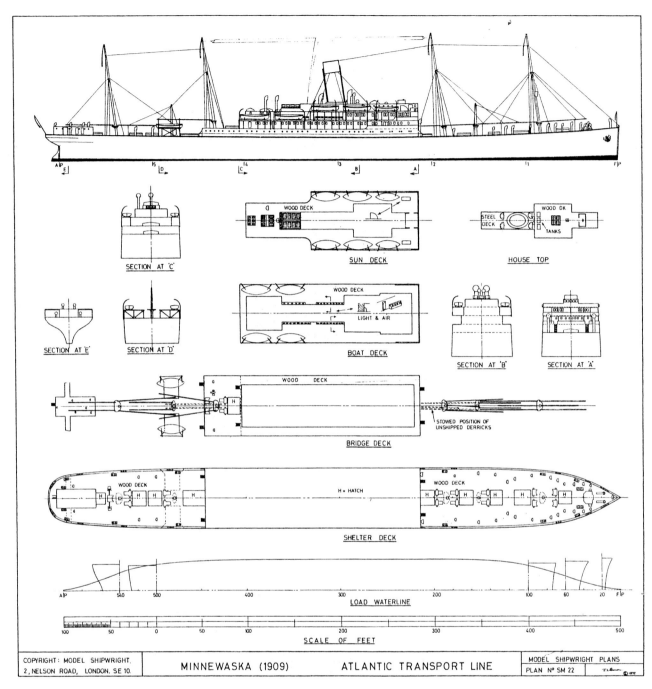

Above: General arrangement.

Deck. With the position of the forward and after perpendiculars marked on the top, bottom and both sides of the hull block, the outline of the Shelter Deck and of the waterline should be marked on their respective surfaces. The profile of the stem, which has a very slight forward rake, and of the counter stern should be marked on each side of the block. With the forward and after perpendiculars as marked enables these to be aligned correctly on each side. The ends of the block should be cut to these profiles, taking great care at the stern to maintain the sharp line of the knuckle. It is better to keep the initial cut just a fraction clear of the

marked line to allow for final trimming. That done, the hull can be carved to shape and sanded smooth. There are several points to watch when so doing. The rectangular bar stem (12in x 3.5in or 300mm x 90mm) is extended some 2.5ft, or 760mm, above deck level. From the stem to a point abreast No.3 hatch there is a knuckle in the side plating some 12in, or 300mm, below the deck edge. Above this knuckle line the side plating is vertical. This can be formed, after the hull has been fully carved, by very gently sanding the edge of the deck with a piece of well worn sandpaper wrapped on a flat piece of wood and held vertically when sanding the deck edge.

With the basic hull completed it should be secured to a working baseboard with two fine brass wood screws put in through the board from the underside, and with a thin distance piece between board and hull. The screws should be positioned on the centreline and about an inch, or 25mm, from each end of the hull. The purpose of the distance pieces is to prevent a build up of paint along the bottom edge of the hull were the hull block is secured directly onto the baseboard. The long deckhouse on the Shelter Deck amidships is made of a strip of wood the width of the hull and 0.75in, or 2mm, thick. The ends should be finished before the strip is glued and pinned in place, after which the sides must be sanded flush with the hull. Before going on to prepare the other deckhouses and deck cards the short pieces of shaped plating at the forward and after outboard corners of this house should be fitted, and the bulwark across its fore end added. Note that there are two openings in it for access to ladders down to the deck below. At this point holes should be drilled in the Shelter Deck for the bollards and masts. The hull can then be finish-painted black from deck to waterline and red below the waterline. The sides of the midship deckhouse are painted white, and the portholes added. The superstructure should be built up deck by deck. The sides and ends of the houses should be painted white and any doors, windows and portholes added before gluing in position. The edges of the overhanging Boat and Sun Decks are fitted with a 12in, or 300mm, deep curtain plate. This can be simulated by using card of that scale thickness for the deck cards, and painting the edges white. It may be necessary to reduce the thickness of the wood used for the deckhouses slightly in order to keep the deck-to-deck height overall correct. After fitting the poop hose and hatches the rest of the deck fittings should be added. The lifeboats, whose covers appear to be without the usual triangular lashing tabs, are stowed on chocks on the deck, and are handled by radial type davits. These davits are fitted outside the deck edge curtain plates, with the heel sockets for the boats on the Boat Deck secured to the side just below the edge of the Bridge Deck. The aftermost boat on each side is stowed on a light spar deck. As can be seen on the plan this deck does not extend right across the ship, and is supported solely by pillars and crossbracing.

The heels of the derricks are attached to a large oval-shaped platform on each mast, located about 8ft or 2.1m above the deck, and supported by shaped brackets attached to the mast. The great length of several of the derricks made it necessary for them to be unshipped and stowed on deck when at sea. Apart from the large funnel and four tall raked masts another noticeable feature of these ships was the number of large cowl ventilators.

COLOUR SCHEME

Hull: black, red below waterline. Narrow (probably 6in, or 150mm, wide) red ribband around hull immediately below edge of Shelter Deck

Superstructure: white, but lower half of sides and ends of midship house on Shelter Deck stone colour

Decks: wood-sheathed

Hatches: deck fittings light brown

Windlass and winches: black

Masts and derricks: mid brown

Boats and davits: white, boat covers light grey

Ventilators: white, but the four large ventilators close to the funnel black. Inside of all cowls - red

Skylights: light brown, but large one abaft funnel black

Funnel: rich reddish-brown and black

Miniature Marine Carving

CREATING INTRICATE FIGUREHEADS AND FRIEZE WORK

by Lloyd McCaffery

I am a professional artist and sculptor, specialising in large-scale and miniature ship models, and miniature sculpture. I have been creating full time for over forty-five years. This unusual profession is the result of the development of my natural proclivities, talents, and interests. I like wood, miniature objects with fine detail, ships, and working with my hands. To attain this level of skill I think the key attributes are: excellent close focus, fine and precise motor skills, and an attention to detail – and an overriding passion for 'getting it right'. To this must be added an innate aesthetic sense and eye for what is pleasing. I have cultivated and trained these attributes on a regular basis over a long span of time, resulting in the work seen here.

One of the most visible and important aspects of models of old ships are the many miniature carvings required. These range from figureheads to frieze work along the topsides. In this article I will give some information on what is required to do this type of work, describe my approach to teaching, the research, materials, tools, and techniques involved, and end with some thoughts on aesthetics.

I do not believe in a step-by-step approach to teaching, instead I subscribe to the idea of individual responsibility. I

Opposite: Starboard stern quarter of *Britannia*, 1682. Scale 1:192 (16in = 1ft).

Above: An assemblage of figureheads and marine carvings in small to large scales. L-R: Joseph Conrad, 'La Mer', figure of Isaac Fowle, *Tecumseh*, stern arms of *Royal Charles*, 'Fly Away', Sir Francis Drake.

see it as a good idea to question authority and think for oneself. Only in this way is it possible to develop an active approach to solving the myriad problems faced when creating art. My approach is to teach basic principles and specific approaches and techniques, and let the student puzzle through how to apply these to their own projects. Ultimately, teachers must make themselves irrelevant to the student. This way the resulting work is truly the independent statement of a mature artist. Someone once referred to my book as, essentially, an exercise in problem solving, and I think this neatly sums up my approach. The teacher is not cast as an authority figure, but someone who imparts knowledge, understanding, and wisdom to the student, and helps them to achieve maturity.

ATTRIBUTES

Miniature carving requires talent, fine hand control, superb close focus, and an 'eye'. There are two aspects to this last factor. On the physical level, it is the ability to focus without strain within about 5in to 8in. When I was first starting out, I measured my focal length at around 5½ inches, though it has since fallen off somewhat. I use a binocular visor of 10 dioptres, giving, if I understand it correctly, about 3½ power. I also

Above: Port side of Barge of Napoleon I, *c.*1810, apple planking, boxwood carvings. Scale 1:24 (½in = 1ft).

use a stereo microscope, giving around 5 to 100 power. It is essential to have stereo or binocular vision for magnification, as the three dimensionality of the carving must be realised. The depth of field falls off with increased magnification, as well as focal length, and this means the most difficult work is that which is done under extreme magnification.

The other aspect of an 'eye' is what Thomas Hoving, former director of the Metropolitan Museum of Art in New York talks about in his many books. It is the refined taste that is honed to a superb degree through intense observation of many works of art. Hoving refers to what is called '*grand goût*' as this almost mystical sense of what looks right and what is superb design.

Above: Stern of Prince Frederick's Barge, 1732. Scale 1:24 (½in = 1ft).

TRAINING AND EDUCATION

Generally speaking the necessary attributes are found naturally and form a 'package' of proclivities I alluded to earlier. As to training, knowledge is power in this as any other field. Art classes are essential, beginning with what are known as the foundation courses. This includes drawing, composition, colour theory, and perspective. Drawing is the most important skill an artist can develop. Drawing is a technical skill, and is largely concerned with learning to see correctly. If you can see things as they really are, you can draw them. Life drawing class, working from the nude model, is the most helpful. (Tell your wife it is your new hobby!) Learning to draw also helps to understand and develop both hemispheres of the brain, since most schooling is linear and cognitive. The right brain is largely concerned with the intuitive and subjective abilities needed for drawing and carving. I highly recommend the book *Drawing on the Right Side of the Brain* by Betty Edwards. It is the best course I have found for developing these skills. There is no getting around the fact that you

Above: Close up of Prince Frederick's Barge, 1732. Egg-and-dart carving on rail diminishes in size and spacing towards the stern, along with spacing of motifs.

learn to carve in miniature by making a lot of mistakes, then thinking about what has happened and making corrections. The necessary abilities come only through painful experience over a long time of application. The theory learned as described above must be put to use in the real world of carving. I cannot stress enough that this activity is a solitary effort; only the individual can learn to see their work clearly and determine what needs to be done.

RESEARCH

Ship modelling is a derivative and imitative art form; hence it is necessary to have accurate information of the subject. But research goes well beyond this. We must try to understand and recreate a lost culture; this I call the nautical zeitgeist. Ship carvings had meaning to those who made and used them, and we must try to understand what motivated them as well as the techniques they used. Most carvings I have seen on modern ship models do not ring true to the originals and this is, I think, because modellers have not learned to immerse themselves in the subject and appreciate how and why the originals were created.

Research cannot be done simply by looking at pictures in books. It is essential to visit the original carvings and models, and this means spending much time in the museums and other locations where figureheads have been preserved. It is astounding how much material must have been lost, but we should be grateful for what we have left. From an ancient Turkish galley to the original stern arms of the *Royal Charles*, we have a rich trove of material to study. Many trips to museums, using the skills of observation and visual memory developed through practice, will be required to develop the storehouse of data and understanding needed. Take time to study the techniques, aesthetic norms, and proportions of the work. If at all possible measurements should be taken, using triangulation to fix points in space. This is one of the most difficult aspects of three-dimensional work to be learned, as no drawing, no matter how accurate, can possibly define a figure in space.

Most of the major holdings for Western subjects are in Europe, though the US naval academy museum and the Museum of Fine Arts, Boston, also have major collections. Hunting up individual figureheads, whether in the US or Europe is great fun, and some surprises may result. Richard

Above: Stern arms of *Royal Charles*, 1664. The original is in the Rijksmuseum. Scale 1:48 (¼in = 1ft).

Hunter has amassed a huge trove of information on figureheads, and there is at least one major collection of dockyard models in a private collection in the USA.

One important note: ship draughts often include what is called the space for the figure. This is a drawn shape at the bow defining the basic outline of the figurehead, and the carving should not extend outside these limits, save for the odd extended arm, spear, or drapery. I sometimes see modern drawings and even ship models with the figure stuck on outside this space, and it spoils the line of the stem.

MATERIALS

My natural love and affinity for wood makes this the natural choice for a medium. There is only one choice for miniature carvings: Boxwood (*Buxus semperivens*). This shrub grows everywhere as a hedge plant. It has a tawny yellow colour, diffuse porous fine grain, and superb working characteristics. I use a 'thumbnail test' to check the density. I simply scratch the surface of a smooth piece with my thumbnail, and check the resulting score with a 15X loupe. There should be barely any penetration. I have heard of some commercial stock called Castello (*Calycophyllum multiforum*) which is not

boxwood. I do not use it for carving as it is too coarse and fibrous. I obtain most of my stock of boxwood from private sources, which I find by word of mouth and mail. Ideally the stock should have grown wild without pruning; this results in trunks up to 12in diameter, with long, straight, relatively knot-free wood. I know of some trees in a coastal village in Connecticut that are up to a foot in diameter. A long time ago I was able to find some logs from the old Sharpe estate near Lake Oswego, Oregon. Beware of buying stock sight unseen (or unscratched!). The seller may not understand the requirements.

Pearwood is sometimes used on dockyard models for carvings, but I find the pear much too coarse for carving. Apple can be all right, but the heartwood is much too dark. I would only use it for large-size carving. These two woods do, however, make ideal material for bases and plinths, as the photographs show. The dark heartwood makes a nice contrast with the light yellow of the figure. I must add that the cultivated pear tree is not the same as the wild pear. I do not know the botanical reason for this, but whereas apple works well for bases, the pear tree that bears fruit is no use for modelling. Also, if you are contemplating using pear for structural work on a model, it should be unsteamed.

Above: How it all starts: using a bandsaw to slab logs in miniature lumber.

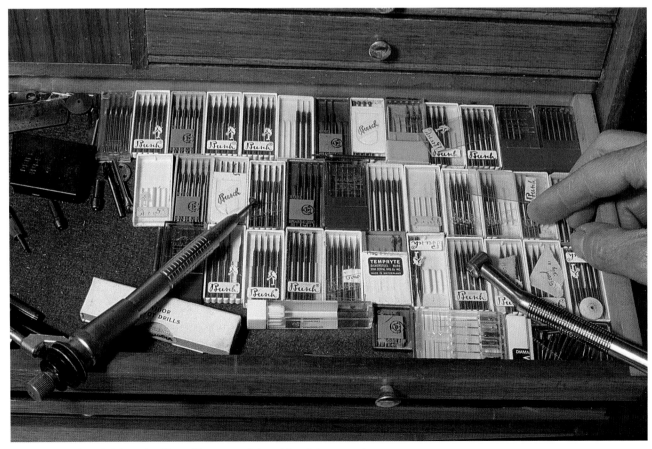

Above: Tool chest holds stock of burs. Two types of dental handpieces are shown.

Above: Beginning to carve 'La Mer', a miniature mermaid.

Above: Burs used while working on the miniature of *Royal George*, 1756.

Above: Large (1:48) and small *Royal George* figureheads.

Virtually all European pear is treated this way, eventually to stabilise it, and it turns fibrous, brittle, and a dark reddish brown colour.

TOOLS

The major stock reduction is done with the usual woodworking tools. I use a jointer to establish a working face and edge on the log, and then cut down if needed using a bandsaw. I must say this tool is far superior in every way to a large table saw. Usually the problem with boxwood is how to obtain pieces large enough, so cutting down is not on the agenda. Since I rarely use patterns or even drawings on the block, I just attack the material with various saws to do major removal. I do not like the idea of mass wasting using large rotary bits. It creates a lot of noise, sawdust, and the results can be obtained much more nicely with saws. I use fine toothed backsaws for straight cuts, and the ubiquitous jewellers saw for curves. If front and side cuts need to be made, sometimes I make one cut, then tack glue the piece back on so I have 'land' to make the side cut.

Then there is the question of 'power carving'; if carving is done with a rotary handpiece, is it power carving? No, because the artist guides the tool. The ancient Egyptians had lathes and drills. The motive power was supplied by humans, but the result was a self-powered tool that was simply guided or used by the human operator. There is no difference between this and an electric motor turning a modern handpiece. If that is power carving, then the ancients had power tools! The term to use is 'machine carving', such as would be done by CNC milling machines or a duplicator. It is also very important to realise that any machine fabrication is a mechanical replica, not an original work of art. The result is evident in the spirit of the work, as Thomas Hoving explains in his books.

All that said, I have a professional belt-driven dental handpiece, far superior to the inexpensive versions, with planetary arm and no whip to the handpiece. This machine takes $^3/_{32}$in burs. I also have an air turbine tool taking $^1/_{16}$in burs. This is only for very fine stock removal. I try to use carbide burs as much as possible, as they last far longer that HSS. Diamonds are very useful for the final fine abrasion of the surfaces. I make miniature pointed burs for minute detailing by grinding down old broken points. The slightly rough surface is enough of an abrasive to achieve the miniscule details needed.

I have some miniature carving tools by Dockyard Model Co. The large gouges and chisels are adequate for some excavation, but the shanks on the smallest sizes are too thin, and they flex too much for critical control. I make extremely small chisels with flat and skew edges by simply grinding flats on old worn burs. They can be honed using 2000 silicon

Above: Close up of bow of *Britannia*, 1682, based on the reconstruction by Frank Fox, Battine, and paintings and drawings by the Van de Veldes. Scale 1:192 (1in = 16ft).

carbide paper and hard Arkansas stone. I do not bother with the whole process of hardening and tempering these chisels, as they are quick to make and the HSS is hard enough for my needs. Various grits of aluminium oxide and garnet papers can be used judiciously to smooth some areas, but great care is needed to avoid rounding off adjacent sharp edges and projections.

TECHNIQUES

There seems to have developed a trend, particularly in making miniature ship models, to imitate carved work by simply daubing some sort of strange gloop onto the model. I find the results a very poor substitute for actual carving. I have carved wood down to the scale of 64ft = 1in, using magnification, and consider the painstaking effort worthwhile. So here is my approach.

First, I establish the overall proportions of the subject. I do lay out centrelines, but for the most part do not draw on the block or make patterns to overlay on the stock. I have been doing this for so long that I have developed the ability to 'see' the finished figure in the material. This is a key point. It is of course necessary to do the drawing when just learning to carve, but a major aspect of achieving 'mastery' is to develop the ability to 'become' the material and the subject, and simply find the shapes within the material by comparing what I know and want to what material is there, and understanding what wood needs to be removed.

A kinaesthetic empathy with the subject being carved is also necessary. I remember one drawing teacher stating that, if you are painting a man digging a ditch, your own back should ache, or at least you should have a muscle response to what the figure is doing. I relate all parts of the figure to each other, comparing the size, length, and angles in three dimensions as I work. As I stated before, this involves switching back and forth between left and right hemispheres of the brain to figure out what to do. The right brain tells me something does not feel right, and I need to kick in the left, cognitive functions, to analyse what it is I need to do to fix things. It is all about finding the figure in the material. I carve the whole figure all over, continuously removing material a little at a time, much like peeling layers away from an onion. This keeps my eye attuned to what is occurring with the proportions. Is the face sticking out too much? If I decide it is, I need to jump on it and decide what to do. I gradually work down to the finished surface, never cutting right down to what I think should be the final point of an elbow or the maximum extension of the hair, because my eye may be thrown off by excess material next to this area, and thus I may take off more wood than will allow for the final details. I

allow extra material for projections such as belts, buttons, or nipples. As I approach the final surface I spend more time looking and thinking about what needs to be done than I do carving.

Now there are many hints and tips I can pass on about the actual process of carving. For example, say I need to locate the end of an elbow within a projection of wood. I do not try to measure with dividers or a ruler from another point. I gradually reduce material, moving the block in all directions, so I get a feel for where I am going in relation to what I sense is the final location of the elbow. This, of course, also involves an understanding of how thick the arm is in cross section, the length of upper and lower parts of the arm, and how all this relates to the figure as a whole. The brain circuits definitely get a workout.

A very important principle, that becomes a technique, is understanding how light and shadow define form. I want a light source that I can manipulate, changing direction and angle of the light, and even intensity, to throw certain details into relief, or wash out certain details and focus on others. Another very valuable trick is to continuously turn the figure to reveal ever-changing profiles. I compare what rotates into view with what I know must be the right profile. This works particularly well for faces. Material that stands out too much is readily seen, and can be reduced accordingly. A completely fresh view can be obtained by viewing the work in a mirror. The reversed image will reveal errors the eye has become used to. Occasionally I turn the work upside down in a mirror for even more fun.

Sometimes I need to check for symmetry, or to see if more material needs to be removed, and the view is not clear because another part of the figure is in the background. An example is looking down on the face from above, with the chin against the background of the chest. I cut a small piece of card stock to fit under the chin, thus isolating the part needed from the background. This card is painted black or left white as needed.

When considering the costume and accessories to add, I make use of my store of knowledge, as well as research. For the figure of the *Bounty*, for example, she had a 'pretty figure of a lady in a riding habit'. We have actual riding habits from the period of 1789 preserved in the textiles departments of museums, along with paintings from this era showing these costumes. Even the type of material and the colours can be determined.

A special amount of care needs to be devoted to the carving of hair, such as for the various heraldic beasts and human figures used as figureheads. The modern tendency is to make the cross sections just convex, whereas the actual figures and miniature carvings of them on old ship models

Opposite: Bow of Barge of Napoleon I, 1810, showing polished boxwood carvings.

use both concave and convex forms. The flowing lines on the old carvings follow to some extent what has been called the line of beauty, which is a re-curved line with a tightening of the radius at the terminus. This adds interest, and is more to the spirit of the prototype. This gets into the matter of personal style versus absolute fidelity to the original.

This is always a judgement call, as straying too far puts a modern gloss on the work, but an artist must express what they feel about the subject or the result is a cold, mechanical replica. This also touches on the matter of controlling the speed with which the eye moves over the work, particularly in the hair. It is possible to manipulate the viewer's response to the material in the visual field through careful design of such lines in the figure. This is something that must be studied and applied through much practice.

There comes a time when I consider the details done, and the final finish must be considered. In certain areas I may smooth the surface with various papers. Extreme care is needed here to avoid rounding off other details such as projecting buttons. I tear minute pieces of paper, fold them into sundry shapes, and use a tweezers to hold these little abrasive tools. It is slow and careful going.

For finishing I use a dilute polyurethane gloss varnish, but I do not allow a coating to build up on the surface. I let the thin varnish soak in, and wipe off with a tack cloth after a few minutes. Individual lints must be picked off with tweezers. This approach allows the finish to bring out the richness and colour of the wood, without a thick coating which would gum up details. The finish is entirely in the wood. Boxwood is a wonderful material for polishing, but in certain areas I may simply roughen the surface to imitate fur, or the texture of cloth. This variety of surface texture adds interest to the finished carving.

The old dockyard models were usually given a coating of gloss varnish, but the large scale and size of the work meant that this approach was acceptable. The gloss varnish creates very strong highlights on the convex projections, creating more apparent depth and interest. I have taken to polishing certain areas with wax, to create a slight sheen on such areas, but this must be done conservatively or it will overpower the carving.

This brings me to another area of concern: painting. I create the free-standing figures illustrated in this article as part of a collection of representative figureheads. I want them all to have the same appearance, and the natural colour of the boxwood lends unity to the display. Of course there are times when figureheads for ship models must be painted. But beware. For most of the eighteenth century these decorations were painted yellow ochre. This is an iron oxide earth pigment. It cannot achieve the bright yellow colours of modern paints. They did have what is called Naples yellow (Lead Antimoniate) but this was a pale, light value pigment, again with none of the saturation of modern formulations.

The chromes did not come on the scene until about 1797, and then just in small quantities for artists' use. They were fugitive; that is they would fade and change hue over time and exposure. The earth pigments were very stable. The cadmiums finally gave us permanent bright yellows, but this was not until around 1849.

Most figureheads of ships in the Royal Navy were painted white. The remaining decorations and rails were yellow ochre. Towards the middle of the 1700s we begin to see some figureheads painted in natural colours. This is particularly evident in the paintings of John Cleveley. Jean Boudriot has done a lot of research on this matter, and L.G. Carr-Laughton refers to the subject in his book on old figureheads.

The important thing to remember about colours is the need to understand what pigments were available for the period in question. It does no good to talk about this or that 'colour' if the result is not consistent with the physical materials available back then.

MOUNTING AND DISPLAY

For carvings made for a model it is necessary to plan very precisely how the finished carving will fit the complex curves of the hull. It is best to get this out of the way before starting to carve. This saves having to cut away part of the figure afterward. For straddle figures I make an initial cut up the centreline with a saw and then work outward with files and burs. I undercut the interior, and thus only the front edge needs to have a precise fit. The stem is often tapered in thickness, which means the piece of wood for the stem should be tapered first, with the slot in the carving cut to fit.

For individual figures made as part of my collection, I mount them on bases of apple and pear, as the figures show. These dark woods make a nice contrast with the boxwood, and allow the carving to be the centre of attention.

ART AND ACCURACY

I have seen a lot of discussion in ship modelling circles about whether or not this activity is an art form, or some type of craft. It depends on who does it, what their motivation is, and their level of talent and accomplishment. A noted authority on antique furniture once said: 'In any given age, in a certain population, for a specific art form, there are only a very few people who are superbly talented. These are the ones who create the works of art.' I realise this may outrage a lot of people who are involved in ship modelling, but people can make up their own minds by examining the results shown here. I do, however, believe that the results I have achieved cannot be done as a hobby. There is simply too much study, research, and learning about ships, wood, tools, techniques,

Above: British Lion of early-to-mid 1700s.

Above: *Bounty*, based on space for the figure on the original draught and paintings by George Moreland.

Above: A coy mermaid for Prince Frederick's Barge (see page 149).

Above: Old and recent work: L-R: *Morning Light*, USS *Constitution*, John Paul Jones, large and small *Royal George*, *Tecumseh*, Lion, Nelson, *Bounty*, *Glory of the Seas*, and 'Ancient Victory'.

and aesthetics to be able to master the subject only on a part time basis. I have been creating full time for over forty-five years, and am still learning things. I have major works and even collections planned in my head, and now have aquired the level of competence that enables me to achieve them.

There is one further question, that of art 'versus' accuracy. Some say a model is simply a technological artefact, and if all parts are cut and fitted according to the plan, then that is all that is needed. Some believe that introducing aesthetics means compromising accuracy. This need not be so, and I invite close contemplation of the photographs here. Ultimately creating a ship model as a work of art involves both the left, cognitive functions, as well as the right, intuitive aspects of our sensibilities.

Virtually all of the thousands of old ships and their decorations are gone. We have evidence of them in drafts, writings, and the occasional preserved relic. If we attempt to create replicas of them in miniature, they deserve our best efforts. Anything less is an insult to our historical legacy.

Editor's note

Lloyd McCaffery is the author of *Ships in Miniature*, (Conway Maritime Press, 1988) and many magazine articles. His work can be seen in a number of museums. The Combs Collection, consisting of thirteen models built by Donald McNarry and eight built by Lloyd , was recently donated and placed on permanent display at the headquarters of the International Yacht Restoration School and Museum of Yachting in Newport, Rhode Island.

REFERENCES

Edwards, Betty, *Drawing on the Right Side of the Brain* (Tarcher, 1989)

Esterly, David, *Grinling Gibbons and the Art of Carving* (Abrams, 1998)

Friend, David, *Composition* (Pitman, 1975)

Henri, Robert, *The Art Spirit* (Lippencott, 1960; IComm books, 1988)

Hoving, Thomas, *Art for Dummies* (IGD Worlwide, 1999)
– *King of the Confessors* (Simon & Schuster, 1981)
– *Making the Mummies Dance* (Simon & Schuster, 1993)

Lucchesi, Bruno, *Modeling the Figure in Clay* (Watson-Guptill, 1980)

Masatoshi, *Art of Netsuke Carving* (Kodansha, 1981; Weatherhill, 2002)

Norbury, Ian, *Techniques of Creative Wood Carving*, (Scribner, 1985)

Stone, Irving, *Agony and the Ecstasy*, (Doubleday, 1961)

Two Yachting Dioramas

BASED ON PLANS FROM FRED W. MARTIN'S 1901 ALBUM OF DESIGNS

by John Pocius

FRED W. MARTIN

The following is a brief history of Naval Architect Fred W. Martin by Steve Wheeler (see References), on whose published plans the models in these dioramas have been based:

'Fred W. Martin…is one of those people who, while he had far-reaching effects on the boatbuilding industry in his day, is now largely forgotten. Born in Canada in 1860, he seems to have had formal training in naval architecture, although records of his schooling are very sketchy. His first known work is a canoe he designed and marketed in 1882, the drawings for which are unfortunately lost. Martin worked for a time in Waukegan, IL and Clayton, NY, where his designs 'to scientific principles' propelled the St Lawrence River Skiff, Canoe, and Steam Launch co. to prominence. He moved to Racine, WI in 1891 and was instrumental in creating a boatbuilding industry there that spanned five sep-

Above: Diorama 1, based on four Fred Martin designs. Scale is 1:64 (³⁄₁₆in = 1 ft).

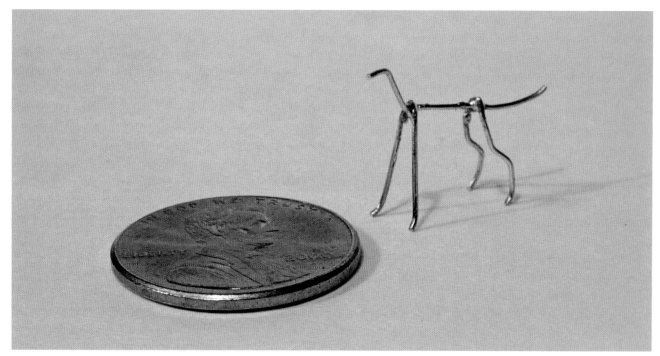

Above: The brass wire armature for the Dalmatian.

arate boatyards and more than fifty years building literally thousands of hulls in the process. Fred Martin worked in Racine and later, again, in Waukegan for only twelve years, from 1891 until his death in 1903. In that period he designed and published, in four design catalogues he called "Albums of Designs", the drawings for some 160 individual boats (more than one design per month). They were powered by steam, gasoline, sail, and oars and paddles; in size and complexity they ranged from small punts to large river steamers, and covered just about everything in between. Those four design catalogues represent a priceless time capsule of nearly all the types of boat in use on the Great Lakes at the turn of

Below: The finished sculpture of the Dalmatian. The ears are small pieces of tracing paper glued on.

Above: The seven carved figures before paint and final shaping.

the twentieth century. As can be seen from the models shown here, most of his designs are true classics. It is fascinating to speculate where he could have taken his career if his early death had not intervened.'

DIORAMA NO.1

Designs for the four boats in this diorama were published in the Second Edition, 1901 *Album of Designs for Boats, Launches and Yachts* by Fred W. Martin. The catalogue contains plans for seventy-three vessels, from a 12ft punt up to a 120ft passenger steamer.

Design No. 1: Punt
Length overall: 12ft
Beam overall: 3ft 6in

Design No. 13: Runabout Catboat
Length overall: 18ft
Beam overall: 6ft 3in

Design No. 20: Shallow Draft Cruising Catboat
Length overall: 29ft
Beam overall: 7ft

Design No. 33: Knockabout Cruiser Sloop
modelled as a pond yacht

THE SCENE

The scene depicts a summer day in 1901 on a calm inland lake in Wisconsin. A family consisting of a father, mother, daughter and a tabby cat are aboard the large cruising catboat, being followed by two young men and a dog in the smaller runabout catboat. The two catboats are cruising past

Below: The young boy.

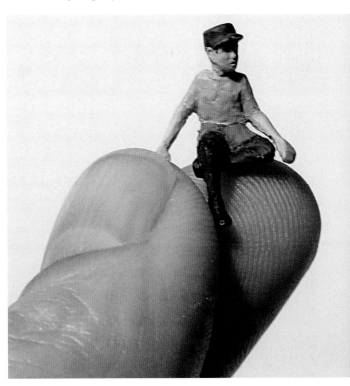

Above: The pond yacht, the sails are made from cigarette paper.

a father and son in a punt who are sailing a pond yacht. Their attention is taken by the Dalmatian in the small catboat. The Dalmatian's gaze is fixed on an unknown object in the distance. The young girl in the large catboat is watching the activities of the occupants of the punt.

MODEL CONSTRUCTION
The models are built to a scale of 1:64 ($^3/_{16}$in = 1ft). The hulls were built using the plank-on-bulkhead method. Pear wood was used for the bulkheads and planking. I used the same techniques as covered in my article about the Open Catboat of 1901 in the February/March 2008 issue of Seaways' *Ships in Scale*.

The pond yacht was carved from solid pear wood. Mast, gaff and boom are brass wire. All rigging is 0.002in nichrome wire that was painted with Floquil. Diluted white glue was used to attach the rigging. The sails were made from cigarette paper; the seams were drawn in with a 4H pencil. Deck planking and margin planks were drawn on with a sharp 2B pencil. The flag is cigarette paper painted with watercolour.

The water was created using Super Sculpy® modelling clay; after baking Super Sculpy is harder than regular Sculpy, allowing finer detail to be carved. It is stronger and I found it shrinks less than the regular Sculpy during baking. First I rolled out the clay with a marble rolling pin. I pressed down on the rolling pin as I rolled until the Sculpy was about $^3/_8$in thick. Since the scene is portraying a calm inland lake, I kept the water fairly flat. The shapes of the hulls were cut into the Sculpy and then the bottom of the finished hulls were covered with clear plastic wrap, gently pressed in to fit and then removed. The wakes were shaped by adding on small pieces of clay and then sculpting and smoothing them in. The clay was then baked in an oven for 15 minutes at 150°C. The baked clay water was cut to size on a table saw using a fine tooth blade to avoid chipping. Then I glued it to a piece of $^1/_2$in Baltic Birch plywood using Weldwood carpenter's glue. I like to use Baltic Birch for the bases as it is not prone to warping. The openings for the hulls had to be refitted after the Sculpy was baked. The wavelets were carved in with a U-shaped wood gouge. The foam for the wakes was made by pressing on some Magic Sculpy and then rubbing my finger across the top to rough it up a bit. I primed the water with Liquitex Gesso using a large, soft bristle brush. When dry, I sponged on Liquitex matte gel medium to give a stipple effect. After this was dry, different shades of blue and green were sprayed on by airbrush. Lighter shades were airbrushed on the wakes, since water appears lighter in a wake due to more light passing through the water. Lighter shades were also sprayed around thee openings for the boats to simulate the reflection of the hulls through the water. A couple of coats of clear semi-gloss Poly Scale paint were sprayed on. White paint was dry-brushed on the wake to simulate water

foam. The boats were glued in with carpenter's glue and then matte gel medium was flowed into any gaps with a brush.

Seven human figures were sculpted for the boats. For the clothing, I studied old photographs and books on period clothes found at my local library. They were all constructed on brass wire armatures that were soldered together. I have switched to using brass instead of copper wire as it is a bit stiffer. For these figures, I used #28 Gauge brass wire. The armatures were fitted into the boats first. Then Magic Sculp epoxy modelling clay was pressed onto the armatures, and when set hard the figures were carved to shape. The Magic

Below: Cruising catboat. Sails are Strathmore 300 series transparent light weight tracing paper painted by airbrush with opaque pro white and water colours. Seams are drawn in with a sharp 2B pencil.

Sculp is slightly translucent and I find that it is difficult to see where you are at with the finer details until a first coat of opaque paint is applied. I find that after the first coat of paint there is always more work to be done on the figures. The figures were carefully checked for fit in the boats while carving. The Magic Sculp is a bit brittle and care must be taken when handling while carving is being done. It is easy to add on additional Magic Sculp, or glue on a broken piece with 5-minute epoxy glue. I use a sharp #11 X-acto blade for most of my carving, I also have a #11 blade that has been ground down to a chisel, and a hand-made miniature spoon gouge. The figures were painted by hand using a sable hair brush with Vallejo Acrylic Model Color. These paints are formulated for painting figures and come in a large variety of colors. The figures are held into the boats with small drops of epoxy glue.

DIORAMA NO. 2: A SCHOONER AND A SKIFF

This is set in 1901 on a warm summer day on Lake Michigan, off the shores of Chicago, Illinois, USA. The skiff is heading out from the protected waters of a harbour into deeper water. On board there are two fishermen; one is showing off his catch of a lake Salmon to the crew of the schooner. His fishing pole is set beside him, the line still in the water waiting for the next catch. The schooner crew consists of a man, boy, girl and a cat.

The schooner and skiff designs were also published in the Second Edition, 1901 *Album of Designs for Boats, Launches and Yachts* by Fred W. Martin.

Design No. 39: Cruising Schooner
Length overall: 34ft

Above: Cruising catboat. The tabby cat was carved from a solid piece of Magic Sculp.

Beam overall: 9ft

Design No. 2: Skiff
Length overall: 13ft
Beam overall: 3ft 6in

The models are constructed to a scale of ³⁄₁₆in = 1ft, or 1:64.

There were two drawings of the schooner reproduced in the catalogue. A sail plan that was about 3.5in wide and a lines and deck plan that was 5in wide. The plans for the schooner were scanned and scaled on a computer. The first thing I noticed after comparing the two drawings side by side was that the masts and cockpit/cabin location on the lines and deck plan did not match their location on the sail plan.

The location was further aft on the lines and deck plans. I decided to use the lines and deck plan drawings. These were reproduced in a larger scale in the book and had more detail than the sail plan. Also on the sail plan the tiller was quite far forward, and it would have been awkward for the pilot to reach it. This required me to create different dimensions for the sails. I printed out a copy of the lines and deck plan and redrew the masts, booms, gaff and sails to fit the new dimensions. I then worked out all of the dimensions for rails, deck planks, margin planks, coamings, etc. in decimal inches for reference.

There were no problems with the skiff plans. I had a copy that was produced in a larger size from an earlier Martin catalogue. I printed them out and marked the dimensions of all the scale numbers that were needed.

Above: View of the runabout catboat's cockpit. The deck would have been covered with canvas and painted.

Above: The pond yacht and punt.

The schooner was built using the plank-on-bulkhead method of construction. It was built upside down, and planked with pear wood. I followed my usual construction techniques, making pear wood bulkheads and centre keel piece. The location of the cockpit and cabin depth was marked on the keel piece so that I could cut this out later. After the hull was planked and sanded I glued on two thin pieces of pear wood to form the deck base. The cabin and cockpit areas were marked and cut before application. After this the cabin and cockpit areas were cut out. The inside of the hull was then coated with epoxy for strength. When the margin plank and deck planks had been fitted to the deck base, I made the deck railing. This was tapered from fore to aft. To make the rails I temporarily glued together two pieces of pear wood, cut to the correct thickness, with Duco cement. To make the scupper holes the piece was marked and slots were made by running it through a table saw set at the height of the scupper opening. The slotted piece was then tapered slightly oversize, soaked in acetone to separate the pieces. These were cleaned up and bent to the deck profile using a hot hair curling iron. They were then glued on to the top of the margin plank. When dry the rails were sanded to the correct height and taper. A cap rail made of apple wood was glued to the top of the railing. Since I had decided to show the cabin door and hatch in an open position the cabin interior would need to be fitted out. There were no cabin or cockpit details beyond the top view showing the profile. I made the cabin interior based on similar size boats in the Martin catalogue that showed inte-

rior layouts. Even though the cabin interior is barely visible on the finished model, I think it adds interest and draws the viewer in for a closer look if the cabin doors and hatch are slightly open.

I polished all the brass parts using FLEX-I-FILE brand sanding pads. These are foam-backed pads that come in a variety of grits. I work my way down from medium, fine, extra fine and then a final polish with their polisher/finisher. I apply a coat of matt lacquer to all polished parts to keep them from tarnishing. I usually do this after the parts have been attached to the model because it allows me to clean up any glue spots or blemishes before coating.

The bands on the spars are made from 0.002in thick brass shim stock. I begin by marking the width on the brass, and then tape it down on to a cutting board. Using a metal straight edge as a guide, strips were then cut off with a very sharp #11 X-acto blade. There is some roughness to the edges after the strip is cut; which I remove by burnishing a strip with a smooth, round rod such as the shank of a drill bit. Holding the strip against a backing it is polished using the FLEX-I-FILES. Individual pieces are cut off for the bands. To fit the bands I wrap the strip around the spar, and then gently pinch the free ends together with a flush cutting nipper. When the strip is snug against the spar and aligned I cut the ends off flush. The band is then glued on with either cyanoacrylate or epoxy glue. A pilot hole is drilled at the seam so a photo-etched eyelet can be glued in place.

The photo-etched parts were formed by creating artwork on a computer. I like to use Adobe Illustrator for the drawing.

I made multiple copies of the parts to fill the sheet. I had extra space on the sheet so I created parts that could be used on other models. The file was then sent to a local graphic arts service to have a piece of negative film made. I sent the film to a professional photo-etching source for the etching.

For attaching the various small parts I used a small drop of 5-minute epoxy glue. Parts such as the cleats are pinned to the boat with 0.06in diameter brass wire. I use a #90 (0.0087in diameter) drill bit to make the pilot holes; this gives a small amount of clearance for the glue. I also mark and drill all the holes in the sails with a #90 drill; this makes it easier to get the threads through the material. Holes made just by poking with a sharp point tend to close up slightly, and it is difficult to get a line through them.

The paint colours were custom mixed using Floquil Model Railroad Colors. Since the model was to a small scale, all of the colours were muted to achieve the appearance that they would have when viewed from a distance through the atmospheric haze. A small amount of grey was added to all the colours.

The stripe on the side of the hull was masked and spray-painted with Floquil paint using an airbrush. To make the stripe I put a piece of Tamiya brand masking tape down on a piece of glass that was taped down to a drawing board. The width of the stripe was marked on the masking tape, then cut with a very sharp #11 X-acto blade held against a stainless steel T-square. Cutting on the glass gives a very clean edge to the cut tape; blades have to be changed often since cutting against the glass quickly dulls them. A piece of tape was then applied to the top

of the cut line to hold the two pieces of tape together when they were pulled off. I cut a strip of tape, ⅛in wide, and applied it to the hull following the sheer. The tape piece with the stripe was butted against the first piece of tape applied to the hull. When burnished firmly in place, the tape holding the two pieces together was peeled off and then the centre stripe piece of tape was peeled off. The rest of the hull was taped off and the stripe was spray-painted. After the paint was dry to the touch the tape was pulled off. When doing a line like this I get a cleaner edge if the tape is pulled off before the paint is fully dry.

The name on the stern of the schooner is a decal made using Toner Transfer paper. This paper was designed originally for making photo-etched circuit boards. This material is a laser paper that is treated with a water-soluble adhesive; when it is soaked in water the toner image is released from the paper backing. The artwork for the lettering was created on a computer and printed out on a laser printer using the Toner Transfer paper. A wet coat of matt clear lacquer was sprayed on to the surface and left to dry for about 15 minutes. Then the name was cut out cropping close to the edge of the printing. The paper was then soaked from behind with tap water using a brush and when saturated the decal was slid off onto the model. The decals are very fragile and great care must be taken when applying them. After the decal was dry, I sprayed multiple coats of clear matt lacquer over the area. I sanded lightly before the last coat was applied to make sure that no edge between the decal and surface would be visible.

The rigging blocks were made from a stick of wood shaped to the profile and width of the block. First the length of the block was marked on the piece. Then the location of the sheave hole was marked on both sides and the hole for the eyelet was marked on the end with a sharp point. The hole for the eyelet was drilled with a #96 (0.0063in diameter) drill. Then I drilled half

Above: Another view of the finished diorama.

Above: Detail of Diorama 2. I studied photographs of boats in motion to achieve the correct effect of the schooner pushing through the wa

way through each side with a #90 (0.0087in diameter) drill bit for the sheave hole. I always drill from each side for the sheave hole. If the hole is drilled from one side only the drill will wander and the hole will not be straight. A slot is made on each side for the sheave using a broken piece of a jeweller's saw blade held in a pin vice. The block is then shaped with 800 grit sandpaper. The sheave hole is darkened with a sharp HB pencil to give the effect of depth to the slot.

The sails are made from Strathmore 24lb artist's transparent parchment paper. Sizes and seams were marked and drawn on with a sharp 2B pencil. This was done on both sides. The sails were then taped down to a piece of ¼in foam board. Thus was done to keep the paper from warping from the water-based paint. They were spray-painted with a mixture of Pro White brand opaque watercolour mixed with transparent yellow ochre and black. I painted test patches on a scrap of paper until I was satisfied with the colour. I then spayed on the paint slightly dry so there was a texture. After one side was done, the sails were turned over and the other side painted. When dry they were cut to shape.

The flag was made using white inkjet decal film. The artwork for the flag was created on a computer using Adobe Illustrator software. Both sides of the flag were set up so that after the decal was printed it could be folded in half. Multiple flags were set up on the sheet so I had extras. I printed out a test on inkjet paper then, satisfied with the size, printed it out on the decal film. Immediately after printing the sheet a coat of Microscale brand liquid decal film was sprayed on with an

Below: The rigging of the schooner was done in silk, cotton and nylon thread. Liquitex brand matt polymer emulsion was used to stiffen lines where they needed to have a sagged appearance.

Above: The fisherman in the skiff is showing his catch to the crew of the passing schooner.

Above: The figures were painted with a 00 Windsor & Newton brush using Vallejo acrylic paint.

Above: The deck of the schooner is planked in boxwood with apple wood margin and king planks.

Above: Cockpit cabin doors are made from pear wood; door knobs were turned on a lathe from brass.

Above: Top view of the diorama.

airbrush. This has to be done immediately after printing to seal the ink and also to prevent the ink colours bleeding together. One flag was cut out of the sheet, then scored down the centre so it would fold correctly and easily. It was soaked from behind with water and slid off. It was folded in half very carefully so both sides were aligned. The flag was left to dry, then cut out. I wrinkled the flag and gave it a coat of matt lacquer.

WHERE TO FIND FRED W. MARTIN CATALOGUES

The four Martin design catalogues are all available. The Racine Heritage Museum (701 S. Main St, Racine, WI 53403) has a photocopy of Martin's *Racine Yacht & Boatworks* catalogue from 1895 and an original of his first *Album of Designs* (1897). They will make copies of both. The museum also has a reprint of his second *Album of Designs* (1901), which they sell for $5.00. The Cleveland Public Library has original of the second *Album* (1901) and Martin's *Supplement to the Second Edition Album of Designs* (1903). They will make copies.

REFERENCES

Wheeler, Steve, 'The Racine Hardware Manufacturing Company', *Nautical Research Journal*, Vol. 45, No. 2, June 2000.

Wheeler, Steve, 'The Racine Boat Manufacturing Company', *Nautical Research Journal*, Vol. 46, No. 2, June 2001.

Wheeler, Steve, 'The Racine Boat Manufacturing Company, Conclusion', *Nautical Research Journal*, Vol. 46, No. 3, September 2001.

Wheeler, Steve, 'The Racine Boat Manufacturing Company of Muskeogon', *Nautical Research Journal*, Vol. 47, No. 2, Summer 2002.

Wheeler, Steve, 'Fred W. Martin's Yacht Designs', *Nautical Research Journal*, Vol. 48, No. 2, pp.67-84, Summer 2003.

Wheeler, Steve, 'Racine Boat Company: The end of an Era', *Nautical Research Journal*, Vol. 48, No. 4, Winter 2003.

The Gunner's Table

INVESTIGATING THE HISTORY OF A SEVENTEENTH-CENTURY ARTEFACT

By Richard Endsor

Three hundred years after her loss in 1703, shifting sediment and sand, which had for so long entombed the wreck of the 70-gun third-rate ship *Stirling Castle*, began to move revealing parts of the ship. During the summer of 2002 the sediment on the gun deck toward the stern began to erode away causing part of the upper deck to collapse. Divers from the Seadive Organisation who monitor the site investigated the exposed area. They noticed on the port side, a little forward of the third gun port from the stern, a swingleg table (later known as gateleg) still standing on its feet. Near it, and a little

Above: The table in place on the wreck. *(Robert Peacock, Seadive Organisation)*

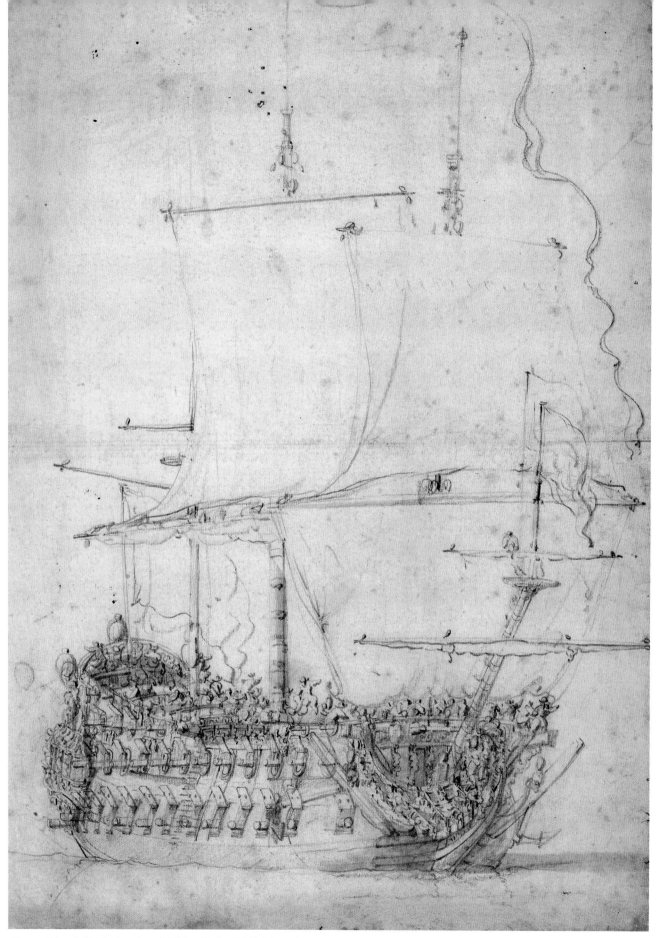

Above: Van de Velde drawing of *Stirling Castle. (British Museum)*

further inboard, was a Surgeon's chest. Above, and in imminent danger of crushing the table, was an upper deck gun. The uniqueness of the find was evident to the divers, who, over the next two months, carefully recorded the table in great detail.

Ship construction techniques of the seventeenth century are little understood today mainly because of the lack of good contemporary manuscripts or printed works. My work into the subject included investigating the archaeological remains of ships like the *Stirling Castle*. This work culminated in my recent book, *The Restoration Warship* (Conway, 2009). [Interested readers will find a brief assessment of Richard's book in Book News. Editor] Over the years Mr Robert Peacock of the Seadive Organisation has kindly brought interesting finds to my attention, including the earliest archaeological evidence of a ship's steering wheel (published in *Mariner's Mirror*, Vol. 90, No. 1), and now here the meticulous work he carried out in recording the swingleg table. Such was the accuracy it was possible to produce a drawing showing such features as the wood grain. The ship's table is, as far as I know, unique, although many civilian swingleg tables survive from the seventeenth century. It is one of countless artefacts from the *Stirling Castle* that are rapidly disappearing as the ship erodes away. These artefacts and the ship itself are as interesting and important as the *Mary Rose*.

STIRLING CASTLE

Stirling Castle was built at the Royal Dockyard at Deptford by the master shipwright John Shish and launched on 28 July 1679. She was part of the great thirty shipbuilding programme of 1677 intended to make the small English battle fleet of King Charles II the equal of the French and Dutch navies. These ships were so successful that by 1700 England was the world's leading maritime power. When the ship was completed Charles himself attended the launch and lavish celebrations were held not just for him but also the workmen who were amply provided with food and drink. Charles made it part of the celebrations to meet and talk with the workmen. So much money was spent by Shish on the ceremonies that the Admiralty held an inquiry and ordered that no such expenses should be made in future without their particular orders.[1] After her launch *Stirling Castle* joined the rest of the fleet 'in ordinary' at Chatham until 1690 when war broke out with France. She fought as part of the Red Squadron at the defensive battle of Beachy Head in 1690 that prevented a French invasion. The next and last battle of the war was the great victory at Barfleur-La Hogue in 1692 where she fought as part of the Blue Squadron. The French fleet never again put to sea during the war and *Stirling Castle* spent her time escorting merchant ships to and from English

ports. The war ended in 1697 by which time the timbers of the ship had worked loose and parts of her were rotten. Along with many other ships in similar condition, *Stirling Castle* was taken apart and rebuilt in 1699 at Chatham. Her dimensions hardly altered during the re-build but the work would have ensured she was in as good condition as new.[2]

Amid fears of French plans to assemble an invasion fleet, *Stirling Castle* (Captain John Johnson) was part of Sir George Rooke's fleet put to sea in the middle of August 1701. Their orders were to cover the French fleet making ready at Brest and escort to safety a squadron bound for the West Indies. The voyage was uneventful and they returned to St Helen's on 20 September where Rooke received orders to take the fleet into the Downs and end the year's expedition. While most ships in the fleet made ready for their winter refit, on 2 January 1702 *Stirling Castle* sailed for Plymouth, where she was to have her winter refit. Once in the Hamoaze she was docked and refitted and she sailed again in mid February for Spithead where, on 9 March Sir George Rooke came aboard and hoisted the Union Flag at the main topmast head. He brought news of the death of William III and the accession of Queen Anne who quickly ended the uncertainty of hostilities by declaring war against France and Spain on 4 May 1702. Plans were laid for a decent on Cadiz and in mid June *Stirling Castle* sailed as part of an expedition of twenty-eight ships under Sir Stafford Fairborn with orders to cruise off Cape Finisterre until the main Anglo-Dutch fleet under Sir George Rooke arrived to join them.

The whole fleet arrived in the Bay of Bulls at the entrance to Cadiz and on 13 August the troops were landed. After taking Rota, a small village on the north side of the bay, they advanced about 5 miles south along the shoreline to take Port St Mary's. Here progress slowed, not least because of the plunder of goods and wine, and eventually, due to stiffening Spanish resistance and allied indecision, ground to a halt.[3]

On 23 August *Stirling Castle* together with the similar sized *Northumberland* and *Eagle* were ordered by Rooke to cruise between Cape St Mary's and Cape Spartell to look for enemy ships. During the three weeks they were out it was decided to abandon the Cadiz expedition. Rooke ordered the ships out cruising to return into the bay to replenish their water before the return voyage to England.[4] They rejoined the fleet on Thursday, 10 September. After only three days, advancing Spaniards occupied the landing place and beat off the boats. Unable to fill her casks, *Stirling Castle*'s boats were used in the evacuation of British troops from the coast.

THE GUNNER

In the midst of all the turmoil and activity, one of the boats found time to exchange the Gunners of the *Stirling Castle* and

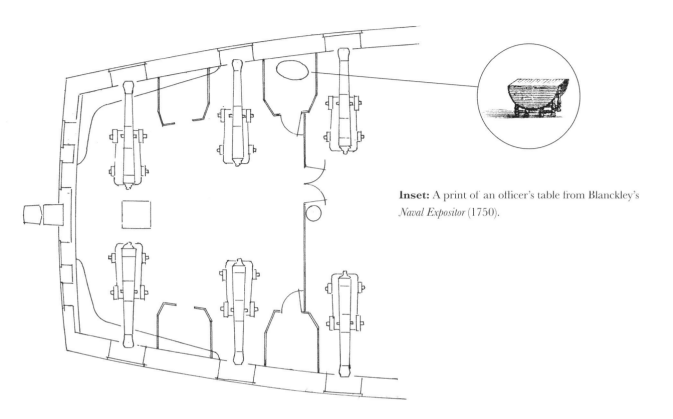

Inset: A print of an officer's table from Blanckley's *Naval Expositor* (1750).

the 80-gun third-rate *Boyne*. The Gunner was one of five permanent warrant officers appointed to each warship and was retained in service even when laid up in ordinary. As well as keeping records of ordnance stores he was responsible for the state and efficiency of the guns so they would perform well in action. He also undertook the vital task of looking after the gunpowder in the forward and aft magazines and the making of cartridges. It is difficult to understand why the exchange of Gunners was carried out at that time but John Laws and Thomas Browning, his servant from the Boyne, replaced Josiah Streater of the *Stirling Castle*.[5]

John Laws and Browning would have made their way to their berth in the gunroom on the lower gun deck abaft the mizzenmast. This area measured about 26ft square and was separated from the rest of the gundeck by a bulkhead[6] enclosing the last two broadside guns on each side of the ship and the aft facing chase ports. As Laws entered his new domain he would have noticed a beautiful, shiny Prince Rupert Patent 32lb Demi-Cannon bearing the survey number 6221 and marked as weighing 49 hundredweight, 0 quarters and 3 pounds, just one of the lower deck battery he now inherited.[7] The tiller swept almost the entire area above

their heads and at its forward end was the gooseneck for the whipstaff. Just aft the mizzenmast was a double-sheaved block for the steering wheel ropes.[8] Between each broadside gun was a cabin made from old canvas;[9] one, against the bulkhead, belonged to John Laws, while another opposite belonged to the Surgeon, William Deas. The remaining two smaller cabins between the aft broadside gunports were for Mates, one who would have been the Gunner's Mate, Robert Jefferson. Amongst the others who shared the gunroom was the Surgeon's servant, up to ten Midshipmen and a Volunteer, Henry Johnson. Forming the lower sill of the four aft facing chase ports was the huge 14in thick wing transom and acting as the upper sill was the port helm transom at the top of the sternpost. Huge fore-and-aft knees connected the transoms to the main wales on the outside of the ship through which they were bolted.[10] For third-rate ships such as the *Stirling Castle* a deal table was provided for the Gunner.[11]

Although a mere detail of cabin fittings it was an important part of an officer's equipment without which life would have been very uncomfortable. The Captain, Lieutenant and Master all wrote their log books on them while the Gunner filled in meticulous ordnance stores lists showing the allocation of stores, the stores aboard and the quantity of stores used to make up to the allocated level (see *The Restoration Warship*, p.163). Swingleg tables are also very adaptable and probably acted as a dining table for the officers and mates in the gunroom. The gunroom table was regarded as important and if missing Commissioners of the Navy would ask the Navy Board to provide one.[12]

Two days after Laws and Browning arrived aboard, Rooke made the signal to weigh anchor. The expedition to Cadiz had been a complete failure. However, following intelligence picked up while *Stirling Castle*, *Pembroke* and five horse transport ships were replenishing their depleted water supplies in Lagos Bay, Rooke sought out and attacked a Spanish treasure fleet escorted by French warships in Vigo Bay. In the ensuing battle six French warships from between 42 and 76 guns were taken and eleven destroyed while seventeen Spanish ships were taken or destroyed and a great deal of treasure and booty seized.[13] While the fleet were fighting the French and Spanish, *Stirling Castle* was fighting heavy seas on her way back to England with a flyboat in tow. On 8 October the heavy seas strained the ship so much that before they were aware of any damage, she had 4ft of water in the hold. This required 3 to 4 hours' pumping with both chain pumps. Then, at the same time the mizzenmast split and two of the mainmast chain plates broke. The next day the sea came over the waist and smashed the yawl. The heavy seas continued and a few days later the tow hit the starboard quarter and broke off some of the quarter gallery. The *Stirling Castle* was in company of the *Eagle* and they continued up Channel to Portsmouth where both ships made ready to enter dock for repair. This was a busy time for John Laws, the Gunner, as he supervised the removal of the guns, carriages, powder, shot and the stores from the ship. Emptied, she entered dock on 7 December for her repairs and cleaning which lasted three days. While at Portsmouth on 4 November the victorious ships that fought at Vigo came in with their treasure and prizes and those aboard *Stirling Castle* joined in the celebrations by firing 21 guns.

By 13 January 1703 *Stirling Castle* was again ready for service and at anchor at Spithead. She was not there long for a fleet of 120 merchantmen needed convoying to Portugal and she became part of the escort squadron of five third rates. She unmoored on 11 February and after surviving very hard gales arrived at Lisbon on the 24th. She remained there while the merchantmen did their business until 28 March. Moving up the coast *Stirling Castle* was detached on 7 April to escort ten merchantmen from Viana into the fleet. Heading home with the wind continually against them, it was not until 14 May before the Scilly lighthouse was seen. A few days later *Stirling Castle*

was ordered into Plymouth to be cleaned by careening. To do this she was emptied of her stores and ballast, John Laws again having to remove all the guns, carriages, powder, shot and his stores, amongst which was probably his table. *Stirling Castle* was then taken alongside the Saudadoes Hulk and hauled over as far as possible on top of her with tackles, exposing as much of the hull underwater as possible. The weed and rubbish was then burned and scraped off and new stuff applied. Each side took a day's work, after which the process began of putting everything back into the ship.

Stirling Castle was ready just in time to join a fleet of 250 sail including seventeen third rates under the command of Sir Cloudesley Shovell bound for the Mediterranean. The main purpose was to aid the Cevenois people against their king on the French south-west coast, to encourage the inhabitants of Sicily against the French and Spanish and to assist Prince Eugene at Leghorn. *Stirling Castle* joined the fleet off Land's End but was detached with the *Swiftsure* to escort a group of merchant ships into Porto and Viana. By 25 July she was again with the fleet anchored off Cascais near the entrance to Lisbon[14] seeing to the safety of trade and taking on water. They stayed until the end of July before setting sail, but were slowed by a Levant wind and only reached as far as Tangier Road by 9 August and Altea Bay by the end of the month. During early September ships were detached from the fleet to escort trade and try to contact the Cevenois people. By 19 September the fleet was off Leghorn where diplomatic contacts got off to a bad start with four days being wasted in a dispute over salutes. The expedition achieved little and the fleet returned home, arriving off the Isle of Wight on 16 November and shortly afterward arrived in the Downs.[15] A short voyage was made by *Stirling Castle* in company with the *Assistance* to meet the *Nassau* which had lost her rudder off Beachy Head but by 22 November she was back in the Downs.[16]

LOSS OF THE *STIRLING CASTLE*

It was a great risk for warships to be exposed to winter gales in the Downs so late in the year. On 26 November the wind began blowing very hard with all the indications of getting worse. Experienced officers veered out a long service 'shot' of two-and-a-half cables spliced together bent to a bower anchor. It seems likely that only a single length of cable on the port side anchored *Stirling Castle*. As the short day drew to a close the WSW wind increased to a tremendous storm driving ships toward the Goodwin Sands. Between two and five in the morning, just after high tide, it became 'a dreadful tempest…the like whereof hath scarcely happened in the memory of man'.[17] *Stirling Castle* may have survived but she was fouled and torn free by the doomed *Northumberland* which

Above: The author's detailed drawings of the Gunner's Table.

had lost her anchors. In spite of the storm some brave souls aboard *Stirling Castle* managed to loose her spare anchor on a single cable. It could not stop her and before other anchors could be deployed or the masts cut away she struck the Goodwin Sands. The *Mary*, *Northumberland* and *Restoration* appear to have been turned broadside on when they hit the sands and smashed to pieces as they rose up and down in the seas. *Stirling Castle* was a little luckier for when she struck the spare anchor, although dragging, managed to keep her head into the storm.[18] The next day the stern was still visible although the numbers of survivors clinging to it were seen to be dwindling. Eventually some brave men from Deal managed to row out the 5 miles to the wreck and save about 70 men, all that was left of 268 onboard.[19]

Among those who died was the Gunner John Laws. The navy worked out Laws' wages to be £47 6s 5d but after deductions to Greenwich Hospital and the Chatham Chest it amounted to £46 2s 9d. Browning, his servant, was more fortunate for he had left *Stirling Castle* in January while she was at Portsmouth for repairs. His wages for the time aboard worked out at £3 19s 5d. Grace Laws, John's widow, later collected both men's wages.[20]

THE GUNNER'S TABLE

The tabletop is oval shaped and just over 3 feet 6 inches in length. The central section is fixed, while the two outer leaves are hinged to fold down vertically. Each section is roughly a third the overall length and measure within an eighth of an inch of each other. It is made of what appears to be pine but may be fir, the materials known in the seventeenth and eighteenth centuries as deal. Beneath the table is a drawer, also made of deal and joined only by pins and probably cow glue. Unfortunately, the supporting board underneath the drawer is missing although a slot cut into the back panel indicates its presence and size. Also missing is the supporting rail at the front of the drawer. It is therefore conjectural exactly how this rail and the drawer supporting board were joined. All the metalwork is corroded away including the drawer handles and the table hinges. However, the size and position of the hinges and the nails that held them are indicated by impressions made in the wood. The deal parts of the table, it would polite to say, are workmanlike, in complete contrast to the turned oak bobbin legs and rails that are beautifully and precisely made. The lower rails between the legs have a small moulding on the upper surfaces that on the end rails show considerable wear. The wear was clearly caused by someone sitting at the table and resting their shoe on it. Also of interest are the remains of about forty or fifty copper and silver coins in the drawer. They were in an extreme state of decay and disintegrated at the slightest touch. They were

drawn using photographic evidence made shortly after they were discovered.

There were eight deal tables allocated to each third-rate ship. They belonged to the Master, Lieutenant, Minister, Second Lieutenant, Boatswain, Carpenter, Purser and Gunner.[21] The Commander of *Stirling Castle*, Captain Johnson, also had a table but his was made entirely from oak.[22] A large oval table with benches was also provided for the area known as the steerage where officers usually dined on the upper deck just forward of the Captain's cabin.[23] It is clearly not this table as it was much larger and made in one piece.[24] Of the eight officers who were entitled to a deal table, those belonging to the Master, Lieutenant, Minister and Second Lieutenant were probably two decks above on the quarterdeck while the Purser's was down below on the orlop. It is also unlikely to belong to either the Boatswain or Carpenter for their cabins were on the deck above against the quarterdeck bulkhead and 15ft further forward. Their cabins were also very small for such a relatively large table. Only the Gunner had his cabin on the gun deck where the table was found. Not only that but the Surgeon's chest was found within feet of it and the Surgeon and Gunner's cabins were on opposite sides of the ship in the gunroom.[25] Both the Surgeon's chest and the table were found about 8ft further forward than the position of the gunroom bulkhead but during the process of wrecking they could easily have moved there. Considering the evidence it must be reasonable to assume the table did indeed belong to the Gunner, John Laws.

It is easy to imagine Laws sitting in his cabin working at the end of the table with the two folding sections closed down to save space. His foot would be on the rail wearing down the decorative moulding to its present state. The wear suggests the table was a good number of years old and made before the *Stirling Castle* was rebuilt in 1699. If so the table, along with the guns and other fittings almost certainly belonged to the ship long before her rebuild. They were first allocated to her at Chatham in 1690 just before she fought at the battle of Beachy Head.

By the greatest of good fortune, one contract exists for eighty tables and dates from the precise period in 1690 when *Stirling Castle* was being fitted out.[26] It was a contract made between the pious Commissioner at Chatham, Edward Gregory[27] and Henry Ward, a joiner of Chatham. Not only do the dimensions agree but the contract states the top should be of deal with legs of oak. There is a difference in that the contract states the rails should be of deal where in actuality they are of oak. The contract may also suggest only one part of the table is hinged whereas in actuality there are two, as was almost universally the case. If the contract relates to the table and quite possibly it does, remarkably, both the man who used it and the man who made it are known to us today. The contract reads:

Contracted and agreed this 1st February 89/90 with the Honourable Edward Gregory Esq. one of the Principal Officers and Commissioners of their Majesties Navy for and on behalf of their Majesties by me Henry Ward of Chatham joiner and I do hereby oblige my self at my own proper cost and charge, and with my own materials well and seasonably to make finish and deliver into their Majesties stores at Chatham in good and workmanlike manner within six weeks from the date hereof (that is to say 1/3rd part thereof in 14 days, 2/3rd part thereof in one month and the residue by the time exprest) the tables and hencoops under mentioned for the ships now ordered to be got ready viz:

	Feet	No	
Tables	3 ½	20	With legs of oak, deal tops, deal rails 1/3rd part
	3	20	of the top to hang with hinges with a swing leg to retain it and a drawer to each at 8s 6d each
	2 ½	40	After the same manner at 8s each
Hencoops		20	Each to be 6 feet 2 inches long 2 feet 7 inches High 1 foot 9 inches broad at bottom 1 foot 8 inches broad at top–The tops and ends to be Whole deal and the back slit deal with a Trough at 16s each

To be paid for the same at Chatham upon passing a regular bill as is usual–

Henry Ward

A warrant 3rd February 1689
A copy
Edward Gregory

NOTES

1 BL ADD MS9322, f56v.

2 Brian Lavery, *The Ship of the Line, Vol. 1*, Conway Maritime Press, 1983, p.166.

3 Josiah Burchett, *Transactions at Sea*, 1720, p.619-623.

4 *The Journal of Sir George Rooke*, Navy Records Society, 1897, pp.183, 208.

5 Pay Book of *Stirling Castle*, TNA, ADM33/230.

6 Joiners work for Guersey 1696, TNA, ADM106/3541, Part 1.

7 The Rupertino gun, serial no. 6221, was raised by the Seadive Organisation in 2000 and is now being conserved.

8 Richard Endsor, 'Loss of Stirling Castle', *Mariner's Mirror*, Vol. 90, No. 1 (2004), p.92.

9 Sir John Tippetts orders 1678, TNA, ADM106/331, f272.

10 Contract of Yarmouth, TNA, ADM106/3071.

11 Cabins and Tables of each Ship 1686, TNA, ADM49/123.

12 Robert Lee to the Navy Board 1678, TNA, ADM106/330 f328.

13 Josiah Burchett, p.628.

14 Captain's and Master's log book of *Stirling Castle*, TNA, ADM51/4355 and ADM52/291.

15 Burchett, pp.646-656.

16 David Chamberlain, Bygone Kent (2005), p.349.

17 Burchett, p.656.

18 Endsor, (2004), p.93.

19 Ibid., p.92.

20 *Stirling Castle* Pay Book, TNA, ADM33/230.

21 Cabin and Table Establishment 1686, TNA, ADM49/123.

22 Thomas Riley Blanckley, *The Naval Expositor*, 1750, p.167.

23 Robert Lee to Navy Board, 1678, TNA, ADM 106/330, f328.

24 Edmund Dummer, Section through a First Rate, *c.*1680, Pepys Library 2934 and Phillip's print of a first-rate ship *c.*1690.

25 Cabin and Table Establishment 1686, TNA, ADM49/123.

26 Contract with Henry Ward, 1690, TNA, ADM106/3069.

27 Journal of Edward Gregory, Author's Collection.

Prospector BA25

MODELLER'S DRAUGHT

by J. Pottinger

This boat is an example of the numerous wooden fishing boats built by Alexander Noble at his yard at Girvan, on the Ayrshire coast in Scotland. His boats have long been admired for their shapely design and workmanship, being true examples of the art of the builder of wooden boats. The earlier dainty cruiser stern boats were especially of pleasing appearance. They also impart their own readily identifiable characteristics on craft which have to withstand the rigours of the hard life of any fishing boat. An enduring recognition feature has been the proud Scottish Thistle emblem carved

Above: *Prospector* ready to be launched. Her shapely lines can be seen here, and it also shows the original towing gallows aft and an early type of power block crane. (*John Murray, Girvan*)

Above: Alexander Noble climbs aboard to have a last check before launching. The immaculate planking and careful carpentry are immediately evident. Note the arrangement of foremast tripod and bracing. *(John Murray, Girvan)*

Above: The boat making her way proudly after launching, with owners and friends in Sunday best for the occasion. The rather elaborate arrangement of derricks rigged for pair trawling is prominent. The draught aft can be seen as just less than 9ft. (*John Murray, Girvan*)

on, and adorning the nameboard, on each bow. Many of the boats had varnished hulls, which left no hiding place for anything but perfect hull planking. Starting from a bare green field site in Girvan in March 1946 the yard was expanded gradually to cope with the increase in size, type and complexity of fishing boats, with additional slipways, workshops, drawing office and building sheds progressively erected.

The founder of the yard was born in Fraserburgh, and served an apprenticeship at a local yard building a variety of types of fishing boats, yachts and launches of carvel and clinker construction, an experience enhanced by that of working on all kinds of repair work. Further experience was gained in a boatbuilding yard in Donegal, where he first undertook the design of some boats, and later in a yacht building yard on the Clyde which was heavily engaged on Admiralty work during the Second World War.

The *Prospector* was completed in September 1973 as Job No. 73 and fitted with a Caterpillar diesel engine, later replaced by a Volvo Penta unit. She was designed originally as a ring net boat and, in contrast to earlier boats of this type, had a transom stern instead of a rounded cruiser stern and

was fitted with the specialist rig and gear peculiar to that mode of fishing. It is possible that she was the last of that rig to be built at the yard.

Ring netting was a speciality of the lower Clyde and the area around the entrance to Loch Fyne, Kilbrannan Sound and around the island of Arran. Ring netting was originally a shore-based operation, but with the advent of powered fishing boats equipped with winches, dependence on the inshore operation was eliminated. The basic method afloat, when worked from a pair of boats, was for one end of the net to be attached to the stationary boat whilst the other went round the shoal of herring in order that the net formed a ring, hence the term 'ring netting'.

With this method of fishing now gone this boat has been modified over the years to operate as a trawler, and most recently as a scalloper. Whilst retaining her original name she has borne the successive port numbers BA 25 (Ballantrae), TT 25 (Tarbert) and now N1, representing Newry in Northern Ireland. I have chosen to depict her as a trawler and rigged accordingly with trawl winch and towing gallows aft.

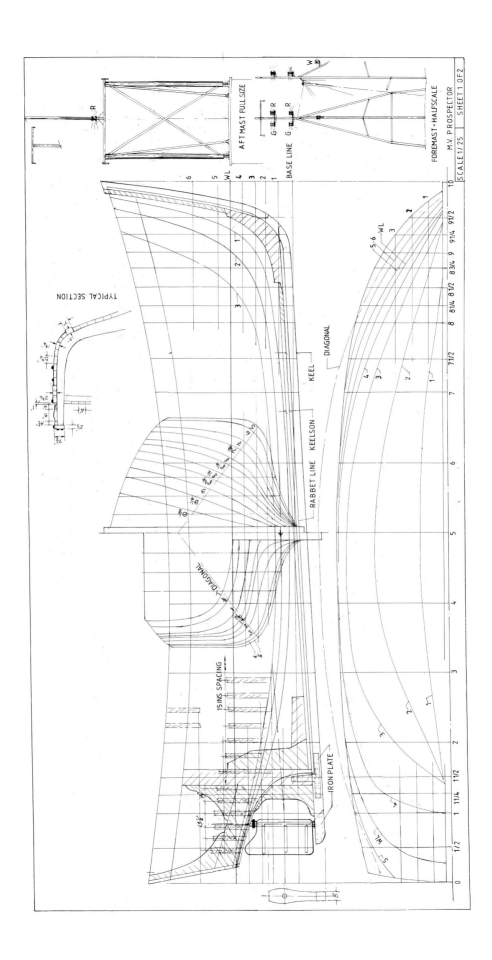

TYPICAL SECTION

15 INS SPACING

IRON PLATE

DIAGONAL

RABBET LINE   KEELSON

KEEL

DIAGONAL

AFT MAST FULL SIZE

BASE LINE

FOREMAST - HALFSCALE

M.V. PROSPECTOR

SCALE 1/25   SHEET 1 OF 2

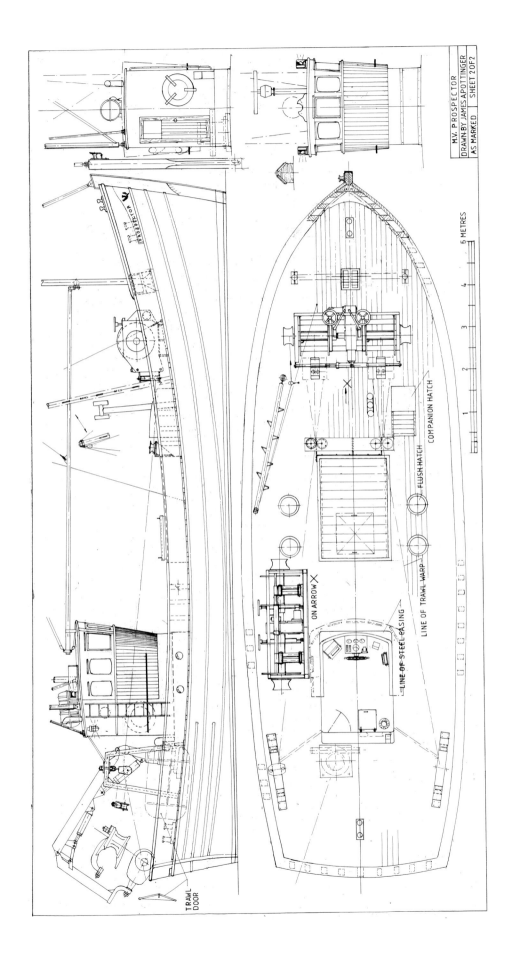

M.V. PROSPECTOR
DRAWN BY JAMES APOTTINGER
AS MARKED   SHEET 2 OF 2

5 METRES

1   2   3   4

COMPANION HATCH

FLUSH HATCH

LINE OF TRAWL WARP

LINE OF STEEL CASING

ON ARROW

TRAWL DOOR

PROSPECTOR

Left: Fully rigged she is trawling in this shot. Over the years a number of modifications have been carried out to the arrangement of the radar scanner, various aerials and rigging. *(Peter Drummond)*

Below left: A typical power block and crane, as fitted to a twin rig prawn trawler. This power block has an additional hydraulic ram to actuate the angle of the power block itself.

Below: A trawl winch as fitted to a twin rig trawler, with three drums to handle the two wing and centre warps. The guide-on gear is actuated by a horizontally mounted hydraulic ram similar to the arrangement shown on the model plan, the winch being of similar design to that in the photograph, without the centre drum.

The lines show a boat whose hefty lines are perhaps belied by the sweeping sheer and dainty appearance on the water. The hull is beamy with fairly flat slack hull bottom sections with a very sharp and hard turn at the bilge. I have shown on Sheet 1 a detailed section of the typical arrangement of planking and bulwarks, note the thicker planking just below deck level and a heavier plank under the bilge. Some wood boatbuilders fit two planks instead of one at this point. These thicker planks extend for about three quarters of the length of the boat, but have the ends tapered into the thickness of the rest of the planking. Nowadays most wooden boat builders dispense with the shaped centre plank on the bulwarks and fit plain timber planking instead.

The camber of the deck is about a half inch per foot of beam, thus on the plan would result in a height of 9mm at the centre. I have also shown some of the main structural elements of the hull, such as frames, sternpost, deadwood and apron, for anyone interested in knowing more about the construction of the vessel. This also gives some indication of the complexity, amount of large timbers and the shaping work entailed in ensuring the integrity of a wooden vessel of this size. Also indicated is the steel half round protective bars on the hull side planking and on top of the bulwark rail. Note that the steel keel band extends from the top of the stem post all along the length of the keel and terminates at the steel shoe which encapsulates the extreme aft end of the keel.

As stated above, I have shown the boat rigged as a trawler, with a trawl winch, power block and gallows aft; note the roller sheaves positioned at the forward end of the hatch coaming to ensure a fair lead of the warps to and from the winch to the hanging blocks on the gallows. The warps are guided on to the lower side of the winch barrel by means of a hydraulic ram, which pushes the cage with horizontal and vertical rollers at the aft side of the winch back and forth to ensure that the warp wires are laid on evenly on the barrel without overriding turns. I have shown the trawl gallows as formed from H-section steel bar. Note that a different design and construction of the gallows are shown in the photographs. In fact when launched *Prospector* was fitted with gallows made from tubular steel, but the detail shown here is typical of many boats of this size and rig.

The outer gypsy barrels can be clutched in as required, and on this deck arrangement would be used to hoist the fall from the cod end derrick by means of suitably located lead blocks at the foot of the derrick, and brakes are provided to lock each barrel as required. Incidentally, it is unusual to have this cod end derrick mounted on the port side instead of on the starboard side; this may be a hold over from her ring net

days when she may have been working with a pairing boat. When rigged for trawling the main fish hold hatch is closed off apart from a small opening with a lift-off cover just large enough to pass through a fish box.

As the crew accommodation is forward, a wooden access hatch with a sliding cover and a glazed opening skylight is fitted on the fore deck. Note the protective bars over the glazed skylight lids, with galley stove funnel further aft; usually the top half could be detached during fishing operations to avoid fouling warps etc.

The circular flush hatches on each side of the deck had been used to pass the herring catch down to the hold when ring netting, but were probably sealed off when converted to trawling or scalloping.

The forward part of the wheelhouse is wood planked and sits on a raised steel coaming. The after part of the wheelhouse is also made of steel, and is thus more able to support the various appendages attached on top and also the bracing to the trawl gallows. I have to admit that I was never a fan from a purely aesthetic point of view of this builder's arrangement of different types of wheelhouse windows, I assume the square wooden framed windows were of the railway coach type, able to be dropped down to open.

It will be noted that the length of the engine exhaust outlet pipe has been greatly extended above the wheelhouse in later photographs of the boat. The foremast is of tripod form of relatively light tubular construction. The derrick heel pivot is mounted on the cross beam which is just above head height. As will be shown in the accompanying photographs many alterations to fittings, rig etc. have been carried out over the life of the boat to reflect her changing roles and fishing methods. The modelmaker can use his discretion as to how many of these to incorporate.

COLOUR SCHEME (SUGGESTED)

Dark blue: upper hull, power block crane, towing gallows, guide rollers

Light blue: trawl winch, main hatch, bollards, steel casing under wheelhouse

White: waterline cutwater, port number, wheelhouse top

Pale red: hull underwater, masts, derricks, inside of bulwarks

Varnished wood: fore part of wheelhouse, name board on each bow, companion and skylight

Light brown: after part of wheelhouse

Black: panel on sides for port number

Yellow/gold: name, ribband at lower edge of bulwarks

SS *Great Britain*

BRUNEL'S FAMOUS IRON SHIP

by John York

BACKGROUND

Following a holiday in the UK in May 2006, during which I was able to pay a second visit to the *Great Britain* lying in her original dry dock in the Great Western Dock in Bristol, I decided to build a model of this famous iron ship. The history of Brunel's masterpiece, her salvage and subsequent restoration has been well recorded elsewhere so will not be covered here.

Below: Port bow view of finished model.

THE MODEL

The *Great Britain*'s length was 289ft and beam 50ft. The model was built to a scale of 1:96 (⅛in = 1ft).

The model was based on information contained in *The Iron Ship*, supplemented by various other books and photographs I had taken of the ship. The hull was built in the conventional method of slotting the frames into the keel, cutwater and sternpost assembly, which were of 3mm

Above: Hull planking started.

plywood, with external parts added after the planking was in place. The hull was double planked. After the first layer had been laid it was sanded smooth. The final layer of planking was put on and aligned to follow the ship's iron plates. These plates were etched in later. There are about 500 plates on each side of the hull, each one being approximately 6ft x 2ft in size (1.83m x 0.61m).

The extension to the keel abaft the sternpost, which would house the heel of the rudder stock, was about 1in long. It consisted of a piece of 2mm diameter stainless steel wire sandwiched between two pieces of 2mm x 4mm timber planks connected into the main keel.

The next consideration was the 15ft diameter propeller. This was not a casting but of composite construction. I used sheet copper cut to shape for the blades, which were soldered into slots cut in the end of the propeller shaft (for which I used part of an old brass water tap). This had been shaped to represent the propeller boss. With the blades firmly in place they were adjusted to the correct pitch.

The rudder was made from 4mm plywood, with 2mm copper wire for the pivot points.

The plywood deck was cut slightly oversize and sanded to fit. It was painted a light grey colour then, using a 2H pencil, marked to represent the deck planks with a scale width of 1.5mm. The internal planking of the bulwarks above the deck was then finished. The capping rail was cut to shape from 2mm plywood in two pieces, one for each side of the ship, sanded, and fitted in place. The shape of the rail was marked on the plywood and the cutting done on a bandsaw fitted with a fine-toothed blade. To prevent the plywood laminates from chipping when being cut, clear adhesive tape was put on both sides in way of the areas to be cut. It was removed prior to sanding and gluing the rails in place on top of the bulwarks.

The hull was now almost complete and ready for painting. After receiving a final sanding it was given a primer undercoat. This was lightly rubbed down when dry ready for

the final coats. When all the other parts of the hull painting were complete a band of white enamel was applied in the area where the dummy gunports would be added. After masking the white area I applied two coats of black enamel, followed by more masking prior to painting below the waterline with two coats of a red/orange mix of enamel to simulate anti-fouling composition.

The positions of the false gunports were marked using office quality clear adhesive tape. This gave me much sharper edges than the ordinary tape. The ports were then painted black, and the tape removed when the paint was dry.

Most of the deck fittings, skylights (Figure 5), companion-ways and hatches were made from 2mm plywood. The curved tops to the companionways were made from two pieces of 1mm wood veneer glued together as they were being fitted. The funnel was made from a length of 20mm diameter copper water pipe, with the cooling fins at the base consisting of a length of cored solder.

Four of the masts were hinged at the base, apparently for adjusting the sails. I have shown my method of constructing these hinged masts in Figure 1. As the making of masts, spars, blocks and deadeyes, and the methods of installing shrouds, stays and rigging has been well covered in other articles, I will not go into this here. Suffice to say that I

Below: The finished model.

Above: Overhead view of after end.

Above: Showing scored hull plating.

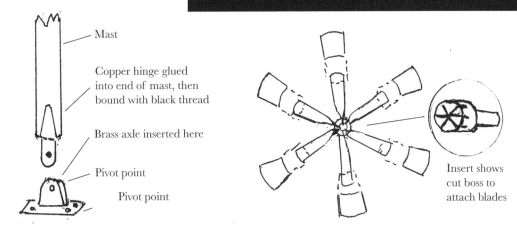

Mast

Copper hinge glued
into end of mast, then
bound with black thread

Brass axle inserted here

Pivot point

Pivot point

Figure 1. Detail of mast hinges.

Insert shows
cut boss to
attach blades

Figure 2. Construction of propeller.

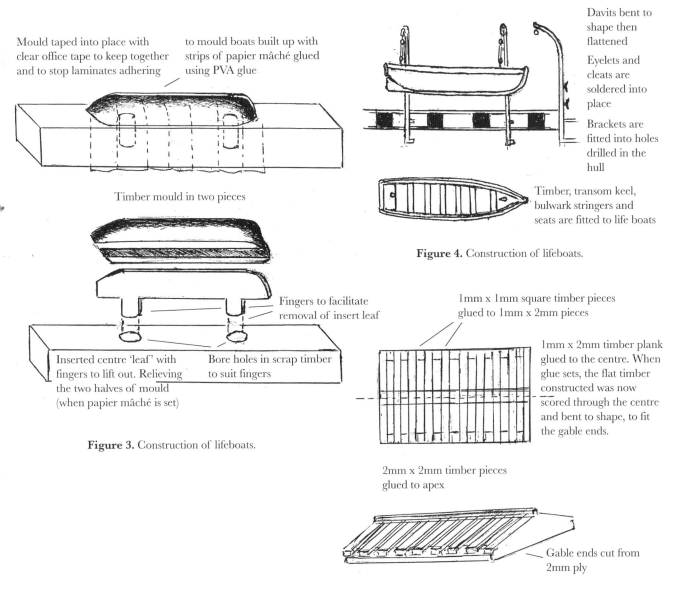

Mould taped into place with
clear office tape to keep together
and to stop laminates adhering

to mould boats built up with
strips of papier mâché glued
using PVA glue

Timber mould in two pieces

Fingers to facilitate
removal of insert leaf

Inserted centre 'leaf' with
fingers to lift out. Relieving
the two halves of mould
(when papier mâché is set)

Bore holes in scrap timber
to suit fingers

Figure 3. Construction of lifeboats.

Davits bent to
shape then
flattened

Eyelets and
cleats are
soldered into
place

Brackets are
fitted into holes
drilled in the
hull

Timber, transom keel,
bulwark stringers and
seats are fitted to life boats

Figure 4. Construction of lifeboats.

1mm x 1mm square timber pieces
glued to 1mm x 2mm pieces

1mm x 2mm timber plank
glued to the centre. When
glue sets, the flat timber
constructed was now
scored through the centre
and bent to shape, to fit
the gable ends.

2mm x 2mm timber pieces
glued to apex

Gable ends cut from
2mm ply

Figure 5. Method of making skylights.

Above: Showing midship area layout.

followed accepted practices when doing this work on the model.

LIFEBOATS

The lifeboats were made of papier mâché on a mould or plug to simulate metal construction. Wood thwarts and bulwarks were added, see Figures 3 and 4.

GUARD RAILS AND STANCHIONS

Stainless steel dressmaking pins were used for the stanchions, they were roughened to make sure they held in place when glued in holes drilled in the bulwark rail. The rails were made of continuous lengths of polyester thread, correctly spaced on the stanchions, and held in place with a coating of white enamel. The rails and stanchions were then covered with hammock netting.

ENGINE MAIN CHAIN WHEEL

The plastic cap from a pill container was used as the base on which to build a mock-up chain wheel, which could be seen

Above: Stern detail.

through the engine room skylight. Spokes and piston rods, made from wood, were glued in place. The centre shaft was a length of dowel. A length of chain was added.

Above: Starboard quarter view of model.

ELECTRIC WINCH
This was a purchased item which was then greatly modified to represent the one on the ship.

TRAIL BOARDS AND TRANSOM DETAIL
The information on which to replicate these was obtained from the book SS *Great Britain*. This was laid out at scale size, painted in the appropriate colours and glued in place on the model.

REFERENCES
Corlett, Ewan, *The Iron Ship: the story of Brunel's SS Great Britain*, (Conway Maritime Press, 1974 and 1989) ISBN 085177 531 4

Book News

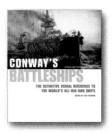

Conway's Battleships: The Definitive Visual Reference to the World's All-Big-Gun Ships
Revised and Expanded
Edited by Ian Sturton
Conway, 2008
Hardback, 240 pages, profusely illustrated, some in colour, with photographs, paintings and line drawings. £30.00
ISBN 978-18448-606-28-5

This is a revised and expanded edition of a book first published over twenty years ago. The new, larger format allows the photographs to be reproduced at a larger size, thereby allowing more detail to be extracted; particularly useful for the modeller. The content is divided logically by country in alphabetical order, following an extensive explanatory introduction by the editor.

The majority of the profile line drawings of every individual or class of battleship and battlecruiser that entered service are reproduced to a common scale of 1:1250, although in exceptional cases some are to the scale of 1:1500 in order to fit the profiles on the page. However, there is a major scale discrepancy in the profiles of HMS *Hood*. These are marked as being to the scale of 1:1500, but have not been printed accordingly as the three profiles – as completed, after her 1941 refit and the *Anson* design of 1919 – show three different lengths, whereas the first two at least should be identical!

There is a specification table for each class of battleship and battlecruiser listing salient statistical data. These tables precede summary design development and career histories of the individual ships or ships within a class, with each being supported by large photographic images showing both the ships as a whole, and close-up details, including some rare and previously unpublished shots.

The power and majesty of these incredible warships, some of which were obsolete whilst still on the drawing board, continues to generate awe, particularly in those, like this writer, too young to have witnessed them in person. It is difficult, however, to appreciate the reality that several of the early capital ships were in fact no larger than some modern frigates and destroyers, even if these definitions no longer mean what they originally did. It is probably the sheer visual impact of the size of barrel necessary to support the firing of an 11in shell, or larger, that creates the sense of power and awe, when today the largest gun used by the Royal Navy, at 4.5in, looks so insignificant in comparison!

Complementing the black-and-white photographs are a number of full-colour reproductions of paintings and photographs, with those by W. L. Wyllie being particularly noteworthy – demonstrating his ability to successfully portray the power and majesty of the battleship in one of the most delicate of painting mediums – watercolour.

This book will appeal to the modeller of twentieth-century warships, and for those interested in the relatively short-lived technology of the big-gun battleship and battlecruiser.
Michael Leek

Kongo Class Battlecruisers
ShipCraft 9
by Steve Wiper
Seaforth Publishing, 2008
Paperback, 65 pages; profusely illustrated in full colour and black and white (photographs, paintings, illustrations and line drawings, etc).
£14.99
ISBN 978-1-84832-004-8

This A4-sized volume is number 9 in Seaforth's *ShipCraft* series and follows the successful formula and layout of previous volumes, including the quality of paper and production, much of the latter being in colour.

Even though there has been some determined and successful research into the design, construction and layout of warships of the Imperial Japanese Navy, particularly in Germany, the fact that the Japanese deliberately destroyed many of their records when they realised defeat was inevitable has not made the task of the researcher easy. It is, therefore, always welcome when a new study is published which provides yet more insight into the Japanese Navy's way of thinking and this volume, aimed specifically at the model maker, provides much that will be of interest.

Considering the self-destruction the Japanese imposed on themselves it may come as a surprise that so much material did survive, particularly in the case of the *Kongo* class battlecruisers, but then they were designed and built in the UK and the original builder's model fortunately still exists. This has now provided plastic kit manufacturers with the opportunity to produce, in some cases, highly detailed models comparable to many an exhibition-standard model. This has been made possible particularly due to the additional aid of highly detailed accessory sets, many of which are included and listed in this volume. The range of models of these formidable looking warships currently available is extensive, from 1:2400 to 1:350 scales.

Many of the completed models shown in the 'Modellers Showcase' section could easily be mistaken for larger scale non-plastic models, such as might be found in a museum collection, so high is the level of craftsmanship shown, enhanced by the use of brass and resin detail sets. Indeed, some of the amateur-built plastic models are far more realistic and convincing than the original Vickers builder's model, with its brass fittings and too immaculate finish. Full colour photographs of the Vickers model are also included in this volume.

Probably the most outstanding model in the book is the 1:150 scale full hull model by K Okamoto, considered the leading authority on the *Kongo* class. This model is not from a kit, but is entirely scratch-built. As with the work of so many Japanese warship modellers this is a notable and incredibly detailed model.

Supporting the modeller, the book also contains very detailed line drawings, colour profiles and some superb photographs of various ships from the class during their careers, including some highly detailed close-ups.

Books such as this, regardless of the emphasis on plastic kits, are a ship modeller's dream. It is highly recommended.

Michael Leek

production the same applies here as it does to the *Kongo* book.

For anyone interested in modelling one of these two famous and beautifully proportioned battleships this volume has to be considered one of the prime reference sources, even if the modelling focus is on the construction of one of many plastic kits. The fact that the focus is on plastic kits in no way undermines the quality of the content, as the author has gone to considerable lengths to ensure the approach to the modelling is about accurate scale representation, such as one would expect from any scratch-built miniature ship model.

The detail contained within is exemplary. It commences with succinct design and career histories to an evaluation of available kits and detail accessories. This is followed by 'Modelmakers Showcase'; a visual compilation of seven completed models by different modellers, some of which are clearly to exhibition standard, and at various scales, thereby showing the scope of detailing possible to those with the necessary skill and patience. This is followed by four pages of outstanding colour schemes of both ships at different points in their, albeit short, careers. For the purposes of accuracy (and to avoid confusion) these colour profiles and plans show the colour schemes in their initial, pristine conditions. Some may argue that this is not how the ships actually looked but the inevitable grime and weathering resulting from operational service may be seen – and applied by modellers – using the photographic evidence of the ships themselves, of which there are many reproduced in this volume. Coming after the colour profile section are 'Differences and Appearance Changes', a number of detailed drawings of various structures, armaments and fittings, and a list of 'Selected References'.

This is an excellent model maker's guide. Not only is it a prerequisite for modellers of the *Bismarck* and *Tirpitz*, but it is also useful for anyone interested in the former Kriegsmarine or Second World War North Atlantic Naval operations in general. We can only hope that the publishers continue to expand the series, adding even more detail as the subject allows.

Michael Leek

Bismarck and Tirpitz
ShipCraft 10
by Steve Backer
Seaforth Publishing, 2008
Paperback, 65 pages; profusely illustrated in full colour and black and white (photographs, paintings, illustrations and line drawings, etc).
£14.99
ISBN 978-1-84832-005-5

Following on from the preceding review, this is volume number 10 in Seaforth's *ShipCraft* series. In respect of the quality of

Warship 2009
Editor: John Jordan; Assistant Editor: Stephen Dent
Conway; 2009.
Hardback, 208 pages, profusely illustrated with photographs and line drawings. £30.00
ISBN 978-1-84486-089-0

Warship's success is due very much to the breadth of content and this volume continues a concept so admirably set by the late Anthony Preston, the founding Editor. *Warship 2009* has the usual mix of articles, notes and reviews but commences on a sad note with the obituaries of two stalwarts of *Warship* history: D.K. Brown and Dan Harris.

Articles are profusely illustrated, primarily with photographs and line drawings. The quality of the paper used means even historical photographs retain sufficient contrast and depth for even the smallest of detail to be studied, though understandably in a volume of this nature some photographs are included because of their historic significance of the events they show rather than the quality of the photographs themselves. Featured articles which might interest the ship modeller include the Royal Navy's submarine designs in the immediate post-Second World War period; a fine piece examining *Ise* and *Hyūga*, Japan's hybrid battleship-carriers, complete with some excellent illustrations and plans; a heavily illustrated assessment of the Italian Navy's fast coastal forces; an excellent article detailing the impact of the First World War upon John Brown & Co. shipbuilders on the Clyde; and much, much more. There is the annual review of current naval developments in 'World Navies in Review, 2008'; Warship notes and a pretty hefty book review section. As always with *Warship*, you get a lot for your money and there is a lot here of interest to the warship modeller.

Martin Robson and Michael Leek

The Frigate Surprise: The Complete Story of the Ship made Famous in the Novels of Patrick O'Brian
by Brian Lavery and Geoff Hunt
Conway, 2008
Hardback, 144 pages, profusely illustrated in full colour (photographs, paintings and illustrations), including maps, charts, draughts, line drawings and diagrams etc). £30.00
ISBN 978-1-84486-074-6

Shipwright is about the researching, making and presentation of accurate scale models of ships, boats and vessels of all periods and types, from anywhere in the world. Underpinning the success of any model is the quality and relevance of reference material from which to construct as accurate a model as the skill of the model maker allows. This book provides not only the reference material necessary, but also the historical context in which this fictional Royal Navy frigate operated.

Patrick O'Brian's success in his naval stories about the career and exploits of Jack Aubrey (accompanied by his friend Dr Maturin), and his eventual captaincy of the 28-gun frigate *Surprise*, are probably well known to many readers. O'Brian's stories are more than just Aubrey and the actions fought by the *Surprise*, but include much about the life and organisation on board the frigate. Taking the research O'Brian has used in his novels to ensure historical accuracy a stage further, the noted sailing navy historian Brian Lavery, formerly of the National Maritime Museum (NMM), and the internationally accomplished marine artist Geoff Hunt, former President of the Royal Society of Marine Artists, have put together this volume wherein they successfully present the real, factual context in which O'Brian set his fiction. It is important to stress that the historical context is not mere supposition but underpinned by the archives and resources of the NMM, HMS *Victory* and numerous others; and not just exclusively from the UK either.

Brian Lavery's text is, as one has come to expect from such a renowned historian, authoritative, and his juxtaposition of historical fact with the fictional voyages of the *Surprise* works very well. The informative text is supported by numerous illustrations, not the least being the beautiful paintings by Geoff Hunt, many of which were commissioned specifically for the dust jackets of O'Brian's novels. There is even a section on how Hunt arrived at his compositions and the research he used to ensure accuracy in how the *Surprise* might have appeared in different conditions. This particular section is a worthy inclusion as it is rare for any book which contains so much on marine art to cover the working designs and drawings of the artist.

In addition to the works by Hunt, there are photographs of models, preserved vessels, charts and maps, contemporary illustrations and portraits, and reproductions of original ship's draughts, including a superbly rendered longitudinal section of the French frigate *La Seine*.

For the model maker there is a set of draughts of the *Surprise* by the noted marine draughtsman Karl Heinz Marquardt (whose work has previously been published in *Model Shipwright* and in a number of Conway's *Anatomy of the Ship* series). These scaled draughts, which include complete deck plans, a comprehensive lines plan, and sail and rigging plans, are more than sufficient for a model maker to construct an accurate model of the *Surprise* – which would also be a typical representation of a late nineteenth-century 28-gun frigate (in this case one taken into Royal Navy service following her capture from the French). Marquardt's draughts are supported by detailed line drawings of the ordnance and ship's boats.

Obviously complementing Marquardt's draughts are the photographs taken on board preserved ships and the many paintings by Hunt. Collectively this means the model maker, or indeed the aspiring marine artist, should have no problem interpreting the information in this book to produce an accurate three-dimensional or two-dimensional representation.

As a possible subject for a frigate model the *Surprise* has the advantage that, being a 28-gun frigate, she is not as large as the heavy 44-gun frigates. This means the overall size, even at the traditional 1:48 scale, will not be too cumbersome or space hungry as her much larger sisters.

This is one of those books which will delight and inform from so many different angles, and as such should appeal to a wide readership, even if building a model of that most romantic or glamorous of Napoleonic vessels – the frigate – remains a mere dream! The publishers are to be congratulated on producing a book to a format that allows the most to be made of Geoff Hunt's paintings. Indeed, the overall production is excellent and in these increasingly austere days it is encouraging to see a book produced to such a high standard.

The authority of Brian Lavery's text, Geoff Hunt's paintings and Karl Heinz Marquardt's draughts are supported by appendices, endnotes, comprehensive bibliography by chapter, a list of original sources, a subject bibliography and a glossary. This book is highly recommended.

Michael Leek

Reconditioning an Eighteenth-Century Ship Model:
Valkenisse Retourschip of 1717
by Rob Napier
SeaWatch Books LLC, 2008
Hardback, 237 pages; profusely illustrated in full colour, with numerous line illustrations, maps and a number of large scale plans, etc.
$68 ISBN 978-0-98205-790-2

In this day-and-age it is indeed rare to come across a new book devoted to such a specialist subject and for the said book to be produced to such an excellent standard, reflecting as it does the outstanding reconstruction work of the author in his preservation of the model of the *Valkenisse*, 1717, held in the Museum of Fine Arts in Boston, MA.

The *Valkenisse*, a *retourschip*, was built in 1717 for the Dutch East Indies Company. She was typical of the period, sailing from The Netherlands to its colonies in the East, returning with mixed and valuable cargoes of peppers, cloves, cinnamon and nutmeg, amongst other exotic goods. After a career of only seventeen years she was wrecked in 1740. The model of the ship, on which this book is based, was, it is believed, made to be exhibited in the headquarters of the Dutch East Indies Company in Middleburg where the ship was built. The complete provenance of the model is not known, but it surfaced in New York early in the last century and was eventually gifted to the Museum of Fine Arts in Boston.

The model is 1.75m (5ft 4.4in) long, excluding bowsprit and rigging, so it is important to understand that this was a major and not insignificant restoration project.

Since the model's acquisition by the Museum in 1932 nothing had been done to ensure its preservation, partly because it was not on regular public display. This situation was rectified in 1993 when the author, Rob Napier, who had already confirmed his credentials by previously restoring a number of other models in the collection, was asked to restore the *Valkenisse* to its former standing. Ten years later the restoration was complete. The model will soon return to public display in the revitalised Museum's Ship Model and Maritime Arts Gallery.

This beautiful book is about the restoration of the model; from initial opportunity and research through to the restoration itself. In this writer's experience it is probably the most comprehensively detailed record of a single ship model restoration to have been published in the English language. As a record of an outstanding craftsman's ability and perseverance it is unsurpassed.

Every stage of the restoration is covered, from the establishment of the scale of the model (a far more complex process than might seem to be the case), its transportation to the author's workshop, through to every part of the model from keel to mainmast truck. Nothing is left out and the author goes into great detail to explain his rationale for decisions taken and materials used. Not only does he go to some lengths to explain even very small and possibly un-noticed restoration actions, but he illustrates his techniques with photographs and line drawings, the majority of the former being in full colour.

Considering the age of the model, its obviously hand-made status, the author nevertheless used modern digital technology, such as Photoshop, to support his own craftsmanship. This mix between two very diverse and opposite ends of the creative process will probably set a standard for future ship model restorations.

In addition to the numerous photographs and line drawings which fill almost every page, there are many tables and a number of appendices, one of which is a comprehensive list of contemporary models and graphic art representations of Dutch East Indies and related vessels. This very useful list may be used as a statistical comparative study confirming the origins of the *Valkenisse* model vis-à-vis other known examples from the same period.

Significantly too, the author does not rely on guesswork where answers might not be immediately forthcoming but refers to established and, whenever possible, empirical reference sources to support his decisions. These reference sources are clearly identified throughout the text and at the end of each chapter, thereby confirming in this writer's opinion that this book is not only a reference source on the restoration of this model but will become a standard text on the restoration of any other models from the seventeenth and eighteenth centuries. The combination of craftsmanship and scholarship by Rob Napier, the author, is outstanding.

Concluding the book in a separate pocket inside the rear cover is a set of finely detailed ship's draughts.

This is an outstanding volume. It will appeal to anyone with an interest in ship model making, regardless of period or preferences, and it will appeal equally to the maritime historian because of the depth the author goes into, drawing to details many would inadvertently ignore, yet which add more to the knowledge of western European ship design and construction from the early eighteenth century. Anyone contemplating building a model of a comparable vessel, at any scale, will not want to be without this book!

Michael Leek

The Restoration Warship: The Design, Construction and Career of a Third Rate of Charles II's Navy
by Richard Endsor
Conway, 2009
Hardback, 256 pages, profusely illustrated, some in colour, with photographs, paintings and line drawings. £50.00
ISBN 978-1-84486-088-3

This lavish book represents the culmination of a quarter of a century's worth of research, writing and intellectual development on the part of the author. The Restoration warship of the title is the 70-gun third rate *Lenox*, the first ship to be completed of Charles II's 1667 thirty shipbuilding programme. *Lenox* was a run of the mill workhorse and had a largely unspectacular career but, by placing her at the centre of his narrative, Endsor provides a window into the world of Restoration England.

A simple chronological structure underpins the entire work, allowing the author to begin the work by examining the debates behind the evolution of the third-rate warship before examining the minutiae of her construction and her active career. Throughout this we see the importance of personalities, Charles II, Samuel Pepys, the shipbuilding dynasties, the shipwrights, the patronage, the corruption and the grind of daily life. Out of this emerges a wonderful assessment of the shipbuilding art and hence, there is much here of interest to the ship modeller. From ship particulars, to timber details, ship's boats to decoration, sails and rigging to anchors, fittings and armament: in fact everything about *Lenox*, from keel to top – and everything in between. All beautifully illustrated with plans, drawings, paintings and a

colour plate section – the majority of which were completed by the author himself. Probably the best way to describe this book is akin to a Conway *Anatomy of the Ship* volume – but writ large. It is a huge book, based on exhaustive primary research, and the author is to be commended for seeing the project through.

This is a remarkable book, large scale, weighty, full of scholarly endeavour, professionally presented and will certainly delight those interested in building model ships – it does have to justify a hefty price tag. Moreover, it will not just interest those with a passion for warships from the Restoration era, but all those who are fascinated by the art of the shipbuilder.

Martin Robson

British Destroyers and Frigates
by Norman Friedman
Seaforth Publishing, 2008
Hardback, 352 pages, 200+ illustrations. £45
ISBN 978-1-84832-015-4

This massive, very well produced book is basically a very thorough technical and design history of the ships which, during the period in question, have come to form the backbone of the Royal Navy. Now commonly described under the generic term 'fleet escorts', they have at various times been called destroyers, frigates, sloops and corvettes. Beginning in the late 1930s with the 'Tribal' class destroyers, Norman Friedman takes the story through numerous challenges in peace and war right up to the present-day Type-23 frigates (the brand new destroyer HMS *Daring* evidently appeared after the book had gone to press and barely features). The rationale behind each design is clearly explained: it is a complex, intriguing tale and overall the impression is gained of a great deal of respect being due to the ships' designers and builders, who were usually having to contend with at least two, and frequently more, conflicting requirements. The author, a noted US naval analyst, explains clearly not just how, but why, these ships were built the way they were. The publishers, in a welcome change from the currently common practice, place explanatory footnotes on the relevant page, rather than in some dense and unwieldy section at the back of the book. (That said, because they are frequently quite long, they are also typeset so small as to be very hard to actually read.)

From a ship modeller's point of view the book is of slightly mixed value. A.D. Baker III's superb line drawings are numerous, covering just about every design featured (including some for export, and from Commonwealth navies), and reproduced clearly and at a good size, not split or lost down the gutter. The outboard profiles are excellent for general arrangement, although there are not nearly so many deck plans, meaning anyone looking to model one of these ships would need to consult other sources as well. (It is a pity that for some reason the small number of drawings done by Alan Raven and others have been reproduced noticeably less well.) The majority of the many well-chosen photographs are of equally outstanding quality. As well as the usual ship portraits, these include many detail shots, particularly useful when they feature radar and other electronics – surely in modelling terms the modern day equivalent of the rigging of sailing-era ships: the really difficult, fiddly bit.

A hefty book, with an equally hefty price tag, it is nevertheless excellent value, containing an absolute mass of detail, presented in a generally clear, well thought out manner, and so for anyone interested in the modern Royal Navy it is pretty much essential.

Stephen Dent

Building a Miniature Navy Board Model
by Philip Reed
Seaforth Publishing; 2009
Hardback, 144 pages, about 400 images, colour. £25.00
ISBN 978-1-84832-017-8

The superb Navy Board ship models of the seventeenth and eighteenth centuries have long been considered as the ultimate in the art and craft of ship model construction. Finished in such a way as to show how a proposed ship would appear, and by omitting sections of planking, the method of internal construction was also visible. Fortunately many examples have survived, and are to be found in museums and private collections in the UK, America and Europe.

In this book the author takes a modeller step-by-step through the construction of such a model, basing the work on a model of the *Royal George* of 1715. The author describes the essential practices of what has become known as the Navy Board form of planking and framing. Every stage of the work is described and illustrated with numerous colour photographs hull and deck framing, internal and external planking, the stern with its windows and galleries, and the mass of carved and decorative embellishment on the stern sides and bow, including the magnificent figurehead, always a prominent feature.

This is an invaluable book, and one which should encourage anyone contemplating the construction of such a model to hesitate no longer.

Michael Leek

Chatham Dockyard, 1815-1865: The Industrial Transformation
Edited by Philip MacDougall

Ashgate, Navy Records Society, 2009
Hardback, 410 pages, £30 (annual membership)
ISBN 978-0-7546-6597-7

This, the latest offering from the Navy Records Society, is an assessment of how the far-reaching technological developments that transformed shipbuilding and naval administration and, ultimately, warfare, impacted upon the running of a major naval dockyard, in this instance Chatham. The period under consideration witnessed fundamental changes, from timber ship construction to iron-hulled ships and the utilisation of steam power. With increased industrialisation came changes to working habits and skill sets; those at risk most were shipwrights who had to adapt to working with iron instead of traditional timber.

For those unfamiliar with the publications of the Navy Records Society the emphasis is to provide access to documents within the chosen field. This volume follows the traditional approach with chapters, in this case organised thematically, prefaced by a short introductory section to contextualise the primary source material that follows. Subjects covered are shipbuilding and repair; improving the shore-based facilities; the move to steam; storage, security and materials; economics, customs and the workforce; and central and local management. The documents themselves are mainly culled from The National Archives and The National Maritime Museum and provide a wealth of useful information. With the model shipbuilder in mind those chapters dealing with shipbuilding and repair and the introduction of steam power might prove the most attractive. There are some useful ship descriptions in the sources but, as with all such Navy Records Society volumes, there are no images, photographs or plans: a frustrating omission for the modeller. I suspect that most ship modellers would be content to obtain this volume from a good library.

Martin Robson

Ship Models from Kits
by David Griffith
Seaforth Publishing, 2009
Hardback, 245 x 185mm, 200 colour photographs. £25.00
ISBN 978-1-024-6.
[We regret that this book, together with Philip Reed's *Building a Miniature Navy Board Model*, arrived too late for an in-depth review. Editor]
In this book the author describes, step by step, the construction of 1:350 to 1:700 scale ship models either in injection moulded plastic or resin. Covered, too, are subjects such as rigging, painting and display, as well as the use of materials like photograph –etched brass. The text is illustrated with some 200 colour photographs.

Shipwright Gallery

SOYA

Mark Slota, whose models have previously appeared in *Model Shipwright*, feels that readers may be interested in this example of the latest generation of high technology plastic kits. This 1:350 scale version, in full hull form, of the Japanese Antarctic research ship and icebreaker *Soya*, comes complete with scale drawings, photographs and booklet of colour details. The ship was launched in 1938 as an order from the Soviet Union, but was retained for use by the Imperial Japanese Navy, and eventually overhauled in 1956. In the period 1956 to 1962 she made six voyages to the South Pole. The package includes some interesting colour photographs taken during those voyages. Although the instruction sheets are in Japanese, the step-by-step diagrams are clear and easy to follow. Paint diagrams and rigging details are also included. The kit is for a full hull model, but for Mark

Above: *Soya*: close-up of after end detail.

Above: The completed model of *Soya*.

Slota's diorama the part below the waterline was cut away. Most of the approximately 200 parts supplied were used, but commercially prepared laser-printed colour sheets for the decks were also used. Both the scale and colour of the sheets can be altered to suit in a copier. The guard rails and stanchions were made from wire. The 1:350 scale figures were commercially photo-etched ones which were thickened up with glass paint (obtained from a craft shop). The two tractors were white metal, but the two helicopters were scratch-built. The snow is talcum powder, filler and paint over white card. At 1:350 scale the model is approximately 9in (230mm) long.

Above: *Empress of Britain*. Midship area seen from above.

EMPRESS OF BRITAIN

Roy Chapman has recently completed a 1:384 scale model of the Canadian Pacific's *Empress of Britain* (1930). Construction generally followed the methods described in his previous articles in *Model Shipwright*. Even so, it was not an easy model to build. Apart from the repetitive nature of some of the work, which is an inherent aspect of building models of large passenger ships, there were the many oval portholes to overcome. Furthermore, there was a mass of ventilation, other machinery and fittings in the vicinity of the funnels which had to be made and fitted. As well as information from articles published in the technical press at the time of her completion, and many photographs of the ship the main data source was a set of shipbuilder's large-scale general arrangement plans. Photographs available from the Scottish Record Office, Edinburgh, include a series of excellent overhead shots of her as she lay in the fitting-out basin of John Brown's, near Clydebank, where she was built.

Above: The finished model of *Empress of Britain*.

HMS *Daring*

THE PORTSMOUTH FLOTILLA WELCOMES THE TYPE 45 DESTROYER
TO THE FLEET, 28 JANUARY 2009

By Lt Cdr F. Evans RN and Robert Fosterjohn

The Royal Naval Philatelic Society has produced a commemorative limited edition 410 covers to celebrate the arrival of the new Type 45 destroyer, HMS *Daring* to the Portsmouth Flotilla. The new *Daring* class ships will replace the Type 42 class destroyers which have been in service since the 1970s, and will offer a far greater capability due to technical advancements in several areas.

These six ships currently planned for the class are all in various stages of construction. Incidentally the bow section of each of the *Daring* class destroyers has been built in Portsmouth Dockyard and floated on purpose-built barges to Scotstoun on the Clyde to be attached to the rest of the ship. After HMS *Daring* come HMS *Dauntless*, *Diamond*, *Dragon*, *Defender* and *Duncan*. Although much larger and about double the tonnage of the Type 42's the ship's complement required to operate them is considerably less. Further economies are achieved with the fuel system where the propulsion is all-electric and therefore 'greener'. The range of this class is 7,000 nautical miles compared with 4,000 nautical miles of the Type 42's and sea trials in HMS *Daring* showed a 75 per cent saving in fuel usage. The size of the ships allows for a high standard of accommodation for the ship's company. Junior ratings will have six-berth cabins with a separate mess area. Senior ratings will be in single or two-berth cabins and officers will be in single cabins. Facilities are available to embark up to 60 troops or Special Forces with their domestic requirements. The main armament is the Principal Anti Air Missile System (PAAMS) which sets new standards in air defence and incorporates the Aster missile and the UK designed Samson tracking and fire control radar. Several sophisticated anti-ship missiles can be engaged at the same time and some other nations are planning to use the same system it will provide for interoperability when required. A 4.5in medium-calibre gun is mounted for use in shore bombardment and there are close-range guns and Surface Ship Torpedo system.

A Merlin or Lynx helicopter will normally be operated but the size of the flight deck allows for a Chinook-size helicopter for such things as troop-carrying. The ships can also control and direct other aircraft for attack and defence over large areas.

HMS *Daring* is the seventh ship to bear the same name in the Royal Navy, and details for each one are listed here.

Above: The Type 45 destroyer, HMS *Daring*.

Type	**Gun Brig**
Builder	Jabez Bailey
Yard	Ipswich, Suffolk
Ordered	June 1804
Laid down	June 1804
Launched	October 1804
Completed	Chatham between 18 October and 11 December 1804
Commissioned	November 1804
Dimensions as built	80ft 2in, 65ft 10.75in x 22ft 6.75in x 9ft 5in, 178 beam
Displacement	178 tonnes
Armament	12 x 18-pdr
Complement	50
Fate	On 27 January 1813 she was burnt to avoid capture by the 40-gun *Le Rubis* off the Kos Islands, West Africa.

Type	**Sloop**
Builder	Joseph Wight
Yard	Portsmouth
Launched	2 October 1844
Displacement	426 tons
Armament	12 guns
Fate	Broken up 1864

Type	*Fantome* **class composite screw sloop**
Builder	Wigram
Yard	Blackwall
Launched	4 February 1874
Completed	1874
Displacement	940 tons
Dimensions as built	160ft x 31ft x 12ft 6in
Machinery	1 shaft John Penn 915ihp = 10.63 knots
Armament	2 x 7in MLR 2 x 64-pdr MLR
Complement	125
Fate	Sold to be broken up 1889

Type	**Destroyer 1892 ORDER: Thornycroft 26 – knotters**
Builder	Thornycroft
Laid down	July 1892
Launched	25 November 1893
Completed	February 1895
Displacement	280 tons
Dimensions as built	185ft oa x 19ft x 7ft
Machinery	Twin shaft 4-cylinder triple-expansion design 4000ihp = 27.5 knots
Armament	3 x 18in TT (one fixed bow tube, two single deck tubes)
Fate	Broken up 1912

Type	**C and D Class Destroyer**
Pennant number	H53
Builder	J. I. Thornycroft & Co.
Yard	Southampton
Launched	7 April 1932
Displacement	1375-1400t standard
Dimensions as built	317ft 9in pp 329 oa x 33ft 12ft 5in
Machinery	2 shaft Parsons geared turbines, 3 Admiralty 3-drum boilers 36,000shp = 36 knots
Fuel capacity	461–473t
Armament	4 x 4.7 QF Mk IX (4 x 1), 1 x 3in HA 2 x 2 pompom, 8 x 21in TT (2 x 4)
Complement	145
Fate	Sunk by *U23* in the first U-boat attack on a Norwegian convoy on 18 February 1940 off Duncansby Head.

Type	*Daring* **Class Destroyer**
Pennant number	D05
Builder	Swan, Hunter and Wigham Richardson
Yard	Wallsend
Laid down	29 September
Launched	10 August 1949
Completed	8 March 1952
Displacement	2830t (actual) standard
Dimensions as built	366ft pp 390ft oa x 43ft x 13ft 7in
Machinery	2 shaft double-reduction geared steam turbines by Babcock and Wilcox, 54,000shp = 37.5 knots
Fuel Capacity	590t
Armament	6 x 4.5in/45 QF Mk V (3 x 2), 6 x 40mm Bofors (3 x 2), 10 x 21in TT (2 x 5)
Complement	278–330
Fate	Broken up 1971

Type	*Daring* **(Type 45 Destroyer)**
Pennant number	D32
Builder	BAE Systems
Yard	Scotstoun
Ordered	2000
Laid down	28 March 2003
Launched	1 February 2006
Displacement	7205t (Light Seagoing), (8092t Deep Load).
Length	152.4m
Beam	21.2m
Draught	7.4m
Machinery	2 Rolls Royce WR-21 turbines, Alstom electric motors.
Speed	29 knots +
Range	7,000 nautical miles 13,000km at an economical speed
Sensors and Processing systems	SAMPSON Radar S1850M ED Radar
Electronic warfare and decoys	Seagnat SSTD
Armament	PAAMS Air Defence System, 6 x 8 cell SYLVER VLS Aster 15 missiles, Aster 30 missiles, 2 Phalanx (Close in weapons system), BAE Systems 114mm (4.5 inch) Mk8 Mod. 1 gun, 2 x 30 mm guns
Aircraft carried	1 x Lynx HMA8 or 1 x Westland Merlin HM1
Complement	190

THE ROYAL NAVAL PHILATELIC SOCIETY

The Royal Naval Philatelic Society (RNPS) is the officially accredited philatelic society for the Royal Navy. Formed in 1972 the Society meets the needs of philatelic enthusiasts around the world who enjoy an interest in naval history. It has an Admiral President and is based in Portsmouth Historic Dockyard, of which it is part. The Chairman is a serving member of the RN/RM.

The RNPS issues limited edition official naval commemorative and/or first day covers through which it seeks to foster a wider awareness of our naval history and tradition.

Each numbered Limited Edition cover consists of an envelope displaying a specially commissioned full colour picture of the event being commemorated, together with a commemorative stamp (or stamps) from an appropriate country. Each issue also contains a unique selection of historic photographs plus, where appropriate, relevant diagram, drawings, details of honours and awards and extracts of reports of proceedings. People involved in

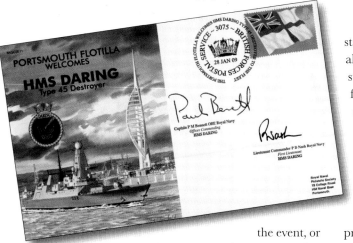

the event, or having a strong relevant connection with it, sign some of the covers. Various editions of commemorative covers feature ship or squadron badges, relevant military emblems and decorations that reflect many aspects of the Surface Fleet, Royal Marines, Submarine Service and Fleet Air Arm. The detailed research involved creates an exclusive philatelic item.

Official covers have the lettering 'RNSC' (Royal Naval Souvenir Cover) at the top of the envelope and should not be confused with covers issued elsewhere. All covers are franked by a one-day special postmark or the daily operational cancellation approved by the Royal Mail, British Forces Post Office or foreign equivalents.

A BRIEF HISTORY OF THE RNPS

On 14 February 1972 a Royal Naval Souvenir Cover (RNSC) to commemorate the 20th Anniversary of the First Deck Landing on HMS *Eagle* was issued by the Fleet Air Arm Museum at the Royal Naval Air Station Yeovilton. This was the first of many and they were numbered as RNSCs in series of 25. They were small, standard size envelopes with stamps as applicable, with illustrations by our naval artist Tony Theobald who still provides our artwork. The information was printed on the front and eventually became so small that a microscope was required to decipher it.

The first five series, which took us up to the end of 1990, were signed by one or two relevant personalities but series six and onwards did not impose any limitation on signatory numbers. For example (6)11 which commemorated D-Day provided a choice of 24 in various combinations. Currently we stick to about five different suitable examples.

We search for appropriate stamps to use on our covers. South Africa, France, Greece, Norway, Hong Kong, Singapore, Ascension Islands, St Helena, Falkland Islands and Gibraltar and, nearer home, Jersey and the Isle of Man have all contributed over the years. This approach means that the stamps we select have been issued at some period before the date of the incident commemorated and therefore the postmark date is not the issue date of the

stamp. We do not aim to produce 'First Day Covers' although on rare occasions this has occurred. For UK stamps we obtain a personalised and numbered postmark from the British Forces Postal Service. Other countries' stamps have to be cancelled in the country of origin.

Series No.6 began in 1991 using a larger envelope which gave more scope for the excellent illustrations provided by our naval artist Tony Theobald, and more room was also available for the proposed increase in signature numbers. The main improvement, however, was to include a large text sheet and photocards which provided details of the subject of the cover and raised the status of the product to a Royal Naval Historical Document.

The year 1991 also heralded the formation of an official Royal Naval Philatelic Society with an Admiral as Patron and a serving Royal Naval Officer as Chairman. A two-tier price structure was also introduced for members and non members.

In January 1994 the RNPS moved from the Fleet Air Arm Museum Yeovilton to Portsmouth Historic Dockyard and became part of the Portsmouth Naval Base Property Trust from where it continues to thrive. We aim to issue four covers per year and are now up to Series No.8, Issue 11.

Newsletters are issued regularly to all RNPS members. New subscribers receive an attractive certificate signed by the Admiral President of the Society. Membership is £20 on joining and a £5 annual subscription thereafter. Monies after cover expenses goes towards the upkeep of the Heritage Area via The Portsmouth Naval Base Property Trust.

Further details can be obtained from:
The Royal Naval Philatelic Officer, 19 College Road, HM Naval Base, Portsmouth, PO1 3LJ
Tel: 023 9281 5494
Web: www.rnphilatelic.org/rnps
Email: enquiries@rnphilatelic.org

REFERENCES

Chesneau, R., (ed.) *Conway's all the World's Fighting Ships, 1922-1946* (Conway Maritime Press, 1997)

Chumbley, S., (ed.) *Conway's all the World's Fighting Ships, 1947-1995* (Conway Maritime Press, 1995)

Gardiner, R., (ed.) *Conway's all the World's Fighting Ships, 1860-1905* (Conway Maritime Press, 1997)

Thomas, D. A., *A Companion to the Royal Navy* (Harrap Ltd, 1988)

Winfield, R., *British Warships in the Age of Sail 1797-1817: Design, Construction, Careers and Fate* (Chatham Publishing, 2005)